TEACHING ABOUT ASIA
IN A TIME OF PANDEMIC

Teaching About Asia in a Time of Pandemic

Edited by
David Kenley

ASIA
SHORTS

Published by the Association for Asian Studies
Asia Shorts, Number 8
www.asianstudies.org

The Association for Asian Studies (AAS)

Formed in 1941, the Association for Asian Studies (AAS)—the largest society of its kind, with over 6,500 members worldwide—is a scholarly, non-political, non-profit professional association open to all persons interested in Asia. For further information, please visit www.asianstudies.org.

Published by Association for Asian Studies, 825 Victors Way, Suite 310, Ann Arbor, MI 48108 USA.

We gratefully acknowledge the generous grant from The Henry Luce Foundation, which helped fund this project.

Cover image, girl releases a medical mask into the sky against a gray brick wall, by Gloomso. Courtesy of Shutterstock.

Cataloging-in-Publication Data available from the Library of Congress

ASIA
SHORTS

"ASIA SHORTS" offers concise, engagingly-written titles written by highly-qualified authors on topics of significance in Asian studies. Topics are intended to be substantive, generate discussion and debate within the field, and attract interest beyond it.

The AAS is exploring new ways of making rigorous, timely, and accessible work by scholars in the field available to a wide audience of informed readers. This new series complements and leverages the success of the pedagogically-oriented AAS series, "Key Issues in Asian Studies" and is designed to engage broad audiences with up-to-date scholarship on important topics in Asian studies.

"Asia Shorts" books:

- Have a clear point of view, a well-defined, and even provocative argument rooted in a strong base of evidence and current scholarship.

- Are written in an accessible, jargon-free style suitable for non-specialist audiences.

- Are written by a single author or a small group of authors (scholars, journalists, or policymakers).

- Are rigorously peer reviewed.

For further information, visit the AAS website: www.asianstudies.org

AAS books are distributed by Columbia University Press.

For orders or inquiries, please visit https://cup.columbia.edu

COLUMBIA
UNIVERSITY
PRESS

ABOUT THE AUTHORS

RICHARD AIDOO is a Professor of Politics at Coastal Carolina University. His research work on China's political-economic engagements with Sub-Saharan African countries, and other economic development issues in Sub-Saharan Africa has appeared in journals, book chapters, as well as several media outlets such as *The Washington Post, CNN, Real Clear World* and *The National Interest*. He co-authored *Charting the Roots of Anti-Chinese Populism in Africa* in 2015, and recently edited a volume titled *The Politics of Economic Reform in Ghana* (2019).

TEJPAUL SINGH BAINIWAL is a PhD Candidate in the Department of Religious Studies at University of California, Riverside. His research focuses on Sikhi, Asian American history, and religion in America. He is also on the board for Asian and Pacific Islander Americans in Historic Preservation and is a researcher/historian for the Stockton Gurdwara (Stockton Sikh Temple). He has contributed to *Religions* and the edited volume *Religious Violence Today: Faith and Conflict in the Modern World* (2020).

GARETH BARKIN is Chair and Professor of Anthropology at the University of Puget Sound. He directs that university's Luce Initiative on Southeast Asia and the Environment (LIASE) Southeast Asia Symposium, and leads ethnographic field-school programs in Indonesia. His current research explores short-term study abroad at U.S. universities, focusing on the representation of Southeast Asian culture and place in an increasingly market-driven pedagogical arena. His work has appeared in numerous edited volumes and journals, including *Visual Anthropology Review, International Journal of Asian Studies,* and *Anthropology & Education Quarterly.*

GWENDOLYN CAMPBELL is a doctoral candidate in the College of Humanities, Arts and Social Sciences at Flinders University. Her thesis explores the converging relationship between the native speaker fallacy, identity development and context. Gwendolyn has a background as an academic educator in the teaching of ESOL and TESOL topics at undergraduate and postgraduate level at Flinders University from 2009 to 2017. She collaborated in the design and initial implementation of the Chinese Corner/English Corner Tandem Language Learning Program at Flinders University and has since become interested in the potential of synchronous online peer partnerships to facilitate interactive learning between geographically dispersed pre-service teachers. Other research interests include computer-mediated research in applied linguistics and the changing dynamic of pre-service teaching in TESOL arising from COVID-19.

KIN CHEUNG is Assistant Professor of East and South Asian Religions at Moravian College. He researches Contemporary Buddhism, including Buddhist-based meditation's effects on the brain and senses of self, the practical implications of Buddhist ethics, the relationship between Buddhism and mindfulness, and the involvement of Buddhist institutions in China's stock market. His next major project is a case study of a contemporary Chinese American religious healer. His work appears in *The Journal of Buddhist Ethics*, *Studies in Chinese Religions*, *Meditation and Healing* (2016), *Handbook of Ethical Foundations of Mindfulness* (2018), and *Buddhism and Medicine: An Anthology of Modern and Contemporary Sources* (2019).

LUCIEN ELLINGTON is UC Foundation Professor of Education and Director of the Asia Program, the National Consortium for Teaching About Asia for Tennessee, and the Center for Reflective Citizenship at the University of Tennessee at Chattanooga. He is the founding editor of *Education About Asia* and editor of *Key Issues in Asian Studies*. A former high school economics and world history teacher, Ellington's Asia-related books and publications have focused upon Japan, Northeast Asia, comparative education, and teaching about East Asia. His research and publication interests for the past several years include history and economics education with an emphasis upon Taiwan and South Korea. He is a passionate advocate for American elementary and secondary school reform—especially the implementation of rigorous academic content-based standards. Ellington is a Senior Fellow in the Foreign Policy Research Institute's Wachman Center for International and Civic Literacy.

ADAM FRANK is Professor of Anthropology and Performance Studies in the Norbert O. Schedler Honors College at the University of Central Arkansas. He is the author of *Taijiquan and the Search for the Little Old Chinese Man: Understanding Identity through Martial Arts* (Palgrave 2006), as well as numerous articles on Chinese martial arts, race, and identity. A forty-year practitioner of taijiquan (tai chi) and an actor, Frank is also Producing Artistic Director of Ozark Living Newspaper Theatre Company, based in Conway, Arkansas.

NABAPARNA GHOSH is an Assistant Professor of Global Studies at Babson College. She is the author of *A Hygienic City-Nation: Space, Community, and Everyday Life in Colonial Calcutta* (Cambridge University Press, 2020). At Babson College, she offers courses on global studies with a focus on South Asia.

JEFFREY GIL is a Senior Lecturer in ESOL/TESOL at Flinders University, where he is involved in the development, teaching and administration of ESOL and TESOL topics at undergraduate and postgraduate level, and served as the coordinator of the Chinese program from 2011–2014. Jeffrey also has experience teaching

English as a Foreign Language (EFL) and Applied Linguistics at universities in China. He has published widely on applied linguistics topics, including English as a global language and the global use and status of Chinese. He is the author of *Soft Power and the Worldwide Promotion of Chinese Language Learning: The Confucius Institute Project* (Multilingual Matters, 2017).

SARAH G. GRANT is Assistant Professor of Anthropology at California State University, Fullerton. She is finishing her first book length manuscript about the industrial coffee industry in Vietnam and developing a new project—a multispecies ethnography of fertilizer manufacturing, birds, shrimp, and climate change in the Mekong Delta. Her work has appeared in numerous journals, edited volumes, and coffee industry publications including *Education About Asia, Boom California, Standart,* and *Barista Magazine*.

TRISTAN R. GRUNOW is Visiting Assistant Professor of Modern Japanese History at Pacific University. Previously, he was Associate Research Scholar at the Council on East Asian Studies at Yale University, Assistant Professor without Review at the University of British Columbia, a postdoctoral fellow at the Reischauer Institute of Japanese Studies at Harvard University, and Visiting Assistant Professor at Bowdoin College. He researches the urban history of Tokyo, and is the author most recently of "Pebbles of Progress: Streets and Urban Modernity in Early Meiji Tokyo." In addition to organizing the *Meiji at 150 Project*, co-curating the *Meiji at 150 Digital Teaching Resource*, and co-organizing the *Hokkaidō 150* workshop and digital platform at the University of British Columbia, he also produced the *Meiji at 150 Podcast* and is now producing the *Japan on the Record* podcast.

BYRON HAAST is a Classroom Teacher at St Michael's Grammar School in Melbourne, Australia. He specializes in senior years education, teaching senior years Global Politics and Geography. He has a Bachelor of Arts (Political Science) from Monash University as well as a Masters of Teaching (Secondary School) from Melbourne University. He has published articles on population dynamics in Japan and Bangladesh and other articles about teaching practices in the secondary classroom.

JARED HALL serves as Dean of Academic Life at the Hotchkiss School where he teaches courses in history and philosophy with an emphasis on China and global themes. He completed his M.A. in modern Chinese history at the George Washington University and is currently a doctor of education (Ed.D.) candidate at the University of Pennsylvania in educational leadership. His current research focuses on global citizenship education and independent thinking in a Chinese context.

PETRA HENDRICKSON is an Assistant Professor of Political Science at Northern Michigan University, where she teaches classes on international relations and comparative politics, including East and Southeast Asian Politics. She was previously an Assistant Professor of International Studies at Centre College, where she taught South Asian Politics, and an instructor at Michigan State University, where she routinely taught a class on mass killing, including in Cambodia, Indonesia, and East Timor. Her research interests focus on active learning pedagogy, genocide/politicide and youth views of the political transition in Myanmar. She has been published in the *Canadian Foreign Policy Journal, Journal of Political Science Education*, and *Terrorism and Political Violence*.

DAVID KENLEY is Dean of the College of Arts and Sciences at Dakota State University. Formerly Professor of Chinese History at Elizabethtown College, he is committed to the concept of the scholar-teacher. His publications include *Modern Chinese History* (published in the AAS Key Issues in Asian Studies series), *New Culture in a New World: The May Fourth Movement and the Chinese Diaspora, 1919–1932*, and *Contested Community: Identities, Spaces, and Hierarchies of the Chinese in the Cuban Republic* (with Miriam Herrera Jerez and Mario Castillo Santana).

HAN LIN taught Chinese language and Asian environmental politics at Flinders University from 2012 to 2019. She also has experience teaching English as a Foreign Language (EFL) in China and academic communication skills in Australia. Her research interests include sustainable energy policy, climate change mitigation and adaptation, sustainable resource management, sustainable urban living and Confucian philosophy. Her PhD, obtained from Flinders University, proposed an alternative climate change related energy policy for China. She is the author of *Energy Policies and Climate Change in China: Actors, Implementation, and Future Prospects* (Routledge, 2019).

JEFFREY MELNIK is the Managing Editor for *Education About Asia*. He earned his MA in English from the University of Tennessee at Chattanooga and BA in History with a minor in East Asian Languages and Literature from the University of Florida. His research interests include the information technology industry, integrating technology with pedagogy, and the digital humanities.

MINJUNG NOH is a doctoral candidate in the Department of Religion and Advanced Graduate Scholar Fellow (2020–2021) at Center for Humanities at Temple University. Her interdisciplinary research concerns transnational Korean evangelical Christianity and its gendered practice between North America and South Korea. Her work appears on *Journal of Ecumenical Studies, Journal of Korean Religions* and edited volumes including *Buddhism & Medicine: An Anthology Vol 2:*

Modern and Contemporary Voices (Columbia University Press) and *Explorations in Protestant Aesthetics* (Routledge). She was a Louisville Institute Dissertation Fellow in 2018–2019.

PHILLIP O'BRIEN is a Casual Academic and Research Assistant with Deakin University and teaches Humanities at McKinnon Secondary College in Melbourne, Australia, having taught previously in Japan and Brazil. He holds a BA (Humanities/Social Sciences) from La Trobe University and a M.Ed (Studies of Asia) from Flinders University. Phillip enjoys empowering students and tapping into their areas of global interest and background to help foster their engagement with humanities, intercultural communication, and education. He is also an accredited evaluator with the Council of International Schools.

TINAZ PAVRI is Division Chair for Social Sciences and Education at Spelman College and Founding Director of the Asian Studies Program. She is a professor in the department of Political Science. Her research and publication interests lie in the area of security studies and conflict resolution, questions of national identity and globalization in South Asia. She has published numerous articles, book chapters and a co-edited book on these and other topics. Her book *Bombay in the Age of Disco: City, Community, Life*, was published in 2015. She has served as President of the Georgia Political Science Association (GPSA) and is their 2015 recipient of the Donald T. Wells award for outstanding service. She directs Spelman's $1.2m grant project, the Career Pathways Initiative.

MATTHEW ROBERTS is the Social Studies Department Chair at Pine-Richland High School in Allegheny County, Pennsylvania, where he teaches World History, Asian Studies and AP Psychology. He is a regular guest presenter for NCTA seminars including *The Physics of the Samurai Sword* and *The Neuroscience of Buddhism*. Through NCTA, he has traveled to China and Japan and most recently co-led the 2019 Study tour, China: The Space Between Us. His academic interests include curriculum development, educational travel, health and wellness, and traditional woodworking.

MELODY ROD-ARI is Assistant Professor of Art History at Loyola Marymount University. She is also the Southeast Asian Content Editor for Smarthistory as well as an active curator who has organized exhibitions and permanent galleries for the Norton Simon Museum and the USC, Pacific Asia Museum. Her research investigates Buddhist visual culture in Thailand, and the history of collecting South and Southeast Asian art. Her work has been published by various journals and university presses including *Amerasia Journal* and the NUS Press. She has received fellowships from the Henry Luce Foundation, the Andrew W. Mellon Foundation, the NEA, and the NEH.

TANYA L. ROTH is an Upper School history teacher at MICDS, an independent K-12 school in St. Louis, MO. She completed her PhD in history at Washington University in St. Louis and teaches courses in Post-1900 World History and US History. She participates regularly in Asian history and culture courses from the National Consortium for Teaching About Asia and has been a contributor to the journal *Education About Asia*. In 2019 she was part of an NCTA teacher delegation to Taiwan.

THOMAS J. SHATTUCK is a Research Associate in the Asia Program and the Managing Editor at the Foreign Policy Research Institute. Mr. Shattuck was a member of the 2019 class of scholars at the Global Taiwan Institute, receiving the Taiwan Scholarship to conduct research on transitional justice and the legacy of the "White Terror" in Taiwan. He received his BA in History and English from La Salle University in 2013 and his MA in International Studies from National Chengchi University in 2016.

SUSAN SPENCER is a Professor of English at the University of Central Oklahoma, where she served as Director of Global Initiatives for the College of Liberal Arts from 2008–2020. She has taught UCO's World Literature survey course since 1996. She is especially fascinated by Japan's Edo era, a period of isolationist policy when the nation's authors, cut off from outside literary influence, relied upon their creative resources to forge a vibrant vernacular literature that was unique to its time and place. Her essay in this volume explores a different kind of isolation, which challenged her own creativity.

JEFFREY WASSERSTROM is Chancellor's Professor of History at UC Irvine. A specialist in Chinese history and world history, he has written, co-written, edited, or co-edited more than a dozen books including, most recently, the third edition of *China in the 21ˢᵗ Century: What Everyone Needs to Know* (Oxford University Press, 2018), co-authored with Maura Elizabeth Cunningham, and *Vigil: Hong Kong on the Brink* (Columbia Global Reports, 2020). He often contributes to newspapers, magazines, literary reviews, and blogs, regularly speaks to the media about events relating to China, and was a consultant for "The Gate of Heavenly Peace," an award-winning documentary.

JUSTIN WU is a doctoral candidate in Asian History at the University of North Carolina at Chapel Hill. His research interests include nationalism and identity formation, social movements, and pan-Asianism in 20th-century East Asia. His dissertation explores anti-Japan sentiment and the dispute over the Diaoyu/Senkaku Islands in the East China Sea since the 1970s, focusing on protests in Taiwan, Hong Kong, and the United States.

Contents

Section Two: Pedagogical Tools and Methods for a Pandemic

Introduction

Getting Past the Plexiglass

David Kenley

In the early morning hours of October 2, 2020, US President Donald Trump used Twitter to announce he had just tested positive for the coronavirus. "Trump's positive diagnosis," *New York* magazine wrote, raises "unprecedented questions from how he'll handle the duties of the presidency to whether others in the administration have been infected to how voters will react."[1] There were many unprecedented events in 2020. Indeed, "unprecedented" may just be the most overused word of the year, frequently employed to describe our political, economic, and demographic conditions. Certainly 2020 was unprecedented for educators and their students. It started with the near total shutdown of schools in the early spring, followed by hasty attempts to shift online in the late spring, and then it transformed into a long summer of hand-wringing and strategizing. By the time autumn arrived, educators and their students were desperate for a return to what proved to be an elusive sense of normalcy. Residence halls became quarantine centers. Cases dramatically spiked in small college towns. Student athletes sat by as their sports were canceled, restarted, and canceled again. Well-financed private schools provided regular testing, expensive technology equipment, and multiple distance-learning possibilities. More cash-strapped schools plowed forward with limited options, spreading out desks, installing plexiglass shields, and hoping for the best. The year was unprecedented for many reasons.

And yet, "unprecedented" was only one part of our 2020 vocabulary. We incorporated many new expressions into our daily conversations. It is remarkable to think that at the beginning of the year, most of us had never used such terms as "socially distanced," "herd immunity," "PPE," or "coronavirus." Even such common words as "bubble" and "face mask" took on entirely new meanings. In the realm of education, we found ourselves talking about "Zooming it in," chatting about "HyFlex" courses, and discussing the most recent count on our school's "pandemic dashboard."

Teaching About Asia in a Time of Pandemic seeks to make sense of the unfamiliar situation educators and students are facing around the globe. As Sarah Grant explains in chapter 18, "pandemic pedagogy is necessarily rapid response pedagogy." However, as she reminds us, it must not come at the expense of intentionality, sound design, and scholarly curiosity. This volume contains sage lessons and insights from highly respected educators who have been engaged in "pandemic pedagogy." Each chapter is concise and engagingly written by highly qualified authors on areas of significance in Asian Studies. They have reflected on both the unique challenges and opportunities presented by COVID-19 and our transformed educational environment. Rather than succumb to resignation and despair, they challenge all of us to seize this opportunity to broaden our understanding, incorporate novel methodologies, and integrate new Asia-informed lessons into our curriculum.

For those of us teaching about Asia, the year of COVID-19 has been particularly significant. The virus originated in China, quickly spread to Korea and Japan, and proved to be dreadfully lethal in India. It has exacerbated tensions between Taiwan and China and diverted our attention from border disputes in the Himalayas. On a more practical level, missed classes meant teachers had to make difficult decisions regarding what to cut from the curriculum, with topics about Asia becoming often unceremoniously bypassed on the course syllabus.

The pandemic has highlighted many discouraging inequities within our global society. Service workers in the United States, street vendors in India, and migrant laborers in Southeast Asia have all been more likely to contract the disease than their wealthier neighbors. Beyond just infection levels, COVID-19 has highlighted disparities in employment rates, access to health care, digital access, and gender equality. Often these discrepancies correlate with race, providing another stark reminder of ongoing systemic racism. Countries around the world have responded to the pandemic by closing borders, shutting down market access, and stoking xenophobic nationalism. The so-called "China virus" led to a metaphorical pandemic of anti-Asian sentiment, with numerous companies, governments, and individuals infected. The study of Asia and cross-cultural difference has rarely been more important than during this pandemic, and *Teaching About Asia* is a potent tonic.

Section 1 of this volume analyzes how to teach Asian history, politics, culture, and society using examples and case studies emerging from the pandemic. Jeffrey Wasserstrom sets the tone for this segment by challenging all of us to move beyond our assumption that "we've never been here before" and to instead reflect on the past for corollaries and precedents, including, for instance, the 1900 Boxer Crisis in China.[2] Even in the face of global catastrophe—both in 1900 and 2020—local issues and identities remain extremely important. "The world is often imagined to be growing ever flatter [as a result of globalization]," Wasserstrom writes, "but 2020 has convinced me, yet again, that the world remains stubbornly bumpy." Other contributors to section 1 show how COVID-19 can be used to teach Orientalism and exceptionalism in Korea, Buddhist devotionalism in Japan, political economy in India, Chinese foreign relations in Africa, and global politics as manifest in Hong Kong and Taiwan. Some take a more regional approach, discussing the concepts of mythmaking in East Asia or Sikh religious practices in South Asia and the United States. As explained by Susan Spencer in her analysis of medieval Japanese literature, many of the chapters in section 1 "concentrate on the themes of loss, sudden change, and a confrontation with the transitory nature of what one has taken for granted—life events that all of the students, regardless of background, were struggling with."

Whereas section 1 focuses on what to teach in light of the pandemic, section 2 focuses on how to teach it. It includes chapters written by seasoned online instructors as well as those who have recently been forced into an online environment because of COVID-19. Their recommended instructional approaches are applicable to both high school and undergraduate courses. All of the chapters in this section force us to reflect on our own methodologies and how to adapt them to new realities. For instance, how do we utilize kinesthetic, somatic methods to teach about Asia when our students are disembodied images on a screen? How do we promote fieldwork for our students when society is in lockdown? Several authors in this section challenge us to incorporate new tools or rethink how we employ them, ranging from Google Maps to blogs, podcasts, apps, simulations, and, of course, Zoom. Section 2 concludes with specific lesson plans from both respected university researchers as well as expert high school teachers working "in the trenches."

While aspects of the 2020 pandemic might indeed be unprecedented, the pandemic's educational impacts will certainly last well into the future. Even when a vaccine becomes available and we are able to return to "normal," it will most certainly be a new normal. For example, now that teachers have demonstrated the ability to teach remotely, several school districts in the United States have announced the end of the beloved tradition of "snow days." College professors who just a few short months ago were adamantly opposed to teaching online have now become accustomed to attending class in their dress shirts and "Zoom pants." Study abroad in Asia may well take years to recover to pre-pandemic levels. And students may come to see HyFlex as an inalienable right.[3] In short, the relevance of this volume will extend well beyond the arrival of a COVID-19 vaccine.

There are many people to thank for their help with this volume, especially since they worked with great speed in getting it published. In the spring of 2020, William Tsutsui was working with Vinayak Chaturvedi to develop a scholarly volume on the pandemic for inclusion in the Asia Shorts series. Tsutsui quickly realized that the situation called for a companion volume focused on the pedagogical impacts of the pandemic and therefore reached out to Lucien Ellington, the editor of *Education About Asia*, to seek his collaboration. I am grateful for Tsutsui and Ellington's inspiration for this volume, and for their unfailing editorial assistance over the ensuing weeks and months. Their commitment to the scholarship of teaching is admirable. The Henry Luce Foundation also saw the value of the proposed volume and contributed financial support, for which I am very grateful. Members of the *Education About Asia* editorial board offered critical insights, as did several individuals associated with the National Consortium for Teaching about Asia. Jon Wilson, Maura Elizabeth Cunningham, Jenna Yoshikawa, and Hilary Finchum-Sung of the Association for Asian Studies have selflessly provided their expertise in terms of production and promotion. I am grateful to Michael Jauchen for his skilled copy editing and to Columbia University Press for their help with promotion and distribution. Of course, the volume would not exist except for the talented author-educators who contributed their work. I have enjoyed working with each of them. This volume is dedicated to them and to all teachers worldwide working under pandemic conditions.

In the West, it is widely believed that the Chinese word for "crisis" (危机) is a combination of the characters "danger" and "opportunity." While Victor Mair has thoroughly debunked this popular trope, it nonetheless persists precisely because we hope to find meaning in times of difficulty.[4] COVID-19 has certainly created a crisis for educators at all levels, but the contributors to this volume have responded by capitalizing on new pedagogical opportunities. Each approached the contagion crisis with creativity, enthusiasm, and most importantly, sound educational practice. We are all the beneficiaries of their pandemic pedagogy.

Notes

[1] Matt Stieb and Margaret Hartmann, "Trump Tests Positive for COVID-19," *New York Intelligencer*, October 2, 2020, https://nymag.com/intelligencer/2020/10/trump-quarantines-after-aide-hicks-tests-positive-for-covid.html.

[2] According to the Chinese zodiac, both 1900 and 2020 are "Metal Rat" years, which indeed seems a fitting appellation for our current time.

[3] *Inside Higher Ed* explains, "In a HyFlex course, courses are delivered both in person and online at the same time by the same faculty member. Students can then choose for each and every class meeting whether to show up for class in person or to join it online. The underlying design ethos behind the HyFlex Model is flexibility and student choice." See

Edward J. Maloney and Joshua Kim, "Fall Scenario #13: A HyFlex Model," *Inside Higher Ed*, May 10, 2020, https://www.insidehighered.com/blogs/learning-innovation/fall-scenario-13-hyflex-model.

[4] Victor Mair, "Danger + Opportunity ≠ Crisis: How a Misunderstanding about Chinese Characters Has Led Many Astray," *Pīnyīn.info: A Guide to the Writing of Mandarin Chinese in Romanization*, September 2009, http://www.pinyin.info/chinese/crisis.html.

SECTION 1

PANDEMIC CASE STUDIES

1

WE'VE NEVER BEEN GLOBAL

HOW LOCAL MEANINGS MATTERED
IN 1900 AND STILL MATTER NOW

Jeffrey Wasserstrom

The last sun of the century sets amidst the blood-red clouds of the West and the whirlwind of hatred.

The naked passion of self-love of Nations, in its drunken delirium of greed, is dancing to the clash of steel and the howling verses of vengeance.

> — Rabindranath Tagore, December 31, 1900

Sometimes a useful thing for historians to do is to point out when something seems radically new. That is our situation today. . . . In our circumstances, historical analogies can easily become a form of dangerous nostalgia.

This isn't 1914. It isn't 1941. It isn't even 2008.

It is 2020. So expect all hell to break loose.

> — Adam Tooze, *Washington Post*, March 25, 2020

As we strive to make sense of this wrenching year of surprise and sorrow, is it useful to look for parallels to the past? And if so, how far back should we go to find a match?

In struggling with these questions, I keep pondering "We've Never Been Here Before," historian Adam Tooze's tellingly titled op-ed that argues for seeing 2020 as taking the world into uncharted waters.[1] I first read it when it was published in March, at a time when I was supposed to be heading to London for a stint as a visiting professor but was instead sheltering at home in California. Tooze, a specialist in international history who has recently been writing impressively on US-China relations, referred to the tendency of many commentators to point to a specific period as providing a key for understanding the unsettling present moment. Many, he wrote, were "struggling for historical reference points," as though a perfect precursor year was out there to be found. This, he argued, was misguided. 2020 is a year of novel and overlapping crises. Pointing to a year defined by a pandemic, a war, or an economic crisis will not do.

As compelling as I find his essay, I view the situation differently. I remain convinced that looking for parallels for present developments in the past can always be of value, as long as we engage in the exercise in a certain fashion that I have described elsewhere as an "imperfect analogies" approach.[2] We need to be clear from the start that history never repeats itself exactly. We must take it for granted that there will be important divergences between the present and whatever point in the past we go back to, no matter how well the match between two moments seems at first. We have to keep those differences in mind. The goal should not be to find a perfect fit—as that is sure to be a chimerical endeavor—but to figure out if there are moments or periods that are particularly suggestive and illuminating to place side by side. The hope is that doing this will help us see things in the present that we might otherwise have missed or that we will see some facet of today's situation in a new way.

What then of my second question—how far back into the past should we look to make sense of a troubled year that seems to have lasted an incredibly long time? My answer, as suggested by opening with lines from Tagore's "Sunset of the Century," is that 1900 is a good place to turn. That century-closing year interests me for two reasons. First, it was a year of overlapping crises. Second, it fell roughly midway through a volatile period, lasting two or three decades, during which the world seemed suddenly to grow smaller. That era shares intriguing features with our current one. I will get to those below, but it is also worth noting that there are some specific echoes of 1900 in the air in 2020. For many weeks, the Internet has been filled with digital equivalents of what Tagore referred to as the "howling verses of vengeance," and we have gotten many reminders of the way virulent forms of nationalism, what the poet referred to as "self-love of Nations," can remain powerful, even in an era that seems to call for broad thinking that rises above parochial concerns.

The cusp between the nineteenth and twentieth centuries is not a period that people in most parts of the world have been mentioning lately. Reflecting this, Tooze does not include 1900 in his list of years that have been suggested as a good match for 2020. The American press as well as publications in other parts of the world have been filled, above all, with commentaries that look back to the late 1910s, the time of a deadly, fast-spreading disease often likened to COVID-19. Since Tooze wrote, as protests against racism have broken out in many locales, 1968 has been added to the list of possible precursors to 2020.[3] There is one place, though, where people have been going back exactly 120 years from 2020 when considering precedents for current events: China, the main country I teach and write about.

Sixty-year cycles, and, by extension, 120-year ones, figure prominently in traditional Chinese numerology. This is because it takes six decades for each animal of the zodiac to be paired in turn with each of the five natural elements. These cycles, and a sense of each year being tied to both an animal and an element, continue to be important in China. This is true even as people in China pay attention to decades and centuries—just as many there now mark two new year moments: January 1, signaling the start of a solar year (in this case, 2020), and a different date a few weeks later marking the start of a lunar year (a Metal Rat Year in this case). It is as natural in China to ponder sixty- and 120-year anniversaries as it is in other settings to consider centenaries and bicentenaries, so 1840, 1900, and 1960 readily come to mind as possible precursors for 2020. There has been some fascination online in China with how often Metal Rat Years (*Gengzi Nian* in Chinese) have been troubled ones (1840 fell during the Opium War, 1900 during the Boxer Crisis, 1960 during the Great Leap Forward Famine).

It is already clear that whatever happens during the rest of 2020, this Metal Rat Year will go down as one when China was hit by domestic problems (a health crisis and an economic one) and its government faced international challenges. Similarly, 1900 could be described that way. It also marked, as 2020 may mark, an inflection point in the history of both Chinese internal affairs and the country's place in the world, due above all in that earlier case to the Boxer Crisis, a complex series of events that reached its apogee during the Metal Rat Year of 1900.

The Boxer Crisis—a term derived from the pugilistic nickname Westerners gave to anti-Christian millenarian militants who sometimes called themselves the *Yihequan* (Fists of Righteous Harmony)—began with religious sectarians launching murderous raids on Chinese Catholic and Protestant villages.[4] The members of the group, who blamed a devastating drought on local gods withholding rain to show displeasure over the polluting presence of Christians on sacred soil, expanded to killing foreign missionaries and sometimes the children of those missionaries as well. In the middle months of 1900, the crisis took on global dimensions when the

Figure 1: A newspaper from "Le Petit Parisien." The Chinese
Boxers destroy a railroad during the Boxer Rebellion.
Source: Wikimedia Commons.

group, backed by soldiers of the Qing dynasty (1644–1912), laid siege to Tianjin
and Beijing, imperiling the lives of foreigners in each case, including, in the latter
instance, diplomats from more than ten countries. The sieges were lifted by an
international military force known in Chinese as the *Baguo lianjun* (Eight Powers
Allied Army) and sometimes called simply "the Allies" in the Western press,
the first time that shorthand was widely used. The soldiers from eight different
nations and empires in that fighting force took Tianjin in July and in mid-August

Figure 2: Boxer Rebellion, 1900. American, British, and Japanese armies storming Pekin Castle, China, August 14, 1900. Artwork by Torajiro Kasai. Courtesy of the Library of Congress. (5/22/2015). Source: Wikimedia Commons.

took Beijing, driving the Qing rulers out of their palaces and into exile in the far western city of Xian.

The Allies then proceeded to carry out reprisals across North China, which were ostensibly to rid the countryside of all remaining Boxers but took the lives of thousands of villagers with no ties to the group. These continued until the crisis ended with a 1901 treaty that allowed the Qing rulers to return to their palaces. In order to gain permission to return to Beijing, the Qing had to make it clear that they realized they had erred in backing the Boxers and agreed to pay an enormous indemnity to make up for all foreign losses.

In China, why is the Boxer Crisis that peaked during one Metal Rat Year worth thinking about in this Metal Rat Year of tragedy and trauma? Radically different answers to this question have been given online, where most of the toggling between 1900 and 2020 has been done. For some, it is because of parallels between the autocratic nature of the Qing dynasty then and the Chinese Communist Party now. This is viewed as having made a bad situation worse in 1900 (when China's rulers made the mistake of backing the Boxers as a sort of renegade loyalist militia to push back against foreigners who had been defeating the dynasty's forces on the battlefields for decades and taking parts of the empire as victor's prizes) and doing the same thing in 2020 (when China's rulers initially suppressed information about a new disease, setting COVID-19 on its way from being a regional to a national and then a global problem).[5] A very different sort of nod back to the time of the Boxers is made by some backers of Xi Jinping. In this case, the parallel lies in the fact that many different countries have mishandled the pandemic, yet some foreigners are talking of requiring the Chinese government to pay an indemnity to make up for losses suffered by other lands—as if the only mistakes have been made in China.

This talk of reparations is seen as uncomfortably comparable to what happened in 1901. The Qing had to pay an indemnity to foreigners, but no comparable penalty was levied on the nations and empires responsible for looting Beijing's palaces and leveling North China's villages.[6] References to foreign powers behaving in 2020 like the *Baguo lianjun* of 1900 have also appeared in some commentaries as Western governments have pushed back against the Chinese Communist Party on issues such as Xinjiang and Hong Kong this year.[7]

My own sense is that there are other reasons to pair 1900 and 2020. Let me explain. When I began sheltering in place this spring, I buried myself in sources related to the Boxer Crisis. As I read letters written by captives of the Beijing siege, I sometimes felt an eerie sense of familiarity. For instance, Sarah Conger, the wife of the chief American envoy to the Qing court, referred to the summer of 1900 as a period of "anxious waiting," as much of 2020 has been for many people. She also wondered if her family had enough of some kinds of food stored away to last them, and she wrote of being unsure how long it would be until she could move about freely again.[8]

I had a similar sense when I read certain news reports. One feature of the 1900 coverage of events in China that particularly interested me as I had 2020 news on my mind was the way that commentators in different settings often used different historical analogies to make sense of specific episodes in the Boxer Crisis. Another was how often these commentators drew connections between the violent events taking place in China and violent actions associated with other conflicts underway in 1900 in other parts of the world—with their choice of where to look across the globe, like their choice of where to look in the past, shaped by their location. This interest in looking back in time and to other parts of the world in locally specific ways to make sense of an event that was affecting people with ties to many different countries feels different when I consider it now than when I considered it before, since in 2020 we find COVID-19 affecting every part of the planet, but discussions of it veer off in varied directions due partly to location. I have already given a hint of what I mean by this in noting that 1900 comes up as a reference point in China but not in Tooze's essay, presumably because he was immersed in news sources in the United States and parts of Europe. I will give further examples below.

I should stress, though, that I do not think that 2020 and 1900 are even close to being completely comparable years. One event that made headlines in America in 1900 was a disease, a variety of plague, that originated in Asia and began causing deaths in the United States early in that century-closing year, but that was a relatively minor news story. The main reason that 1900 was, like 2020, a year of overlapping crises was not because of a combination of an international public health crisis and an international economic crisis, but rather due to three wars with international dimensions. In addition to the Boxer Crisis, fighting raged in the Philippines (between US forces trying to subjugate the former Spanish colony and local ones pushing back against this effort) and in South Africa (between the forces of the British Empire and Boer farmers who wanted an independent state). These 1900 conflicts were not as close to being truly global as was the one in China, but they each had robustly international dimensions. Soldiers from many parts of the British Empire, and other places as well, fought in the Transvaal. The conflict in the Philippines, formerly a colony of Spain, was in some senses a continuation of the Spanish-American War that had begun in the 1890s in the Caribbean, bringing celebrity to Theodore Roosevelt for his charge up San Juan Hill. In general, when it comes to details, the contrasts between 1900 and 2020 are much more striking than the parallels, but there are broad echoes across time that come through in many texts. These cast intriguing light on a major contemporary phenomenon: globalization. And its limits.

In 1900, as in 2020, the world felt to many as though it had recently become much more tightly interconnected, yet in neither case did this mean that localized cultural differences ceased to be important. To put it bluntly, in 1900, the world did not become "flat," to borrow Thomas Friedman's famous term, and it still is not flat now.[9] Even the most global crises of the early twentieth century were often viewed through local lenses using local referents, and this is the case now, too. Local meanings and modes of understanding persist. In both 1900 and 2020, news stories took on richly varied meanings as information (and misinformation) got fed into dramatically different narratives. This is relevant to this volume, as it underscores the enduring value of regional studies broadly defined. The world is often imagined to be growing ever flatter, but 2020 has convinced me yet again that the world remains stubbornly bumpy.

To illustrate what I mean, consider the interconnections, real and imagined, between 1900's three major wars. All of them affected people in more than one place and all sparked debates about, and were shaped by, what we now call "globalization," a word not coined until well into the Cold War era. In *The Birth of the Modern World*, a magisterial work by a leading specialist in South Asian and British imperial history writing on a planetary scale, Christopher Bayly aptly described the late 1800s and early 1900s as witnessing a "great acceleration" in globalizing trends, as well as a dramatic increase in the flow of information across borders. This gave people in widely scattered settings a novel sense of following the same news stories that their counterparts in distant places were following at roughly the same time. Yet, in 1900, people in different places reached to varied parts of the past to make sense of the wars underway and had varied understandings of how the wars related to one another. In part because of this, any notion of a completely shared experience of following global events was illusory.

For example, across the British Empire, commentators continually likened the sieges of Tianjin and Beijing to the sieges that had trapped Britons in the Indian cities of Lucknow and Cawnpore in 1857. In the same newspapers that carried these commentaries, the Boxers were sometimes treated as posing a similar threat to civilized ways as the Boers, with both of the groups being portrayed as using "barbaric," as opposed to "civilized," fighting techniques. The connection between all of these events were emphasized in different ways, including via discussions of literature (new books on 1857 appearing in 1900 were hailed as timely, Britons trapped in Beijing read histories of, and an Alfred Lord Tennyson poem about, Lucknow) and individuals (much was made in English periodicals of soldiers and armaments used in the Transvaal coming to China in 1900). There were even connections made in theatrical works, with Belle Vue Gardens in Manchester, which was known for mounting spectacles linked to current affairs, shifting from putting on one inspired by the lifting of the siege of Ladysmith, a key battle in the Boer War, to putting on one inspired by the lifting of the siege of Beijing, presenting them as though they were chapters in the same basic story.

However, in at least one part of the British Empire, Bengal, the way history came into play was different. The leading foreign-owned English-language newspaper there, the *Times of India*, was filled with articles that likened the Boxers to the Boers and brought up parallels between the 1857 and 1900 sieges. But the vernacular press and a locally run English-language newspaper, *The Bengalee*, brought up a different analogy. The Allied Army's invasion of the Qing Empire, some contributors to these publications claimed, was an action that was similar to events that took place as the last "Hindu kings" lost their kingdoms in the 1700s. The Qing Empire was about to find out, these commentators predicted, what it was like to come under colonial rule.

In the United States, no commentators I know of referred to the "Hindu kings," and while some brought up 1857 parallels, more deployed historical analogies closer to home. One popular approach was to liken Boxer actions to those of Native Americans, such as those by the participants in the 1890 Ghost Dance Rising. This is easy to understand, as the Sioux millenarian militants who took part in that event, like the Boxers a decade later, believed that they could make themselves invulnerable to bullets and call down spirit soldiers to fight beside them against better-armed opponents. While most of those who compared the Boxers to the Sioux in the US context were Americans, including Theodore Roosevelt in speeches given while campaigning for the vice presidency in 1900, not all were. Wu Tingfang, the leading Qing diplomat in America, told US reporters that they should think of the Boxers as Chinese counterparts to those who joined the Ghost Dance Rising. This was a departure from the main historical analogies in play in the Chinese press in the Qing Empire at the time, in which, not surprisingly, the Boxers tended to be compared to militants in China's own past.[10]

When it comes to connections to other contemporaneous conflicts, the American press was less likely to bring up South Africa than to bring up the Philippines. Roosevelt's speeches sometimes included references to the Sioux, the Boxers, and the Tagalog insurgents battling American troops in Southeast Asia as all being similar actors—and, to his way of thinking, all "savage" ones to be dealt with severely. There were other connections to the Philippines as well, as some troops in the Allied Army came to China from Manila, while the head of the US contingent in Beijing, Adna Chaffee, fought Native Americans on the frontier early in his career and came to the Qing Empire from Cuba, where he had seen action in the Spanish-American War. In other words, many observers believed what was happening in the Boxer Crisis had a parallel in the past and a connection to events elsewhere, but they looked back to different years and to different parts of the world depending on their own location.

A single curious event brings much of this into perspective: a 1901 production of the Wild West Show that featured a reenactment of a Boxer Crisis battle. This enormously popular performing troupe was headed by William Cody (aka "Buffalo Bill"), who served beside and became friends with Adna Chaffee when both were cavalrymen in the mid-to-late 1800s. In mid-1900, a journalist interviewed Cody about Chaffee being chosen to head the US contingent in the Allied Army. Buffalo Bill explained that the Chinese would find his friend a formidable adversary, as Chaffee was used to fighting cunning foes, suggesting that the Boxers and Native Americans were similar opponents and also a bit like those his friend fought during the Spanish-American War. The connection was clearer in the battle reenactment. Two of the troupe's most famous previous reenactments had depicted scenes from the 1890 Ghost Dance Rising and from the 1898 charge up San Juan Hill. In each of those, Native American cast members played the enemies that Cody and other white men on horses vanquished. In the spring of 1901, these Native American cast members donned Chinese-style clothing and died on stage not as Sioux or Spaniards, but as Boxers.[11]

One thing to note about the use of historical analogies and comparisons is that there is never consensus, even within a single setting. Consider two examples involving the same famous figure, Mark Twain. Late in 1900, he wrote a scathing "salutation" from the nineteenth century to the twentieth in which he referred to British actions in South Africa against the Boers, American actions in the Philippines, and international actions by the Allied Army in the Qing Empire as all belonging to the same category of immoral activity: brutal "pirate raids" that were dressed up to seem like efforts to protect civilization. In the spring of 1901, he went to see the debut of the Wild West Show's latest incarnation, which ended with the battle reenactment set in China. Twain attended as a guest of Cody, whose show's recreation of life on the frontier he once praised as wonderfully accurate. He left before the climactic battle scene, however, as he knew that he would dislike it, since it would treat the Boxers as villains. The famous author did not want to be in a crowd cheering the defeat of the militant Chinese, for he was one of the rare Westerners who thought that they were "traduced patriots," having once famously said that had he been Chinese, he might have been a Boxer.[12]

One final feature of these diverging analogies is worth noting. In 1900, many people took it for granted that the connections they were making were obvious and self-evident. In the US press, some did not make a case for seeing the Boxers as similar to Native Americans but simply put forward the comparison, just as some cartoonists paired disparaging images of anti-Christian Chinese militants and Tagalog insurgents without explaining the pairing. The British press similarly assumed that readers would find connecting the 1857 and 1900 sieges natural.

I see a similar way of thinking—parochial associations being presented as universal ones—in some commentaries on 2020. This is true of connections between current crises and moves between past and present, via fact and even via fiction. This spring, some commentators referred to people *everywhere* having the 1918–1919 pandemic on their minds, there were articles about the popularity of Camus's *The Plague* around the world, and an article appeared in *Vogue* in May that began as follows: "All of a sudden, *everyone* [emphasis added] seems to be reading Giovanni Boccaccio's *The Decamaron*, a novel published more than 600 years ago" about Italy during a plague.[13] References to 2020 being defined by "two viruses," the new one of COVID-19 and the old one of anti-Black racism, started out as an idea that needed explanation in the American press and then became a standard form of expression used without a gloss. What interests me about this is that in following the news from East Asia as well as the United States, there was a disconnect. In East Asia-based publications, while the 1918–1919 pandemic was certainly mentioned at times, the more recent experience with SARS was more often mentioned. *The Plague* enjoyed a surge of popularity in Japan, but I have seen no evidence that it is being read widely in China, nor that any part of Asia was one where "everyone" was reading stories set in Florence centuries ago. What came to mind for some in Japan (especially those with a particular tie to the locale in question) was how the government response to the pandemic seemed similar to the response to the Fukushima disaster (some referred to a sense of "Fukushima déjà vu"); some people in China saw corollaries between the early efforts to cover up the new disease with Soviet government action in the time of Chernobyl, which led to an increased interest in the 2019 television show about that catastrophe.[14] There have also been multiple ways that the actual virus, so important in 2020, has been likened to metaphoric ones. To cite just one example, when the Chinese official press has referred to there being "two viruses" circulating in 2020, they have sometimes claimed that the second was not anti-Black racism triggering protests, but Hong Kong activism destabilizing society.[15]

***

Just as there are parallels between specific years, so too are there similarities between general eras. The last fifty years or so is another period that can be described as witnessing the sort of "great acceleration" in globalization that Bayly had in mind. Recent increases in long-distance air travel, and the creation and then expansion of the Internet, have had the same sort of exhilarating world-shaking and world-shrinking impact that the rise of steamships, trains, and telegraphy had more than a century ago. The wars of 1900 were not the first events of that earlier period of acceleration to make people concerned about the costs and benefits of the world growing smaller, but they did shine a spotlight on the troubling features of globalization *avant la lettre*. Similarly, the pandemic has made especially obvious the downsides of our own recent moves toward interconnectedness. And in 2020, as in 1900, we have had crises that not only remind us that this period of globalization, like that earlier one, has disturbing features. It also reminds us that when crises take place in such periods, they are often interconnected in complicated ways, as the pandemic and protests of this year have been, and that no matter how much it seems that "everyone" is following the same stories, they end up viewing them through such locally specific lenses that this is an illusion—it was an illusion in the days of the telegraph and is still in this age of the Internet.

Having begun with the best work I have read lately that argues against using historical analogies when considering 2020, I will end with the best work I have read lately about COVID-19 that makes the opposite case. This is an April *Boston Review* essay by Alex de Waal specifically about pandemics: "New Pathogens, Old Politics."[16] While it is tempting with each new pandemic to "scour history books for parallels and lessons," he begins, the "wisdom to be gained" from this often turns out to have been "greatly exaggerated." He goes on, though, to pull a quote from a Barbara Tuchman book that refers to certain "ways of behavior" and "reactions against fate" in varied eras as being able to "throw mutual light upon each other." De Waal continues in his own voice, saying he feels that with the current pandemic, "although the pathogen may be new, the logic of social response is not, and it is here that we can see historical continuities" worthy of attention.

The implication of de Waal's essay is that there is a value in looking backward that is not tied to finding a single perfect precedent. The goal is rather to find one or more past times that are useful partial fits, which can be used on their own or in tandem to alert us to aspects of a current situation we might otherwise miss or that can simply bring a phenomenon into sharper focus. I would argue that applying this argument about pandemic years to those of global crises in general, we find that one recurring "logic of social response" that is definitely *not* new, and hence works against viewing 2020 as thoroughly novel, is precisely the tendency of people faced with unusual circumstances to look to the past for precedents—and to seize on different points in history and different sorts of connections between contemporaneous phenomena to make sense of a confusing world.

Notes

[1] Adam Tooze, "We've Never Been Here Before," *The Washington Post*, March 25, 2020.

[2] Jeffrey Wasserstrom, *Eight Juxtapositions: China through Imperfect Analogies from Mark Twain to Manchukuo* (Sydney: Penguin Specials, 2016).

[3] A July 16 Google search for "1918" and "Déjà Vu" brought up literally dozens of news stories with titles such as "Flu Déjà Vu: UM Closed for Seven Weeks—in 1918" (*UM Today*, a University of Manitoba publication, April 9, 2020, https://news.umanitoba.ca/flu-deja-vu-um-closed-for-seven-weeks-in-1918/) to "What Coverage of the Spanish Flu Pandemic Can Tell Us about Coronavirus" (*Variety*, April 1, 2020) to "The Déjà Vu Virus?" (*Project Syndicate*, May 4, 2020). Searching on the same day for "1968" and "2020" brought up many hits as well, including these three up top: "1968 and 2020: Lessons from America's Worst Year" (*The Atlantic*, May 31, 2020); "2020 is Not 1968: To Understand Today's Protests You Need to Look Further Back" (*National Geographic*, June 11, 2020); and "Why 2020 Isn't Quite 1968" (June 18, 2020—the transcript to an episode of the NPR podcast *Throughline*). One sign of the prevalence of the 1968 analogy is that essays were written specifically to criticize it, and the same thing has happened with the 1918 analogy, as in "The Coronavirus Is No 1918 Pandemic" (*The Atlantic*, March 3, 2020). Note: all URLS listed were last checked on August 15, 2020.

[4] I avoid using the term "Boxer Rebellion," even though it is the standard one now in the West, as the eponymous, martial-arts-loving militants involved expressed support for the Qing dynasty and for a time were backed by that ruling family, which makes it hard to see them as "rebels," a word that tends to describe in the Chinese context those seeking to topple those in power.

[5] See, for example, the collection of materials Geremie R. Barmé introduces and translates under the heading "1900 and 2020—An Old Anxiety in a New Era," in *China Heritage*, April 28, 2020, http://chinaheritage.net/journal/1900-2020-an-old-anxiety-in-a-new-era/.

[6] Grady McGregor, "Trump's Demand that China Pay Coronavirus Reparations Evokes an Ugly History," *Fortune*, May 7, 2020; see also, Ye Jiajia, "Coronavirus and the Boxer War of 1900: Do They Have Something in Common?" *Bitter Winter*, August 14, 2020,

https://bitterwinter.org/coronavirus-and-the-boxer-war-of-1900-do-they-have-something-in-common/.

[7] See, for example, Liu Xin and Wan Lin, "Chinese Netizens, Observers Deride 'Eight Nation Alliance' against China as a Farce," *Global Times*, June 6, 2020. A related reference to 1900 as a time when foreign powers ganged up on the country unfairly appears in an online article describing allegedly misguided foreign suspicion of early moves in China to develop a vaccine for COVID-19: posted on Baidu's Baijiahao platform by Zai Niyan Mouli (pseudonym meaning "In Your Eyes"), "*Zhōngfāng yìmiáo yánfā qǔdé jùdà jìnzhǎn! Xīnbǎn "bāguó liánjūn" yòu láile*" ("China has made great progress in vaccine research and development! But here comes a New Eight Powers Alliance"), July 24, 2020, https://baijiahao.baidu.com/s?id=1673083373636785944&wfr=spider&for=pc.

[8] Sarah Conger, *Letters from China* (McClurg and Co., 1909), see especially one dated July 7, 1900.

[9] Thomas Friedman, *The World is Flat* (New York: Farrar, Straus and Giroux, 2005). For critiques of his argument, see, among other works, my "China & Globalization," *Daedalus*, vol. 143, no. 2 (2014), 157–169.

[10] Documentation on the points above about the Bengali press and the American context will be forthcoming in the book I am writing for Oxford University Press, the working title for which is *The Ghosts of 1900: Stories of China in the Year of the Boxers*; on the importance and prevalence of the analogy between 1857 and 1900 and connections between the Boer War and the Boxer Crisis in the minds of Britons in Asia and Britain, see Robert Bickers and R. G. Tiedemann, editors, *China, the Boxers and the World* (Lanham, MD: Rowman and Littlefield, 2007), and Ross Forman, *China and the Victorian Imagination* (Cambridge: Cambridge University Press, 2013). I have begun to publish short pieces related to the book in progress that supplement the discussion here; see, for example, "'Never Was History So Interesting'—Reading, Writing, and Confinement in 1900," *The American Scholar* online, July 25, 2020, https://theamericanscholar.org/never-was-history-so-interesting/#.XzgWtJNKhok.

[11] Documentation on specific points made here will be provided in *The Ghosts of 1900*, in which I draw on, in addition to newspapers from the time, the excellent general account of the 1901 Wild West Show dramatization of events in the Qing Empire provided in John R. Haddad, "The Wild West Turns East: Audience, Ritual, and Regeneration in Buffalo Bill's Boxer Uprising." *American Studies* 49.3/4 (2008): 5–38.

[12] Twain's reaction to the show is discussed by Haddad in "The Wild West Turns East"; for more details on Twain's view of and references to the Boxer Crisis, see Selina Lai-Henderson, "Mark Twain, The Chinese Boxer," *Stanford University Press Blog*, May 7, 2015, https://stanfordpress.typepad.com/blog/2015/05/mark-twain-the-chinese-boxer.html.

[13] Trish Hall, "Six Centuries Later, The Decameron Is Suddenly the Book of the Moment," *Vogue*, May 5, 2020.

[14] An important resource for Asian responses to COVID-19, including the way that it has been discussed in different settings, is a two-part special feature of the *Asia-Pacific Journal: Japan Focus*, both parts edited by Jeff Kingston: "Pandemic Asia, Part 1," volume

18, no. 14, July 15, 2020, https://apjjf.org/2020/14, and "Pandemic Asia, Part 2," volume 18, no. 15, August 1, 2020, https://apjjf.org/2020/15. Fukushima is mentioned in multiple contributions on Japan; and Chernobyl comparisons are mentioned in Anonymous, "Social Media and China's Virus Outbreak," Part 1, no. 6, https://apjjf.org/2020/14/Anonymous.html. On Fukushima, see also Azby Brown and Sean Bonner, "What the Fukushima Meltdowns Taught Us about How to Respond to Coronavirus," *Bulletin of the Atomic Scientists*, March 13, 2020, which refers to a sense of déjà vu, and that term for connecting the two crises shows up as well in, for example, Hideo Furukawa's "*Ubawareta mono, koeru beki kyōkai*," translated by David Boyd, "What We Lost: COVID-19 Beyond the Numbers," in the May 20, 2020 issue of *Words Without Borders*, https://www.wordswithoutborders.org/article/coronavirus-voices-from-the-pandemic-what-we-lost-furukawa-boyd. On the initial importance and then declining role of the Chernobyl parallel in China (and discussion of the television show's popularity), see Jane Li, "Chinese People Are Using 'Chernobyl' to Channel Their Anger about the Coronavirus Outbreak," *Quartz*, January 27, 2020, and also Olivia Humphrey, "Is Coronavirus China's Chernobyl?" *China Channel* (of the *Los Angeles Review of Books*), March 24, 2020, https://chinachannel.org/2020/03/24/corona-chernobyl/.

[15] Compare, for example, Lisette Voytko, "America's 'Two Deadly Viruses'—Racism and COVID-19—Go Viral Among Outraged Twitter Users," *Forbes*, May 31, 2020, https://www.forbes.com/sites/lisettevoytko/2020/05/31/americas-two-deadly-virusesracism-and-covid-19-go-viral-among-outraged-twitter-users/#911354f5ae3a; see also Helen Davidson, "China Calls Hong Kong Protesters a Political Virus," *The Guardian*, May 6, 2020, https://www.theguardian.com/world/2020/may/06/china-calls-hong-kong-protesters-a-political-virus.

[16] Alex de Waal, "New Pathogens, Old Politics," *Boston Review*, April 3, 2020, http://bostonreview.net/science-nature/alex-de-waal-new-pathogen-old-politics.

2

Sikhi, Seva, and Sarbat da Bhala in a Pandemic

Tejpaul Singh Bainiwal

*I don't know all the principles of their faith, but I know the principles
that they exercise. It's love. It's service. It's selflessness. It's sharing,
sharing and caring. They are just amazing people. They set an
example for a lot of other faiths.*

— San Antonio Food Bank CEO and president Eric Cooper[1]

By April 2020, the COVID-19 pandemic managed to instill fear within people
around the world. As lockdowns were enforced and the virus limited people's
ability to leave the confines of their residence, Sikhs in different countries looked
to their religious doctrines and saw an opportunity to serve their communities.
Through their response to the COVID-19 pandemic, Sikhs find themselves in a
familiar position. Sikhs practice the concepts of *seva* ("selfless service") and *sarbat
da bhala* ("the welfare of all") on a daily basis, and these values are deeply rooted
in the foundation of Sikhi.[2] These two concepts have allowed Sikhs to have a global
impact with regard to the economy and society during the abrupt breakout of
the coronavirus, which caused chaos and panic throughout the world. Through
the practices of their religious beliefs, Sikhs are not only serving many different
communities, but simultaneously teaching the world about Sikhi. By looking at
key concepts of Sikhi, this paper will explore how Sikhs' service during this global
pandemic serves as an educational tool to understand Sikhs and Sikhi across a

wide range of academic disciplines, including but not limited to religion, history, and world civilizations.

Sikhi, Seva, and Sarbat da Bhala

Seva is one of the key tenets of the Sikh faith. The tradition of seva has been practiced by Sikhs for over 500 years, beginning with Guru Nanak, the religion's founder. Sikh historian J. S. Grewal points out that "new religious ideology was needed to become the basis of new social order" as Guru Nanak "denounced contemporary politics, society, and religion."[3] The unjust rule of Afghan rulers prompted Guru Nanak to encourage people to "turn to God, the true king, the king of kings [as] his service alone is true service."[4] However, being of service to God is not simply interior devotion or singing recitations, but it also consists of selfless service to others (seva), which comes in many forms. Guru Nanak exemplified this by defying the Afghan rule and standing side by side with the lowest members of society, bringing forth societal issues and directly challenging the caste system, which has suppressed millions in South Asia for centuries. Grewal notes that Guru Nanak preached "one should cultivate true humility and be of service to others."[5] Guru Nanak's emphasis on service frequently intersects with the concept of sarbat da bhala, which translates to "the welfare of all." Guru Nanak's successor, Guru Angad, institutionalized a parallel practice in the form of *langar*, or a community kitchen. The main purpose of langar is to ensure that no one would be hungry regardless of caste, gender, religion, economic status, or ethnicity. Langar, in its own right, was a revolutionary act against social hierarchies and the caste system.

According to prominent Sikh scholar Kahn Singh Nabha, one of the key elements of a gurdwara (Sikh house of worship) is that it serves as a "storehouse of food for the hungry;" therefore, langar can now be found at every gurdwara across the world.[6] Gurdwaras can be a great resource for the entire community, whether Sikh or not. For example, following the establishment of Stockton Gurdwara in 1912, the Sikh community wanted to ensure that South Asians would not become "charges on public charity." Stockton was the first gurdwara in the United States and served the needs of South Asian immigrants but also fellow Americans when need be. The gurdwara leadership stated that "if a man is hungry and out of funds, we feed him. Our dining room is open at all hours of the day and is closed only for a few hours during the night. The unfortunate hungry American will be as welcome as our own people."[7] The combination of seva, sarbat da bhala, and langar motivated Sikhs and Sikh organizations across the world to mobilize. These values to act selflessly and help others without any reward or selfish intentions are deeply rooted in their faith, with gurdwaras oftentimes being the institution used to highlight these practices.

Figure 1: Gurdwaras across Asia have become reliable sources of food for all—
regardless of caste, gender, religion, or economic status—and the
sole food resource for many. Source: Wikimedia Commons.

New Pandemic-Related Examples

Income inequality and access to health care highlighted the differences between individuals' caste, socioeconomic status, and ethnicity during the pandemic, as several communities were more susceptible to being affected by the virus than others. Looking beyond what makes us different, Sikhs stepped into lead roles where governments failed. They took the initiative to help as many people as possible who were affected by the drastic changes this pandemic brought to society. Although the lockdown in India—which was one of the world's most stringent—bans religious gatherings, gurdwaras across the country remained open to serve millions of people. Gurdwaras throughout the world have remained open through wars and plagues, and this pandemic would be no exception. Religious services at gurdwaras may have temporarily stopped, but this only elevated the importance of langar and the gurdwara as being more than a religious institution. Gurdwaras have become a major source of food for millions of people worldwide during this global pandemic. Although langar has always been a key aspect of the gurdwara, many people are beginning to learn the importance of seva and langar within the Sikh faith. Through Gurdwara Bhagod Sahib, which is along a remote highway in the Indian state of Maharashtra, Sikhs fed two million people within ten weeks. Baba Karnail Singh, the lead *sevadar* ("one who does seva"), states that his

Figure 2: At Gurdwara Bangla Sahib, Sikhs begin their work at 3:00 a.m. daily to ensure 35,000 meals are prepared by 9:00 a.m. for government officials to distribute. Source: Wikimedia Commons.

motivation comes from "the '*marzi*' ('will') of Waheguru (God). We are only his instruments in the service to humanity."[8] Langar has been provided for travelers along this remote highway for decades and continues to be the sole source of food for several hundred kilometers. Even in some of the country's busiest cities, Sikhs play a major role in providing services. The *Los Angeles Times* writes about India's capital: "Bangla Sahib is the largest of New Delhi's 10 gurdwaras, whose kitchens together form a vital part of the city's strategy to feed the poor during the pandemic."[9] Realizing their inability to provide for citizens, the government of New Delhi requested assistance from the Delhi Sikh Gurdwara Management Committee. Sikhs and gurdwaras in New Delhi began serving 40,000 meals per day, which has since increased to 100,000 meals for citizens living on the streets and for those who lost everything as a result of the COVID-19 pandemic.

From a remote highway to the busy streets of New Delhi, the practice of seva and langar for sarbat da bhala has now impacted the lives of millions globally during this pandemic as Sikhs in the diaspora have brought these practices with them. In the United Kingdom, the gurdwara in Slough "responded to the lockdown by reinventing itself as an emergency food operation, delivering thousands of meals a day."[10] Similar work by Sikhs is being done across North America, Europe, Asia, Australia, and Africa. Beyond just langar, certain Sikh communities are creating health kits to distribute to communities in need. Seva continues to take form in many different ways. Just as seva is a significant part of the Sikh way of life, *dasvandh* is equally as important. Dasvandh translates to "a tenth part" and is an act of donating 10 percent of one's livelihood, both financial and in the form of time and service such as seva, to a charitable cause. Not only have Sikhs aided millions of people who have been affected by the COVID-19 pandemic through langar; much of this has been funded by donations from the Sikh community. With gurdwaras in Delhi serving 100,000 meals daily, Sikhs across the globe pitched in to ensure the seva in India continues; however, Sikhs in the diaspora financially support local charitable causes as well to help non-Sikh and non-Asian neighbors. The Sikh Dharamsal of San Antonio raised approximately $250,000 in donations for its local food bank in addition to delivering hundreds of meals.[11]

Figure 3: As medical workers across the world have been extremely busy with handling the COVID-19 pandemic, Sikhs began providing meals to medical workers in an attempt to ease the burden for them during this pandemic. Photo by author.

These practices are nothing new for Sikhs, as they have served those in need throughout history. A prominent example of serving anyone in need came during a battle between the Mughal and Sikh armies in the seventeenth century, when a Sikh by the name of Bhai Kanhaiya gave water to and treated injured soldiers regardless of which army they belonged to. Over the years, Sikhs have continued to serve communities, especially during natural disasters. Many Sikh organizations are founded on the basis of making the world a better place—or sarbat da bhala. The importance of globalization at the turn of the century also resulted in the establishment of two of the most prominent Sikh humanitarian relief, nonprofit organizations, Khalsa Aid and United Sikhs. Both organizations provide humanitarian aid in areas affected by natural or manufactured disasters such as war, floods, and earthquakes. In fact, they have frequently been the first on the scene to help distribute food, water, clothing, and medical and sanitation supplies. Seva has no boundaries, as it continues to aid those in first-world countries as well. In 2017, Hurricane Harvey, a Category 4 hurricane, hit the states of Louisiana and Texas in the United States. The majority of the damage was done to the Houston metropolitan area, with a substantial portion of the city remaining underwater for days and uninhabitable for weeks or months. Sikhs from across the nation immediately took action, pitching in to aid those affected by the hurricane by donating thousands of items, volunteering their time, preparing meals, and delivering food.[12]

With governments across the world burdened by the pandemic for various reasons, the Sikh community provides services for several communities who are unable to access aid from governmental resources for different reasons. For certain communities, Sikhs are the only ones providing services. Through their seva, Sikhs have shown resilience and made a global economic, political, and social impact, with their faith serving as a guide during the COVID-19 pandemic. While many people are now learning about Sikhs through their pandemic seva, Sikhs are simply continuing a 500-year-old tradition started by Guru Nanak. Thus, teachers at all levels can use this unique coronavirus situation to introduce their students to the religious, social, political, and economic importance of both historic and contemporary Sikhi.

Notes

[1] Tom Orsborn, "San Antonio Food Bank Benefits from Sikh Philosophy of 'Selflessness,'" *San Antonio Express-News*, April 26, 2020, https://www.expressnews.com/news/local/article/San-Antonio-Food-Bank-benefits-from-Sikh-15227808.php.

[2] "Sikhi" is used rather than the common term "Sikhism," as the latter is a Western construct and members of the Sikh faith typically use the former. Edward Said notes that Europeans referred to Islam as "Mohammadism" because Mohammad was the founder of the religion; therefore, since the religion of Christ was called Christianity, the religion of

Mohammad should be called Mohammadism (*Orientalism* 60). Muslims were unfamiliar with the terminology; however, Europeans continued to use the Western-created term and impose it onto Muslims. With this in mind, Sikhi is used throughout the article.

[3] J. S. Grewal. *The Sikhs of the Punjab* (Cambridge: Cambridge University Press, 1990), 28.

[4] Grewal, *The Sikhs of the Punjab*, 29.

[5] J. S. Grewal. *Guru Nanak in History* (Chandigarh: Panjab University, 1969), 185.

[6] Kahn Singh Nabha. *Encyclopedia of Sikh Literature,* (India: National Bookshop, 2008), 428.

[7] *Stockton Record*, November 22, 1915.

[8] "81-year-old Sikh Man Feeds 2 Million on Remote Maharashtra Highway," *The Tribune*, May 31, 2020, https://www.tribuneindia.com/news/nation/81-year-old-sikh-man-feeds-2-million-on-remote-maharashtra-highway-92396.

[9] Emily Schmall, "Sikh Kitchens Feed New Delhi's Masses during Coronavirus Lockdown." *The Los Angeles Times*, May 23, 2020, https://www.latimes.com/world-nation/story/2020-05-21/sikh-kitchens-feed-new-delhis-masses-in-virus-lockdown.

[10] Jim Reed, "Coronavirus: The Sikh Community Kitchen Feeding Thousands." *BBC*, June 9, 2020, https://www.bbc.com/news/av/uk-52966810/coronavirus-the-sikh-community-kitchen-feeding-thousands.

[11] Tom Orsborn, "San Antonio Food Bank Benefits from Sikh Philosophy of 'Selflessness.'

[12] Upneet Kaur Aujla, "In the Face of Tragedy, This Is What Sikhs Do." *HuffPost*, September 5, 2017, https://www.huffpost.com/entry/in-the-face-of-tragedy-this-is-what-sikhs-do_b_59af194de4b0b5e53101cae7.

3

Understanding South Korea's Religious Landscape, Patient 31, and COVID-19 Exceptionalism

Minjung Noh

Following its first COVID-19 case on January 20, 2020, South Korea underwent a dramatic shift in its pandemic record. By mid-March, South Korea reported the largest number of confirmed cases—8,236 as of March 15—outside of China. The world watched the exponential increase of the country's patient numbers with anxiety while gauging the threat of the new virus. South Korea, however, succeeded in "flattening the curve" in April. Since then, the country has contained the spread of the virus more effectively than the United States, Italy, Spain, and many other places. As of July 10, 2020, South Korea only added approximately 5,000 confirmed cases over the course of four months while the number of cases in the United States increased from 3,510 (March 15) to 3,233,462 (July 10) in the same period.[1] Considering that the United States has a population approximately 6.4 times greater than that of South Korea, the difference is exceptionally disproportionate. Thus, radically different accounts of South Korea and COVID-19 began to circulate, referring to South Korea's success as "Korean Exceptionalism" in the containment of the pandemic.[2]

The dramatic record of South Korea, including the exponential spread of COVID-19 until March and then the successful control of the virus in the following months, has received a good deal of international attention. Why did the virus spread so rapidly in the beginning, and how did South Korea manage to

Figure 1: A car is parked to protest against shincheonji in Wonil-ro 115beon-gil, Wonju-si, Gangwon-do. Source: Wikimedia Commons.

quell the spread so quickly when other developed countries were still struggling? Within the narratives about South Korea and COVID-19, interestingly, at least two religions were highlighted. First, the Shincheonji Church of Jesus was blamed as a super-spreader during the initial phase of the virus; second, Korean Confucianism was suggested to be the reason for successful containment of the virus.[3]

This essay critically analyzes how national and international observers described and portrayed these two religious traditions of South Korea during the pandemic, while also discussing the implications this has for educators. Popular accounts of both Shincheonji and Confucianism involve perspectives that essentialize the differences between South Korean culture and Euro-American democratic modernity. Within South Korea, media outlets highlighted the irrationality of the Shincheonji "cult" that prioritized religious practice over secular governmental health policy. In doing so, they sought to reassure citizens that their country was a modern democratic nation. Outside Korea, observers frequently offered simplified versions of Confucian "Koreanness," which they claimed promoted conformity and, thus, authoritarian governmental control. Both accounts of South Korea's COVID-19 experience fail to provide a productive discourse on solutions to the global pandemic. Nevertheless, the way in which these religions are portrayed provides educators with an important teaching moment for Korean Studies specifically and Asian Studies generally. By problematizing and scrutinizing popular accounts of South Korea and COVID-19, educators can teach the importance of accurate knowledge and the historical contextualization of the Korean religious landscape. In addition, it is an important case study in which education in Asian Studies and religious literacy translate into student competency in media and information literacy.

Modernity Lagged Behind? Patient #31 of Shincheonji Church

In mid-March 2020, "#patient31" of South Korea trended on worldwide social media platforms, including Twitter. Users inside and outside of South Korea were astounded by the news that patient 31 and her Shincheonji Church of Jesus were responsible "for at least 60% [as of March 18th] of all [COVID-19] cases in South Korea."[4] Called a "super-spreader," patient 31 attended a Shincheonji church service in the city of Daegu with 460 congregants when she had symptoms of the virus. By late February, officials had identified 2,022 cases with ties to Shincheonji churches in the region.[5] Shincheonji church, founded in 1984, is a comparatively small new messianic religious group with origins in South Korean Protestant Christianity. Renowned for its aggressive recruiting methods, secretive membership, and "heretical" doctrines centered around its founder and "messiah," Man-hee Lee (b. 1931), the church has been criticized as a "cult" separate from the mainstream Protestant denominations in South Korea.[6] When the coronavirus cases spread from within the church, South Korean media were quick to condemn the church and its members as symbols of religious irrationality responsible for the rapid spread of the virus.

Based on the church's doctrine that the illness signifies sin, members of the church avoided testing and provided false information to contact tracing officers. In addition, due to strong social disapproval of the church, individuals hid their membership from nonmembers, resulting in more difficulties in contact tracing and testing. The social stigmatization of Shincheonji church members intensified even after the founder, Lee, sent out a message to his followers to cooperate with the health authorities to prevent COVID-19 from further spread. Instead, the media focused on Lee's comment that the virus was caused by "Satan . . . trying to sabotage the growth of the church."[7]

After the South Korean CDC identified Shincheonji church members as the main culprits spreading the virus, criticism of the church went beyond social stigmatization and began to include discussions of banning the Shincheonji church's services in the name of public safety. This in turn initiated a heated debate regarding whether the ban was a violation of the church members' religious freedom as stipulated in the South Korean Constitution. Individuals publicly condemned patient 31 and the church's unenlightened, "fanatical" nature, which threatened South Korea's modern national identity. Here, the mainstream religions of South Korea, including Protestant Christians, Catholics, and Buddhists, highlighted their own modern nature relative to Shincheonji. Unlike the "cult" of Shincheonji, other religions were seemingly well-adjusted to the secular modern national system, particularly in the time of COVID-19, and voluntarily canceled religious gatherings in line with governmental guidelines. Shincheonji quickly became a religion of lagged modernity in South Korea, which had to be revised and subsumed under the banner of modernity.

Despite the alleged dichotomy between Shincheonji and other religions, it is important to note that Shincheonji would not have existed without Protestant Christianity, particularly in the context of Pentecostalism and the evangelical prosperity gospel from the United States. The founder of Shincheonji, Man-hee Lee, was a member of Cheonbugyo (天父教), another Korean new religion founded by former Presbyterian preacher Tae-son Park (1917–1990). Park's Protestantism-derived messianic revivalism influenced the foundation of not only Shincheonji, but also the Unification Church (so-called "Moonies"), leading to the development of rich new religious movements in postwar South Korea. The appeal of these new religions, besides their unique doctrines of salvation based on the Bible, was the promise of spiritual and economic prosperity through religious faith.

The narrative of progress, or what anthropologist Nicholas Harkness calls the "aesthetics of progress" in Korean Protestant Christianity, is associated with a specific form of Western Protestant modernity and economic progress.[8] The backdrop of this Protestant notion of progress is inextricably entangled with the transnational history of South Korea as a peripheral proxy of US hegemony in the twentieth century.[9] Protestant Christianity in Korea was first established in the 1880s through the efforts of Presbyterian and Methodist missionaries from the United States whose theology was founded on conservative evangelicalism.[10] After World War II, the Japanese Occupation came to an end, and Korea was subjected to three years of US military rule (1945–1948). During this period, American missionaries and Korean American Protestants played pivotal roles in the formation of the modern South Korean nation.[11] Syngman Rhee, a Korean Methodist deacon who had lived in the United States for nearly three decades, returned to Korea and became the first president of the South Korean government in 1948. At that time, Christians—Protestant and Catholic combined—represented only 5 percent of the Korean population, but 24 percent of parliamentarians were Protestant Christians.[12]

Protestant Christians in South Korea, a powerful minority, obtained their leverage through their connections to the United States, which aided South Korea

Figure 2: A Notice announcing reduced operation of Seoul
Metro due to COVID-19, April 1, 2020.
Source: Wikimedia Commons.

both financially and politically. These connections helped South Korea become a participating member nation of the Organization for Economic Co-operation and Development (OECD) in 1996. Connections to US-based theological seminaries, Korean American churches, and an affinity for the English language became indispensable for Korean Protestants. As a result, contemporary South Korean Protestant churches have enjoyed unprecedented growth in their scale and sociopolitical influence, signaled by Yoido Full Gospel Church, one of the largest Protestant churches in the world, and its direct connection with Billy Graham (1918–2018).[13] In addition, many scholars of Korean religion boldly and justly argue that Korean/American Protestant Christianity is mostly evangelical.[14]

After considering the historical context of Korean evangelicalism and the Shincheonji church, it is difficult to argue for the clear distinction between "mainstream" evangelical Protestant Christianity and Shincheonji regarding their conformity to secular modernity. For example, on February 22 and 23, in front of Seoul City Hall, amidst the early COVID-19 outbreak, religiously inspired political rallies were held and respectively attended by approximately 5,000 protestors. They were led by Rev. Kwang-Hun Jun, an unwavering evangelical pastor who upholds an ultraconservative political ideology and theology. On February 23, Rev. Jun proclaimed before the crowd: "God will cure us from the virus. You should come out here more often." In the same vein, Shincheonji can also be juxtaposed with conservative evangelical Christians in the United States, who defy social distancing and quarantine guidelines for their religious gatherings.[15] After observing an Ohio evangelical woman's answer to a CNN reporter that she wasn't worried about COVID-19 infection because she is "covered in Jesus's blood," Robert Orsi, an American scholar of religion, called for the exigency of new ways of understanding different religious realities within the contemporary United States.[16] After all, overlooking Shincheonji, evangelical Christianity, and other religious worldviews to be a remnant of an unenlightened past or a "lagged modernity" would be unrealistic, given their durability and prominence in the modern world. Rather, acknowledging the existence of contending worldviews within global contemporary modernity and considering how to achieve dialogues and social consensus provides a much more productive starting point for seeking solutions in a time of pandemic.

Stereotyping Korean Culture through Confucianism

While media outlets blamed Shincheonji for spreading the virus, international observers often turned to Confucianism to explain South Korea's success in controlling COVID-19. As of July 12, 2020, South Korea had 289 cases per million residents, while the United States reported 9,986, the United Kingdom 4,359, France 2,546, and Germany 2,403. International media broadcasted South Korea's comparative success in containing the virus with awe, even calling it "South Korea's COVID-19 Exceptionalism."[17] Byung-Chul Han, a South Korean-born philosopher based in Berlin, claimed Confucianism was the basis of this exceptionalism. Han stated that "Asian states like Japan, Korea, China, Hong Kong, Taiwan or Singapore that have an authoritarian mentality which comes from their cultural tradition [of] Confucianism"[18] are prone to obey the control of the government in a health emergency. In addition, Guy Sorman, a French philosopher of repute, in an interview praising the success of South Korea, mentioned that "[South Korean] Confucian culture also contributed to the selective confinement [of the virus]: they trust intellectuals and experts, the orders are respected, and the individual comes after the community."[19] Sorman also indicated that using mobile phone location data for contact tracing was accepted by South Koreans since "they live in a very surveilled society."[20]

Both arguments by Han and Sorman hinge on the contrast between Korean Confucian (and other East Asian) collectivism and Anglo-European individualism. These analyses are simplistic in that there is no consideration of historical context and the differences between the Confucianism in South Korea and other East Asian countries, and they also presume an inherent difference between East Asian and European cultures.

First, it is true that premodern East Asia was under the dominant cultural influence of Confucianism by way of the imperial Chinese tributary system. Nevertheless, distinctive developments of Confucian thought took place in Korea, Japan, and Vietnam, and this should be taken into account in order to assess Confucian cultural influence in each society. Particularly in the case of Korea, the influence and development of neo-Confucianism propelled the political ideology of the Chosun dynasty (1392–1897), which led social reforms and transformations unique from other East Asian countries. According to Martina Deuchler, one of the decisive characteristics of Korean Confucianism was the reshaping of family norms based on patriarchal hierarchy, which is still prominent in South Korean culture.[21] How can "Confucian collectivism" arguments accommodate the particular historical context of Korean Confucianism? How would the arguments explain the difference in the containment of COVID-19 between South Korea, Singapore, Taiwan, and Japan if they are all susceptible to a "Confucian mentality"? It seems that attributing the success of East Asian countries to a general "Confucian mindset" is a recurring pattern in Western popular—and some academic—debates, as when Anglo-European media appropriated the narrative of "tiger economies" to explain the growth of these countries in the late twentieth century.

Second, the assumption that Korean Confucian culture prioritizes the community over the individual and easily conforms to authority is not only unsubstantiated, but also implies that Koreans do not value individual freedom relative to their Western counterparts, thus perpetuating stereotypes regarding East Asian culture and essentializing the difference between East and West. In this sense, Confucianism symbolizes the irreducible and fundamental differences between cultures. By highlighting the unique "mentality" of the country based on existing stereotypes, Han and Sorman reproduce the Orientalist fantasy of otherness: positing the East as qualitatively different from its observers, i.e., the West. South Korean success, in this context, is an anomaly realized by the odd mentality of Confucianism, which cannot possibly be replicated or learned by others, including Western countries of "proper" democracy. In these accounts, South Korea's robust democracy is readily dismissed.

Teaching Korean Religions in the Time of Pandemic

The COVID-19 pandemic continued well beyond the spring and summer months of 2020. In South Korea, religions such as Shincheonji and Confucianism played significant roles in attempts to understand the pandemic in the society. While it is a compelling reminder of the intertwined nature of religion and society, the discourses created by transnational media inside and outside of South Korea regarding these religions represent the superficial assessment of the phenomena based on a dichotomy between "premodern religions and secular modernity" as well as between "Confucian Eastern collectivism and democratic Western individualism." By reconsidering these dichotomies, educators can foster a heuristic experience for their students. Instructors must consider the concrete historical context of modern Korean religious history and its connection with transnational evangelical Christianity, reexamine the particularity of Korean Confucianism, and lastly, problematize the assumptions of the popular Orientalist discourse. By doing so, they can help their students move beyond the caricatures of isolated incidents in South Korea. Teaching about Asia in a time of pandemic provides an occasion for reflection and analysis, which can lead to a more well-founded understanding of religion and Asian society in the twenty-first century.

Notes

[1] All COVID-19 statistics in this essay are based on the Johns Hopkins University Coronavirus Resource Center Website: https://coronavirus.jhu.edu.

[2] Derek Thompson, "What's Behind South Korea's COVID-19 Exceptionalism?" *The Atlantic*, May 4, 2020, https://www.theatlantic.com/ideas/archive/2020/05/whats-south-koreas-secret/611215/ (accessed September 8, 2020).

[3] In this essay, all romanizations of the Korean language follow the Revised Romanization of Korean released by the South Korean government in 2000. The only exception is the name of the first South Korean president, Syngman Rhee, which is his personal romanization.

For a discussion of Confucianism as it relates to the Western category of "religion," see Anna Sun, *Confucianism as a World Religion: Contested Histories and Contemporary Realities* (New Jersey: Princeton University Press, 2013), 1–14.

[4] Marco Hernandez, Simon Scarr, and Manas Sharma, "2019 Coronavirus: The Korean Clusters," *Reuters*, March 20, 2020, https://graphics.reuters.com/CHINA-HEALTH-SOUTHKOREA-CLUSTERS/0100B5G33SB/index.html (accessed September 8, 2020).

[5] Anonymous, "Ireon hwangdanghan . . . 31beon sincheonji hwakjinja (이런 황당한...31번 신천지 확진자)," *Donga ilbo*, February 22, 2020, https://www.donga.com/news/article/all/20200228/99922875/1 (accessed September 8, 2020).

[6] Jeung-eun Lee, "A Study on the Converted Cause of Shin-Cheon-Ji Devotee," Master's Thesis, Seoul National University, 2013, 2–13. Lee's thesis is the only study on Shincheonji from an academic perspective of the sociology of religion. Other literatures on Shincheonji, albeit informational, are mostly produced from a confessional Protestant perspective that aims at debasing the religion.

[7] Dae-hee Lee, "Sincheonji gyoju imanhui "koronaneun magwi jit" (신천지 교주 이만희 "코로나는 마귀 짓")," *Pressian*, February 21, 2020, https://www.pressian.com/pages/articles/279465?no=279465&utm_source=naver&utm_medium=search (accessed September 8, 2020).

[8] Nicholas Harkness, *Songs of Seoul: An Ethnography of Voice and Voicing in Christian South Korea* (Berkeley: University of California Press, 2014), 7–10.

[9] Ju Hui Judy Han, "Shifting Geographies of Proximity: Korean-led Evangelical Christian Missions and the U.S. Empire," in *Ethnographies of U.S. Empire* (Durham, NC: Duke University Press, 2018), 194–213.

[10] Although a German Lutheran missionary, Karl Friedrich August Gutzlaff (1803–1851), who visited Korea in 1832, is said to be the first Protestant missionary to arrive in Korea, his one-month visit could not establish a continuous Protestant Christianity movement in Korea. Horace Newton Allen (1858–1932), a Presbyterian medical missionary from Ohio, entered Korea in 1884 and built a close relationship with the Chosun dynasty on the peninsula. Following Allen, pioneering figures such as Henry Appenzeller (1858–1902) and Horace G. Underwood (1859–1916) conducted systematic mission work throughout the country. Allen is an important figure not only because he was the first American Presbyterian missionary in Korea, but also because he mediated the first wave of immigration of Koreans to the United States. Su Yon Pak, *Singing the Lord's Song in a New Land: Korean American Practices of Faith* (Louisville: Westminster John Knox Press, 2005), 3–4.

[11] Wi Jo Kang, *Christ and Caesar in Modern Korea: A History of Christianity and Politics* (Albany: State University of New York Press, 1997), 71–80.

[12] Ibid.

[13] Pew Research Center, "6 Facts about South Korea's Growing Christian Population." August 12, 2014, http://www.pewresearch.org/fact-tank/2014/08/12/6-facts-about-christianity-in-south-korea/ (accessed September 8, 2020).

[14] Rebecca Y. Kim, *The Spirit Moves West: Korean Missionaries in America* (London: Oxford University Press, 2015); Timothy Lee, *Born Again: Evangelicalism in Korea* (Honolulu: University of Hawaii Press, 2010); Sunggu Yang, *Evangelical Pilgrims from the East: Faith Fundamentals of Korean American Protestant Diasporas* (Berlin: Springer, 2016).

[15] Hailey Branson-Potts, "Pastor Who Refuses to Cancel Sunday Services Because of Coronavirus Greeted by Police," *Los Angeles Times*, April 5, 2020, https://www.latimes.com/california/story/2020-04-05/pastor-who-refuses-to-cancel-sunday-services-greeted-by-police (accessed September 8, 2020).

[16] Robert Orsi, "Painted into a Corner by the Blood of the Lord," *Contending Modernities*, April 29, 2020, https://contendingmodernities.nd.edu/global-currents/painted-into-a-corner/ (accessed September 8, 2020).

[17] Thompson, "What's Behind South Korea's COVID-19 Exceptionalism?"

[18] Byung-Chul Han, "La emergencia viral y el mundo de mañana. Byung-Chul Han, el filósofo surcoreano que piensa desde Berlín," *El País*, March 22, 2020, https://elpais.com/ideas/2020-03-21/la-emergencia-viral-y-el-mundo-de-manana-byung-chul-han-el-filosofo-surcoreano-que-piensa-desde-berlin.html (accessed September 8, 2020). Translation from original Spanish by Patrick Wintour in "Coronavirus: Who Will Be Winners and Losers in New World Order?" *The Guardian*, April 11, 2020, https://www.theguardian.com/world/2020/apr/11/coronavirus-who-will-be-winners-and-losers-in-new-world-order (accessed September 8, 2020).

[19] Jérôme Béglé, "Guy Sorman : « Le confinement nous fait découvrir qu'avant, ce n'était pas si mal »" *Le Point*, April 27, 2020, https://www.lepoint.fr/debats/guy-sorman-le-confinement-nous-fait-decouvrir-qu-avant-ce-n-etait-pas-si-mal-27-04-2020-2373021_2.php (accessed October 28, 2020). Translation from original French to English is mine.

[20] Ibid.

[21] Martina Deuchler, *The Confucian Transformation of Korea: A Study of Society and Ideology* (Cambridge: Council on East Asian Studies at Harvard University, 1992).

4

DEATH, DISEASE, AND BUDDHIST PATRONAGE IN JAPAN

THE GREAT SMALLPOX EPIDEMIC OF 735

Melody Rod-ari

Smallpox is a highly contagious disease that is transmitted from person to person by infective droplets during contact with an infected individual. Flu-like symptoms, as well as sores and lesions on the body, are physical hallmarks of the disease. While smallpox was eradicated by 1979, the disease had plagued humanity for thousands of years and killed hundreds of millions of people in the twentieth century alone.[1] Smallpox was first introduced to the islands of Japan by merchants and Buddhist missionaries from the Korean kingdom of Paekche in the sixth century CE. Once it reached the shores of Japan, smallpox did not disappear but emerged in waves that were sometimes manageable and were at other times catastrophic. In 735, a second smallpox epidemic afflicted Japan, reducing the population by 30 percent and resulting in labor shortages and declines in agricultural production and tax revenue for the court. A devout Buddhist, Emperor Shomu (r. 701–745) looked to Buddhism as an antidote to alleviate the suffering of his fellow countrymen. By undertaking one of the most ambitious Buddhist patronage projects in Japanese history with the building of the Todai-ji temple (Great Eastern Temple) and the colossal bronze sculpture of the Vairocana Buddha, the emperor also managed to stabilize the economy and social order.

Today, humanity is afflicted by another pandemic, COVID-19, an infectious disease that has killed over a million people globally in less than one year. Until an effective vaccine is developed, communities all over the world have adopted mask-wearing and physical distancing as preventive measures against further spread of the disease. Yet, as social creatures, we seek opportunities for meaningful and intimate connections. To this end, Todai-ji temple and the Vairocana Buddha have been called upon again to help alleviate the suffering of those afflicted by disease through virtual communal prayer.

This article examines how Emperor Shomu looked to Buddhist patronage as a means to reestablish stability and social order during and after the smallpox epidemic that ravaged his kingdom. Specifically, Emperor Shomu understood the importance of Buddhist merit-making as a mechanism to comfort his citizens and to motivate them—while maintaining his political authority—toward a collective effort to remove the evil spirits that were believed to have brought smallpox to the kingdom. For Emperor Shomu, this meant a nationwide effort to appease the Buddha by constructing a colossal bronze image of the Vairocana Buddha at Todai-ji temple (Figure 2). While the emperor sought medical experts and made proclamations about sanitary measures to stem the spread of smallpox, it was his Buddhist policies that ensured a return to political stability after the disease ran its natural course.

Early Buddhism in Japan

Buddhism is based on the teachings of the historical figure Siddhartha Gautama, who lived in India around the sixth century BCE. Its spread and influence throughout the Asian continent can be attributed to merchants and missionaries who traveled along the Silk Road, introducing Buddhism to China as early as the first century CE. As an important political and religious center in East Asia, China was fundamental in bringing Buddhism to Korea in 372 CE, which would later introduce the religion to Japan.

The earliest evidence for Buddhism in Japan comes from the seventh-century Chinese text, the *Book of Liang*, which notes that in 467 CE, Buddhist monks from the ancient kingdom of Gandhara, in present-day northwest Pakistan and northeast Afghanistan, traveled to the main island of Honshu. However, the *Chronicles of Japan*, considered among the oldest and most authoritative texts on Japanese history—albeit with a royalist prerogative—marks 552 as the official year of Buddhism's introduction to Japan when King Seong (r. 523–554) of Paekche sent an envoy of Buddhist missionaries, sutras (Buddhist texts), and a sculpture of the Buddha to Emperor Kinmei (r. 539–571).

Buddhism was not initially welcomed among members of the Yamato court and royal family, whose patronage was imperative for its successful foundation and adoption. Their wealth and influence would be needed to construct new temples, to house and feed Buddhist monks, and to pay for the production of Buddhist images. Because of its foreign origins, many resisted Buddhism, particularly those who advocated for the importance of *kami* (gods) worship, which would later become known as Shinto. The root of the struggle was political rivalry. The Yamato court desired to solidify control over the whole of the country at the expense of influential courtiers, some of whom worshipped kami and others who practiced Buddhism. As translated by William E. Deal in his essay, "Buddhism and the State in Early Japan," in 552, the imperial officials Mononobe no Okoshi and Nakatomi no Kamako, both ardent supporters of kami worship, were asked by Emperor Kinmei if Buddhism should be adopted. They responded that:

> The rulers of our country have always worshipped throughout the four seasons the 180 deities of heaven and earth [kami]. If they now change this and worship the deity of a foreign country, we fear that the deities of our country will become angry.[2]

Another court official, Soga no Inamea, argued that much of the Asian continent had chosen to adopt Buddhism and Japan should also follow suit. Emperor Kinmei granted Soga no Iname permission to worship the gold and silver sculpture of the Buddha sent as tribute from Korea in order to examine its efficacy. After an unspecified period of time, the chronicle notes that an epidemic of an incurable disease (smallpox) killed many people and that Buddhism was to blame. The kami had, apparently, become angered. At the urging of Mononobe no Okoshi and Nakatomi no Kamako, the emperor ordered Buddhist temples to be set on fire and Buddhist statues to be thrown into the Naniwa canal.[3] This act appeased the kami but angered the Buddha, who was said to have caused a fire in the great hall of the Imperial Palace, and smallpox continued to ravage the country throughout the sixth century. Eventually, the *Chronicles of Japan* explains, the Buddha and kami came to live together, and by the end of the sixth century, when Buddhism was largely accepted at court, smallpox is scarcely discussed in the text.

Although there exist many schools of Buddhism in Japan today, it was Mahayana Buddhism, also referred to as the "Great Vehicle," that took hold in the country. Mahayana Buddhism traveled along the Silk Route from India to various parts of Asia around the second century CE. It became the dominant school of Buddhism in East Asia by the ninth century. The self-appellation of "Great Vehicle" was adopted among Mahayana practitioners to express their superior knowledge of sutras, their expansive universe, which included many Buddhas and Buddhist deities, and the movement's focus on transporting all sentient beings from the world of suffering toward enlightenment. Its initial adoption and popularity stemmed, in part, from interpretations of the Buddha as a spiritual sovereign whose job was to care for the world and offer salvation to humanity. This especially appealed to rulers who wanted to maintain their power and authority while at the same time offering their citizens spiritual comfort, whether actual or perceived. By the sixth century, various rulers of China, Korea, and Japan had adopted Buddhism. Their decision to do so was often politically motivated, but their adoption of Buddhism nonetheless offered spiritual guidance to those who accepted the teachings of the Buddha. During times of calamity and epidemic, Buddhism proved itself useful in its promise to bring an end to suffering. Ironically, it was through mercantile trade and religious missions that new diseases were spread from one location to another, turning outbreaks into epidemics, and epidemics into pandemics.

A Buddhist Response to the Great Smallpox Epidemic of 735-737

Beginning on August 12, 735 CE, reports of smallpox in Kyushu, the southernmost island of Japan, began to circulate to the court in Nara, nearly 500 miles away on the island of Honshu, in the region of Kansai (Figure 1). The epidemic began at the port of Dazaifu when a fisherman came into contact with a "barbarian ship" that was infested with the disease.[4] The "barbarians" were thought to be sailors from the kingdom of Silla in Korea. By August 23, the military government of Kyushu submitted a petition to the court, asking for assistance and the relaxation of mandatory rice payments. In their words: "A pestilence characterized by swellings has spread widely in the provinces under our jurisdiction. The whole populace is bedridden. We request exemption from the local products tax this year."[5] The court granted the request, but the devastation was far from over. By 737, smallpox ravaged nearly all corners of Japan, and deaths from the disease reduced the population by a third.[6] These included members of the royal family and high-ranking officials, making the urgency to quell the disease more imperative for the court.

At the height of the epidemic, Emperor Shomu consulted his officials at the Bureau of Medicine. They recommended various remedies and guidelines, including a prohibition against drinking water, an encouragement to eat boiled rhubarb, and a recommendation to apply powdered silkworm cocoons to boils.[7] When these guidelines did not help to quell the disease, Emperor Shomu ordered Buddhist monks and nuns to read sutras to the afflicted and prayers to kami, whom he interpreted to be deities that were part of the Buddhist universe. Eventually the

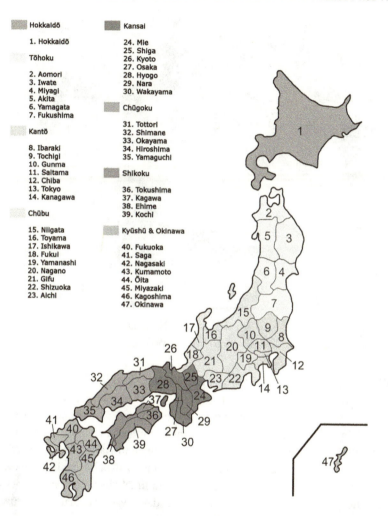

Hokkaidō	Kansai
1. Hokkaidō	24. Mie
	25. Shiga
Tōhoku	26. Kyoto
	27. Osaka
2. Aomori	28. Hyogo
3. Iwate	29. Nara
4. Miyagi	30. Wakayama
5. Akita	
6. Yamagata	**Chūgoku**
7. Fukushima	
	31. Tottori
Kantō	32. Shimane
	33. Okayama
8. Ibaraki	34. Hiroshima
9. Tochigi	35. Yamaguchi
10. Gunma	
11. Saitama	**Shikoku**
12. Chiba	
13. Tokyo	36. Tokushima
14. Kanagawa	37. Kagawa
	38. Ehime
Chūbu	39. Kochi
15. Niigata	**Kyūshū & Okinawa**
16. Toyama	
17. Ishikawa	40. Fukuoka
18. Fukui	41. Saga
19. Yamanashi	42. Nagasaki
20. Nagano	43. Kumamoto
21. Gifu	44. Ōita
22. Shizuoka	45. Miyazaki
23. Aichi	46. Kagoshima
	47. Okinawa

Figure 1: Regions and Prefectures of Japan. Source: Wikimedia Commons.

disease ran its natural course, but it left Japan's population and economy on the brink of collapse. In 741, Emperor Shomu directed court resources to the building of provincial Buddhist temples (*kokobunji*). This would spur the economy and allow the government to assert greater control over the provinces through a shared religious experience. At the same time, temples would become sites of prayer for the stability and restoration of the country and for all the peoples of Japan. He relied on the Buddhist concept of merit, accumulated through good deeds such as feeding monks and nuns, funding temples, sponsoring the production of Buddhist sculptures, and reading or listening to sutras. The accumulation of merit through virtuous deeds was thought to ensure happiness and prosperity.

Figure 2: Vairocana Buddha at Todai-ji Temple, Nara, Japan, 8th century. Bronze, height approximately fifty feet. Photo by Wally Gobetz/Flickr Creative Commons.

With a population that increasingly came to accept Buddhism, the government saw an opportunity to embark on a nationwide effort of Buddhist merit-making while at the same time consolidating political control. In 743, the emperor issued an edict calling all of Japan to help in the construction of a colossal image of the Vairocana Buddha to be housed at the Todai-ji temple in Nara. The construction of the image was intended to bring peace to Japan and to all of humanity. However, one can argue that having been forced out of Nara in 740 by rebellions, Emperor Shomu's edict to have the image constructed at Todai-ji was a calculated maneuver to return to the old capital and to centralize governmental authority.

Emperor Shomu selected the Vairocana Buddha, also referred to as the Cosmic Buddha, who sits at the center of the Mahayana Buddhist universe and oversees a series of worlds where there is only peace and no suffering. The Vairocana Buddha was chosen not only because of its association with stability and prosperity, but also because the emperor wanted to associate himself with Vairocana's central authority in the Buddhist universe. Ultimately, as a devout Buddhist, Emperor Shomu desired to be seen as the Vairocana Buddha incarnate and remembered as a great Buddhist sovereign.

Standing nearly fifty feet tall, the sculpture at Todai-ji is the largest bronze sculpture of the Vairocana Buddha in the world. In order to build such a colossal image, it is estimated that nearly half of the population contributed by donating funds, labor, and materials. The court also instituted mandatory tax payments by every citizen, which brought both hardship and political unrest. With its completion in 749, the sculpture—which weighs an estimated 550 tons—used up all the available copper in the country and nearly bankrupted the court. Moreover, the construction of the temple to house the sculpture led to the deforestation of Japan, taking generations to restore.

After successfully undertaking the largest Buddhist merit-making project in Japanese history, Emperor Shomu abdicated the throne and became a Buddhist priest. In announcing his retirement, Emperor Shomu praised the Buddha for restoring peace to Japan and helping the country avoid even greater disaster during the smallpox epidemic. While smallpox was not eradicated from Japan during his tenure as emperor, it did not return to epidemic levels until 763, well after his death. Emperor Shomu did not invent the ritualization of Buddhism and its deployment during a natural disaster and a pestilence. Such rituals had been described and utilized since the foundation of Buddhism. However, his institutionalization of provincial temples (kokobunji) in 741, with Todai-ji as the central headquarters, was and continues to be effective.

The Vairocana Buddha and Todai-ji Temple in the Age of COVID-19

Over a millennium has passed since the epidemic of 735–737, and modern medicine has developed vaccines that have eradicated diseases like smallpox. After COVID-19 arrived in Japan, Prime Minister Abe Shinzō slowly enacted policies to limit the movement of citizens, including closing schools and institutions. Eventually, his government issued an emergency order effectively shutting down the entire country on April 16, 2020.

While medical professionals continue to research the disease and develop an effective vaccine, religious leaders and practitioners throughout Japan have found succor in ritual and prayer. Not surprisingly, the Vairocana Buddha at Todai-ji remains spiritually important even today. On April 3, before the official government shutdown of Japan, the chief priest and administrator of Todai-ji, Sagawa Fumon, sent out a virtual call on the temple's home page for all Buddhist temples, Shinto shrines, and Christian churches to collectively pray for the quick end of COVID-19. On April 24, leaders from Buddhist, Shinto, and Christian institutions came together on the veranda of the Great Buddha Hall at Todai-ji to pray for the end of the pandemic and the suffering it has caused. These leaders explained that while traditional communal rituals could not be conducted because of the infectious nature of the disease, prayer is a collective action that can be accomplished while social distancing. Videos and images of monks and priests at Todai-ji appeared on various digital platforms such as YouTube and Twitter. In one such video, monks and priests engaged in expiation rituals before the Vairocana Buddha.[8]

As a collective act of Buddhist merit-making, the daily noon prayers can create an incredibly powerful image in the minds of Buddhists of a force field, radiating the latent potential of Buddhahood that exists in all who follow the Buddha's teachings. This field of merit can also be seen as a mechanism to push out the disease and the suffering it has caused. As of the writing of this essay, daily noon prayers continue to take place at Todai-ji, as the Vairocana Buddha watches over the nation and all of humanity, just as Emperor Shomu had intended.

Connections in the Classroom

Although this essay provides a specific example of Buddhist patronage during times of calamity, the Great Smallpox Epidemic in Japan is a useful case study that allows students to make broader connections to religious and governmental responses, both in the past and the present. Specifically, how have non-Buddhist institutions responded to past epidemics and the current COVID-19 pandemic? Or, how have Buddhist institutions and worshippers inside and outside of Asia responded to the pandemic differently? How has the Vairocana Buddha at Todai-ji been used to redirect anxiety into action, and what other icons have similar powers to quell practitioners' fears? Where does its authority come from? Despite the anxiety we are all facing, COVID-19 provides many opportunities for meaningful discussions of these and other such questions.

Notes

[1] World Health Organization, https://www.who.int/news-room/detail/13-12-2019-who-commemorates-the-40th-anniversary-of-smallpox-eradication (accessed on October 11, 2020).

[2] William E. Deal, "Buddhism and the State in Early Japan," in *Buddhism in Practice*, ed. Donald S. Lopez, Jr. (Princeton: Princeton University Press, 1995), 219. For a full English translation of the *Nihon Shoki*, refer to W. B. Aston's text, *Nihongi, Chronicles of Japan from the Earliest Times to A.D. 69*, Volumes I and II (London: Japan Society, Kegan Paul, Trench, Trubner & Col, Limited, 1896).

[3] Ibid.

[4] Ibid.

[5] William Wayne Farris, *Population, Disease, and Land in Early Japan, 645–900* (Cambridge: Harvard University Asia Center, 1985), 54–55.

[6] Ibid, 66.

[7] Ibid, 63.

[8] KyodoNews, https://www.youtube.com/watch?time_continue=20&v=9D7wu33HW7w&feature=emb_logo (accessed June 26, 2020).

5

TAIWAN AND COVID-19

GLOBAL PRESSURE, DOMESTIC SUCCESS

**Lucien Ellington, Jeffrey Melnik,
and Thomas J. Shattuck**

Any essay on COVID-19 that attempts to discern policy responses and reflect upon choices, as the worst pandemic in over 100 years still rages, demands of authors genuine humility, and hopefully what follows honors this obligation. Taiwan's (Republic of China) actions began before the pandemic and since its advent are arguably the world's most effective to date. Microsoft founder and philanthropist Bill Gates effusively praised Taiwan in an April 5, 2020 interview with *Fox News* host Chris Wallace stating, "I don't think any country has a perfect record. Taiwan comes close." Taiwan's success in managing the pandemic was widely reported in Asian, European, and American media as Taiwan garnered more positive global attention because of COVID-19 policies than has been the case for years.[1]

Gates' comment in early spring 2020 was based upon responses to the virus the Taiwanese government had already implemented. Current comparative country data illustrates Taiwan's continued success (Table 1 with select country statistics). Taiwan's gross domestic product (GDP) growth of 3.3% reported on October 30, 2020 makes Taiwan one of the few major world economies to expand this year. This statistic demonstrates that economic recovery comes hand-in-hand with an effective pandemic response. Taiwan's robust high-tech sector including the Taiwan Semiconductor Manufacturing Company (TSMC), the world's largest

Country	National Population	Number of Confirmed COVID-19 Cases	Percent of Population Infected	Total Deaths	Case Fatality Rate (CFR)
Taiwan	23,834,802	675	0.003%	7	1.0%
Australia	25,625,435	27,904	0.109%	908	3.3%
People's Republic of China	1,441,655,170	92,890	0.006%	4,743	5.1%
United States	331,819,261	13.39 million	4.034%	266,877	2.0%
Germany	83,896,205	1,059,755	1.263%	16,312	1.5%
Japan	126,315,717	148,154	0.117%	2,067	1.4%

Table 1: Select Country Statistics on COVID-19 Cases

All data are from November 30, 2020.
Population data from: https://www.worldometers.info.
Additional data from: https://coronavirus.jhu.edu/map.html.
Note: CFR is the percentage of deaths among confirmed COVID-19 cases.

semiconductor contract manufacturer, are doing well, and most Taiwanese, because of the success in fighting COVID-19, are now going about life as usual.[2] Taiwan's situation is definitively unique compared to any other country because the Taiwanese have managed to be highly successful in managing the COVID-19 pandemic thus far while subject to unremitting Chinese pressure and World Health Organization (WHO) barriers faced by no other polity.

Although the 2002–2004 Severe Acute Respiratory Syndrome (SARS) killed far fewer people than expected, Taiwan had the third largest number of deaths from SARS with 73, behind only the People's Republic of China (PRC) and Canada.[3] Taiwan, like many nations, was unprepared for the virus which originated in China and then through human contact came to Taiwan. Unlike other countries, Taiwan was handicapped in addressing the problem because of PRC policies and lack of prompt access to the WHO and the World Health Assembly (WHA), the WHO's decision-making body attended by delegates from all WHO member states.

The PRC has consistently claimed that Taiwan, who was expelled from the United Nations in 1971 when China was also formally recognized by the organization, is a Chinese province and not an independent state and that only the PRC can represent China. Because of its big power status, including a permanent seat on the UN Security Council, the PRC has imposed its "One China Principle" on most of the world. Although China insists that other nations and international organizations follow this policy, most countries, including the United States, have their own "One China Policy." The U.S. view is expressed in the 1972 Shanghai Communique stating, "The United States acknowledges that all Chinese on either side of the Taiwan Strait maintain there is but one China and that Taiwan is a part of China. The United States Government does not challenge that position." The key tenet of the U.S. position is that the United States "acknowledges" the Chinese perspective; it does not "recognize" the PRC perspective.[4]

Since 1971, Taiwan has been barred from membership in UN-affiliated organizations, even though in 2020, despite the PRC's protestations, 15 nations—predominantly located in Latin America, the Caribbean, and Pacific regions—formally recognize Taiwan, and the country has a national government, county and municipal governments, and a standing military—typical characteristics of states as defined by international law.[5] Taiwan also enjoys strong informal ties with a number of countries across North America, Asia, and Europe.

After the SARS virus arrived in Taiwan in early 2003, Taiwan's SARS crisis was worsened by a 50-day delay on the part of the WHO, despite Taipei's requests for assistance. Taiwan, with the assistance of formal diplomatic allies and other concerned nations, had been campaigning to attend WHA meetings and for a "universal application" clause in the revision of UN International Health Regulations (IHR), but PRC representatives blocked these efforts by insisting that the IHR applied to all "Chinese Territory," including Taiwan. PRC representatives also signed a confidential Memorandum of Understanding (MOU) with the WHO Secretariat to enforce its claim. The MOU, later leaked, specified that Taiwan not be allowed to participate under the names "Taiwan" or the "ROC"; if Taiwan was invited, then the PRC must approve in advance all communications between the WHO and Taiwan, and all communications between the WHO and Taiwan must be conducted through contacts in China, not Taiwan. Confronted with this situation, Taiwanese health authorities chose to use U.S. Centers for Disease Control contacts to learn more about WHO information.[6] Taiwan's Ministry of Health and Welfare and its agency, the Centers for Disease Control, also realized they needed to assume more responsibility for enhanced prevention techniques for Taiwan when the next pandemic struck, ranging from travel quarantines to mask supplies and contact tracing. Post-SARS legislation ensured the legal basis for the creation of a Central Epidemic Command Center (CECC) if a potential pandemic seemed likely.

PRC determination to eventually absorb Taiwan and its strong political preferences regarding Taiwanese domestic politics were major factors in Beijing's especially rigid policies toward Taiwan during the SARS era. For at least the last 30 years, the PRC favored Kuomintang (KMT) rule for Taiwan in contrast to its major rival, the Democratic Progressive Party (DPP). The KMT is generally more conservative than the DPP, but more importantly, it is more amenable to business, political, and cultural ties with the PRC. The DPP has been most associated with a desire for formal independence from the PRC and has a disproportionately high number of supporters who trace their ancestry to minority groups in Taiwan and speak other versions of Chinese than Mandarin. Due to its strong historic ties to Taiwan, the DPP puts forward a more Taiwan-centric identity than the KMT. Chen Shui-bian, the first DPP politician to become president, was in office during SARS and was unacceptable to Beijing because of his generally pro-independence stance and his public contemplation on conducting a domestic referendum on a Taiwanese bid for WHO membership. This would have embarrassed the PRC,[7] who was already under international scrutiny for then-Minister of Health Zhang Wengkang's March 2003 guarantee to the WHO that SARS "was well under control" and that the number of cases were declining.[8] PRC leaders, facing a public relations nightmare, fired Zhang, enabled Taiwan to get assistance with masks, initiated some cross-straits contacts, and on May 5, 2003, the aforementioned WHA visit to Taiwan occurred.[9]

The PRC subsequently softened its position regarding Taiwan during President Ma Ying-jeou's 2008–2016 tenure on several issues, including Taiwan's participation in the WHO. Ma, a member of the KMT, made strengthening ties with China one of his key foreign policy priorities. In January 2009, with the consent of the PRC, the WHO invited Taiwan to establish a direct point of contact through the IHS treaty guidelines to exchange information on health issues, and a short time later, the WHO Director General invited "Chinese Taipei" to join WHA meetings as an observer. Even this more open policy was subject to Beijing's control. From 2009 to 2019, Taiwan applied to attend 187 WHO technical meetings as an observer, but due to Chinese vetoes were only allowed to attend 57 of them.[10]

In 2016, Tsai Ing-wen, a member of the DPP, won Taiwan's presidential election. A Hakka minority, veteran of DPP politics, and holder of four academic degrees including a PhD from the London School of Economics, Tsai's candidacy and the population's general discontent with Ma's overly pro-China policies managed to foster for the first time a DPP majority in the Legislative Yuan, the national legislature.[11] China reacted to the second DPP President by putting even more pressure on the international community to diminish Taiwan's influence and coupled this with an increase in military maneuvers to intimidate Taiwan.[12] The WHO and WHA without explanation no longer invited Taiwan to WHA meetings.[13] Throughout Tsai's presidency, China has lured away a number of Taiwan's diplomatic allies and has put immense pressure on the remaining 15 polities (14 nations and the Vatican).

In the latter part of President Tsai's first term, public opinion in Taiwan was affected by the perception that the KMT was too tied to the PRC and by China's increasing pressure on Hong Kong. She was reelected in January 2020 with a record number of votes, just as COVID-19 began to spread throughout Wuhan, China. The pandemic was well underway by Tsai's inauguration in May 2020, but despite more long-term Chinese pressure on Taiwan since the Cold War, Tsai's leadership was already strongly complementing the groundwork of Taiwan's government in reaction to SARS.

President Tsai was well connected with Taiwan's digitally savvy youth. In 2016, Tsai appointed Audrey Tang as Digital Minister. Tang, a junior high school dropout and child prodigy, was reading classical literature at age five, doing advanced mathematics at age six, and programming by age eight. By age 19, she held positions in software companies and worked in Silicon Valley as an entrepreneur. *Foreign Policy* in 2019 featured Tang, the youngest cabinet member in Taiwan's history, as one the top global thinkers of the past decade.[14] Tang's digital creativity and entrepreneurial/management abilities have been critical to Taiwan's success in battling the virus.

COVID-19's Emergence, China, WHO, and Taiwan

On December 31, 2019, Wuhan police announced they were investigating doctors for spreading unconfirmed rumors that threatened the social order while municipal officials released information about a viral pneumonia that infected customers in a seafood market. On the morning of the same day, Taiwan's deputy CDC director received a text message from a colleague in the media monitoring division regarding laboratory reports and warnings about an unusual viral pneumonia in Wuhan. The reports had been deleted within China, but were preserved on PPT, a Taiwanese bulletin board website. The same day, Taiwanese officials emailed their IHR point of contact and the U.S. CDC for more information about the disease but were unable to get satisfactory answers from either source about human-to-human transmission. According to Foreign Minister Joseph Wu, Taiwan's government immediately began performing health checks on inbound Wuhan flights the same night. Chinese officials promptly reported the disease through the WHO IHR point of contact, but the PRC and WHO claimed for well over two weeks that the disease was not contagious and there were no new cases. Xi Jinping later claimed he had initiated an inquiry and response team in the Politburo as early as January 7. During January, as cases were mounting, Wuhan hosted an annual People's Congress of the municipal branch of the Communist Party, including an enormous public banquet of 40,000 families. During this time period, Wuhan officials detained more doctors for sharing warnings about the virus with scientists in Wuhan, Shanghai, and Beijing. Official denial ended on January 20, 2020 as China's most famous epidemiologist, Zhong Nanshan, announced on state television there was no doubt of human-to-human transmission.[15]

Taiwan reacted less than two weeks later on February 6 by imposing a mandatory self-quarantine requirement for Taiwan nationals who had traveled to China, Hong Kong, and Macao. The next day, foreign nationals who had been to the same places were temporarily barred from visiting Taiwan. As outbreaks occurred in other countries such as South Korea, Iran, and Italy, Taiwanese authorities used the same techniques, and on February 10, 2020, Taiwan only permitted flights originating in five Chinese airports to land in Taiwan.[16] Currently, Taiwan's government requires almost all incoming travelers to quarantine in a hotel or apartment for a 14-day period upon arrival with strict monitoring by health officials.

On January 22, following a meeting with Beijing authorities, the WHO chose not to report the seriousness of the virus because of Chinese government resistance. On January 23, Wuhan was placed on quarantine, and by January 24, Hubei Province, which includes Wuhan, was locked down—right before the Lunar New Year holiday. The Chinese government quarantined 50 million people across 15 cities, suspended air travel from Hubei Province to other parts of China, and restricted air travel to major Chinese cities such as Beijing and Shanghai. Meanwhile, the PRC urged other nations to continue their international flights to China. By March 11, the WHO, after outbreaks in 114 countries and 4,291 deaths, finally officially declared COVID-19 a pandemic.

The WHO's excessive deference toward the PRC and the organization's negative comments regarding Taiwan—the WHO criticized Taiwan for restricting flights from China—in the critical first stages of the pandemic warrant further discussion. In the Xi Jinping era, the PRC became influential with the WHO in a way that far exceeded the MOU of the SARS days regarding Taiwan. China actively engaged in attempting to influence WHA member state votes through cultivating relationships with candidates for WHO Director-General, including supporting current Director-General Tedros Adhanom Ghebreyesus of Ethiopia. Confirmed in 2017, Dr. Tedros signed an MOU in support of China's Belt and Road Initiative and traveled to Beijing the same year in order to praise Xi's proposal to create a "medical silk road."[17]

Fighting COVID-19: Exceptional Technological Responses

Citizens of Western countries including the United States frequently distrust big tech companies like Google and Facebook over their handling of personal data and the spread of misinformation online. This attitude has influenced how Americans have responded to the pandemic. In contrast, the trustful relationship in handling sensitive information between the Taiwanese public, the government, and open online platforms has been vital to Taiwan's handling of the pandemic.

Influenced by its experience with the SARS outbreak, and wary of the approaching Lunar New Year when millions of Chinese and Taiwanese travel, Taiwan's government implemented strict procedures based upon early warning data in January 2020 from resources such as Metabiota, an AI-based private health tech company that partners with industries and governments to manage potential epidemics. Metabiota predicted the coronavirus would spread to Taiwan and other East Asian nations. By January 20, the CECC was activated, and the next day, the first confirmed case of coronavirus was reported in Taiwan from a 50-year old woman who had recently traveled to Wuhan. Almost every Taiwanese citizen, approximately 99 percent, is registered for the National Health Insurance (NHI) program, Taiwan's government-run single-payer healthcare program. The NHI database is also integrated with Taiwan's customs and immigration database. On January 27, citizens' travel data was integrated with their NHI identification cards—a process that only took a single day. As a result, the CECC was able to quickly track citizens' recent travel history to determine which individuals were at high risk of infection and required quarantine. On January 30, the NHI database was expanded to include recent patients' information from China, Hong Kong, and Macao. By February 14, the Taiwanese government launched the Entry Quarantine System for foreigners to quickly provide contact information, recent travel history, and log any potential virus symptoms. Travelers to Taiwan could easily access the system's online forms through scanning a QR code on their mobile phones upon arrival in Taiwan.[18]

Taiwanese and foreigners evaluated to be low risk (no travel to high-risk areas, reported symptoms, or positive COVID tests) were sent a border declaration pass via SMS text message for easier travel. For those in high-risk groups, including those who recently traveled to countries under advisory warnings or who tested positive for COVID-19, a 14-day quarantine was mandatory. The government can track these individuals via their mobile phones which can be monitored via location-tracking. Authorities are alerted when quarantined individuals leave their homes or other designated shelter locations—and even when they turn off their devices. These individuals are also contacted twice a day to ensure they are adhering to quarantine protocols and authorities rapidly contact or visit individuals who trigger a warning alert, usually within 15 minutes.[19]

In addition to government-implemented policies, Taiwan's substantial tech-centric community made immense contributions to the distribution and management of vital supplies like face masks. In the years following the youth-driven anti-KMT political protest "Sunflower Movement," a growing community of idealistic, civic-minded programmers and hackers emerged in Taiwan, such as the decentralized, collaborative open source g0v community. These individuals seek to use technology for the public good, make government processes more transparent to citizens, and encourage more active participation in Taiwan's democracy. To achieve these goals, programmers developed platforms, such as Co-Facts, an automated chatbot for LINE—the most popular messaging app in Taiwan—that responds when users attempt to send potential disinformation that has been verified as false, and vTaiwan, an online civil participation platform that enables Taiwanese citizens to interact closely with government officials and elicit public opinion on various issues.

By early February 2020, Taiwan faced a serious mask supply problem. The previous month, the government had announced an export ban on face masks (the ban was lifted in June). Users of LINE swarmed the platform posting information on stores' inventories, but this information was difficult to keep track of as LINE is built for social interaction and not for accurately tracking inventory. A software engineer named Howard Wu quickly developed a website using Google Maps that was constantly updated with crowd-sourced reports coming in from LINE for a much more user-friendly way for Taiwanese to stay informed on available face mask supplies. This quickly proved to be untenable, not only because of the unreliability of crowd-sourced inventory data, but also because of the fees Google charges developers when a certain amount of users access Google Maps through a website or application.[20] It was then that Wu engaged with Taiwan's "civic tech" community through a collaboration tool known as HackMD and caught the attention of Digital Minister Audrey Tang, the architect of vTaiwan and a strong advocate for open data and digital democracy.[21]

Tang met with President Tsai, already a strong proponent of using technology for civic good, to propose a solution to Taiwan's looming face mask supply problem soon after Wu's map exploded in popularity. Tang suggested that the government only distribute face masks through pharmacies associated with Taiwan's NHI healthcare system. The NHI already maintained a database updated in real time of pharmacies' available supplies, far more accurate than ad hoc crowd-sourced information. Furthermore, by tying mask distribution to users' NHI identification cards, the government could prevent mask supply hoarding by individuals and enforce the mask ration system put in place by the government. The mask rationing system, in which individuals could purchase two masks per week, was implemented on February 3, 2020.[22] Tang also proposed that the government make the NHI's database open to the public allowing Tang and other civic-minded, tech savvy Taiwanese to build applications for users to access this information with ease.

Tang's proposals were quickly greenlit, and she made the NHI database available through a channel frequented by Taiwan's civic tech community via the communication platform Slack. Tang also built a web portal where Taiwanese could easily download applications created by Taiwanese developers to track face mask supplies based upon the NHI's real-time data.[23] With the sharing of the NHI's accurate data and the plethora of apps built around it, masks were evenly distributed to citizens throughout the country at pharmacies, and users could easily track inventory data preventing mass hysteria over potential supply shortages. The effort was so successful that Taiwan ended up with a massive surplus of face masks, which the government donated to other nations in need of masks as the pandemic spread worldwide. The strict mask rationing system was loosened as mask production increased. By July 2020, Taiwan had donated over 51 million masks worldwide to over 80 countries including the United States.[24]

Taiwan and the World: A COVID-19 Success but a WHO Pariah

Taiwan's highly successful response to the virus has brought it more international attention than probably any time since the early stages of the Cold War. The Taiwanese government has not only aided many nations around the world by providing medical supplies and critical information, but it has also vigorously pursued soft diplomacy. Perhaps most noticeably, Taiwan has gathered more support for greater access and participation in the WHO and to strengthen informal bilateral ties. A quick visit to its Ministry of Foreign Affairs website includes an English language section titled "The Taiwan Model for Combatting COVID-19" which reads:

> When a SARS-like virus, later named as coronavirus disease 2019 (COVID-19), first appeared in China in late 2019, it was predicted that, other than China, Taiwan would be one of the most affected countries, given its geographic proximity to and close people-to-people exchanges with China. Yet even as the disease continues to spread around the globe, Taiwan has been able to contain the pandemic and minimize its impact on people's daily lives. The transparency and honesty with which Taiwan has implemented prevention measures is a democratic model of excellence in fighting disease. This webpage shares the Taiwan Model for combating the pandemic, as well as links to related international media coverage and video clips. The materials found here also help explain the different aspects of Taiwan's epidemic prevention work, and how Taiwan is helping the international community.[25]

Despite the support of a number of countries, there is no substantial evidence that the majority of WHA member states will accept Taiwan's participation at this time; China's opposition is simply too difficult to overcome. This is evidenced by Taiwan's exclusion from the May and November 2020 WHA meetings despite the strong international support. Nevertheless, limiting Taiwan's engagement with the international health community certainly does not improve the prospects for better global health.

Notes

[1] "Bill Gates: Pandemic is 'Nightmare Scenario,' but National Response Can Reduce Casualties," *Fox News*, April 5, 2020, https://www.foxnews.com/politics/bill-gates-pandemic-is-nightmare-scenario-but-national-response-can-reduce-casualties; Riyaz ul Khaliq, "Taiwan's SARS Experience Helped It Beat COVID-19," *Anadolu Agency*, June 5, 2020, https://www.aa.com.tr/en/asia-pacific/-taiwan-s-sars-experience-helped-it-beat-covid-19-/1830547#!; Dave Makichuk, "Bill Gates Lauds Taiwan's Coronavirus Response," *Asia Times,* April 7, 2020, https://asiatimes.com/2020/04/bill-gates-lauds-taiwans-coronavirus-response/.

[2] Chao Deng, "Taiwan Shrugs Off Pandemic to Deliver Surprise Growth," *The Wall Street Journal*, October 30, 2020, https://www.wsj.com/articles/taiwan-shrugs-off-pandemic-to-deliver-surprise-growth-11604063439.

[3] Ian Rowen, "Crafting the Taiwan Model for COVID-19: An Exceptional State in Pandemic Territory," *The Asia-Pacific Journal* 18, issue 14, no. 9 (2020): 2.

[4] Eleanor Albert, "China–Taiwan Relations," *Council on Foreign Relations*, last modified January 22, 2020, https://www.cfr.org/backgrounder/china-taiwan-relations.

[5] Yu-Jie Chen and Jerome A. Cohen, "Why Does the WHO Exclude Taiwan?," *Council on Foreign Relations,* April 9, 2020, https://www.cfr.org/in-brief/why-does-who-exclude-taiwan.

[6] Rowen, 2–3.

[7] Jacques DeLisle, "Taiwan and the WHO in 2020: A Novel and Viral Politics," *Foreign Policy Research Institute,* May 13, 2020, https://www.fpri.org/article/2020/05/taiwan-and-the-who-in-2020-a-novel-virus-and-viral-politics/.

[8] Simon Shen, "The 'SARS Diplomacy' of Beijing and Taipei: Competition Between the Chinese and Non-Chinese Orbits," *Asian Perspective* 28, no. 1 (2004): 45-47. Accessed November 6, 2020, http://www.jstor.org/stable/42704443.

[9] Ibid., 49–50.

[10] Thomas Shattuck, "The Streisand Effect Gets Geopolitical: China's (Unintended) Amplification of Taiwan," *Foreign Policy Research Institute*, April 14, 2020, https://www.fpri.org/article/2020/04/the-streisand-effect-gets-geopolitical-chinas-unintended-amplification-of-taiwan/

[11] John Franklin Copper, *Taiwan: Nation-State or Province?*, 7th Edition (New York and London: Routledge, 2019), 84–85.

[12] Lucien Ellington meetings with General Shen Yi-ming, Vice-Minister for Policy, Ministry of National Defense, and David Tawei Lee, Secretary-General, National Security Council, June 4, 2019.

[13] Rowen, 3.

[14] Jonathan Tepperman, "Readers' Choices: A Decade of Global Thinkers," *Foreign Policy*, 2019, https://foreignpolicy.com/2019-global-thinkers/.

[15] Rowen, 1–4.

[16] Ankit Panda, "Amid Coronavirus Concerns, Taiwan Takes Measures to Restrict Travel From China," *The Diplomat*, March 3, 2020, https://thediplomat.com/2020/03/amid-coronavirus-concerns-taiwan-takes-measures-to-restrict-travel-from-china/.

[17] Rowen, 3.

[18] C. Jason Wang et al., "Response to COVID-19 in Taiwan: Big Data Analytics, New Technology, and Proactive Testing," *Journal of the American Medical Association* 323. No. 14 (2020): 1341–1342.

[19] Dominykas Broga, "How Taiwan Used Tech to Fight COVID-19," *Tech UK*, March 31, 2020, https://tinyurl.com/y4umo8mq; Anna Novikova, "Software in the Time of Plague: How Innovations Help Mitigate COVID-19 and Other Disease Outbreaks," *Intersog*, March 18, 2020, https://tinyurl.com/y5sbbwv2.

[20] Google would remove fees associated with Google Maps' use later in the year in response to the pandemic.

[21] Andrew Leonard, "How Taiwan's Unlikely Digital Minister Hacked the Pandemic," *WIRED*, July 23, 2020, https://tinyurl.com/y3chvq9e.

[22] Cho-Hung Chiang et al., "Maintaining Mask Stockpiles in the COVID-19 Pandemic: Taiwan as a Learning Model," *Infect Control Hosp Epidemiol*, May 11, 2020, 1–2.

[23] See https://mask.pdis.nat.gov.tw/.

[24] Jay Chen, "Taiwan Donates Over 51 Million Masks to Countries Worldwide," *BusinessWire*, July 22, 2020, https://tinyurl.com/y6cgn2ef.

[25] Taiwan Ministry of Foreign Affairs, "The Taiwan Model for Combating COVID-19," accessed November 6, 2020, https://tinyurl.com/y4kzcxx2.

6

Mythmaking and COVID-19

Asian Alternatives to "Warfare" against Disease

Kin Cheung

Why do some United States officials refuse to follow guidance from the World Health Organization (WHO) and international scientific communities to use the officially designated name for the 2019 novel coronavirus—severe acute respiratory syndrome coronavirus 2 (SARS-CoV-2)—and instead repeatedly use "Wuhan virus," "Chinese virus," and "Kung Flu"? Their motives are not simply to shorten the name, since the WHO uses "COVID-19 virus" in public communication.[1] Rather, these are deliberate attempts to construct a narrative around COVID-19 as something caused by a foreign enemy, against which the country must wage war. A religious studies analysis of this discourse elucidates the process of mythmaking that serves as a foundation for such labeling and continues a tradition of using war metaphors in US history. Asian medical paradigms provide alternative discourses and narratives for educators to bring Asian content into the classroom in light of the 2020 pandemic.

What is at stake in evoking images of war and heroes? The US Surgeon General, Jerome Adams, frames the COVID-19 outbreak as an "attack" on America, calling it "our Pearl Harbor moment, our 9/11 moment."[2] Warfare metaphors—"fighting" and "waging a war" against an "invisible enemy," from which the nation is enlisting "an army of health care workers" who are the "soldiers" on the "front line"

Figure 1: "Heroes work here." A market in central
New Jersey in June 2020. Image by the author.

"battling" in "combat" against this virus—are abundantly used by public officials
and journalists and then circulated on social media. Medical doctors, nurses,
grocery store staff, and workers who provide critical public services are elevated as
"heroes." The Health and Economic Recovery Omnibus Emergency Solutions Act,
better known as the HEROES Act, passed the House of Representatives in May
2020. The bill includes the COVID–19 HERO Act, or the COVID–19 Housing,
Economic Relief, and Oversight Act, which provides medical equipment for first
responders and essential workers. It is clear who the constructed heroes are in this
discourse of war.

This is an example of active mythmaking; creating values and presenting a saga
of good versus evil. The virus is depicted as an alien force, thereby concealing our
collective culpability in this health crisis. Though some resist this characterization,
US political leaders continue to create a narrative of war.[3] To be sure, officials in
other countries, including China, also employ warfare metaphors. However, the US
case deserves attention in how heroes are constructed along an axis of good versus
evil. This dichotomy has a religious basis and is fundamentally different than Asian
perspectives on harmony and disharmony. Educators can take this opportunity
to turn to Asia for alternative discourses in order to expose the complexities of
the current pandemic as well as the process and effects of mythmaking. I use the
contested reception of the germ theory of disease in Kolkata and Hong Kong
during the late nineteenth century as one example of an alternative narrative and
to suggest metaphors of (dis)harmony and (im)balance.

The Politics of Mythmaking

Myths are attempts to explain the world in neat and tidy ways. Religious and cultural studies scholars use myths to glean information on the communities that perpetuate their particular stories and grand narratives. Myths illuminate collective values by establishing who should be considered heroes or villains. The historian of Hinduism and mythology, Wendy Doniger, explains how myths have political meaning.[4] Studying myths elucidates the power to create, interpret, and wield symbols to influence and mobilize people. The processes of mythmaking also deserve attention.

The use of war metaphors in the US is not new.[5] In 1906, William James's speech at Stanford University "was an attempt to explain the paradox that such an ugly and barbaric enterprise as war draws its appeal, in part, by drawing on the best qualities of the people who fight in it."[6] It is an appealing narrative to highlight the strength and courage of heroes uniting to battle a common enemy, who are villainized to represent forces of evil.[7] This discourse can be used for abstract threats. The Cold War was against Communism. American political leaders have waged "War on Poverty," "War on Drugs," "War on Crime," "War on Cancer," "War on Gangs," "War on Inflation," and "War on Terror."[8] Declarations of war continue to provide shortcuts to power that bypass policy deliberation and planning.[9]

Kelly Denton-Borhaug defines US war-culture as "the normalized interpenetration of the institutions, ethos and practices of war with ever-increasing facets of daily human life, economy, institutions and imagination in the United States."[10] Public officials, such as the surgeon general and the commander in chief, employ this discourse to present an image that they are leading the troops to victory. Managing this image is important, and policy decisions are made with an eye on the morale of constituents voting in the next election. Denton-Borhaug explains how leaders evoke a logic of sacrifice to legitimize "violence by covering the activities of killing with a sacred canopy made up of values such as loyalty and freedom."[11] These extreme measures are justified by religious reasoning, as she demonstrates: "Safety becomes the equivalent of salvation in the rhetorical universe that is US war-culture."[12] In addition to lives, civil liberties can be offered as appropriate sacrifices in war discourse.

Mythmaking is the underlying foundation to war metaphors. The mythological battle between good and evil does not allow for middle ground or nuance. This Manichaeistic dualism applies perfectly to warfare: in war, one is either for or against "us." Charles Tilly argues war-making is an essential ingredient to the creation of the modern nation-state.[13] Since war is waged against an *other*, typically a foreign and alien enemy, the use of war metaphors fuels xenophobia and racism.

A crucial ingredient in mythmaking is the control of information and the deliberate use of language, especially names. In comparing the novel coronavirus to foreign attacks on American soil, US Surgeon General Jerome Adams evokes images of Japanese bomber pilots and Islamic extremist plane hijackers. Similarly, President Trump emphasizes the foreign origins of the virus by calling it the "Chinese virus."[14] This phenomenon is not new. The 1918 influenza pandemic is more popularly known as the "Spanish flu" because during World War I, the countries at war censored early reporting of the virus whereas neutral Spain did not. The first documented cases were actually in Kansas.[15]

A Simplified Story

Mythmaking creates a simple story: the world is engaged in a heroic struggle against an alien evil (virus). This ignores the complexities that led to the COVID-19 outbreak and the difficult changes necessary to prevent similar outbreaks in the future. Sonia Shah argues pandemics should not be characterized "as arbitrary calamities but instead as probabilistic events, made more likely by human agency."[16] For instance, the COVID-19 pandemic was partially a function of increased meat consumption. The history of the human domestication of animals for consumption has continuously led to outbreaks and new diseases. Domesticating pigs led to whooping cough; chickens, typhoid fever; ducks, influenza; goats, tuberculosis; ad nauseam.[17] Domesticating cattle likely led to measles and smallpox, leprosy likely came from water buffalo, and the common cold from horses. Scientists and public health experts have continued to issue warnings regarding the rising consumption of animals. The economic pressures to factory farm dramatically increase the chances of new outbreaks. However, this inconvenient truth is hard to swallow. It is more palatable to continue consuming beef, pork, and chicken, accepting the inevitability of swine and avian flu while ethnocentrically condemning the consumption of animals unfamiliar to the Western palate such as cats (linked to SARS) and bats (linked to the Ebola virus).

Changes to consumption and policy can lower the chances of future outbreaks. However, Shah counsels, "doing so will require a fundamental restructuring of the global economy and the current way of life, which rests upon the accelerating consumption of natural resources."[18] Her call for altering consumption patterns is a significantly more challenging and difficult task than waging war on one enemy virus. Pressures for economic growth shape environments that foster outbreaks, but economic values go unchallenged. Warfare, on the other hand, is an engine for making money. Rather than accepting the value of relentless growth, educators can look to Asia for alternative discourses of (dis)harmony and (im)balance. To explain this, I turn to narratives around disease.

Medical Paradigms of Asia

Germ theory can be easily co-opted into a discourse of war. Germs "invade" the body, which requires the immune response as "defense" to resist the "onslaught" from "enemy" microbes. Historians of medicine and science point out how this new paradigm was contested as Asian intellectuals negotiated how to integrate this theory into existing local bodies of knowledge. The British-colonized cities of Hong Kong and Kolkata were zones of informational exchange between Asia and Europe. Though experts in both cities eventually accepted germ theory, they disagreed on the site and location of diseases. The discourse around disease has always been political. As historian Mary Sutphen has demonstrated, local elites in these cities argued "that the most likely place to find bacilli was in the houses, goods, and on the bodies of working-class immigrants, long held to be reservoirs for disease."[19] In Hong Kong, Chinese physicians debated whether epidemics were caused by environmental imbalance through cold-induced factors (*Shanghan* 傷寒 school) or climate changes through warm-induced factors (*Wenbing* 溫 病 school).[20] In Kolkata, experts disagreed on how to interpret bacteriological evidence.[21]

Chinese understandings of medicine, the body, and the universe employ the paradigm of *qi* (psychophysical life force, also romanized as *ch'i* 氣). Disease is caused by imbalance and blockage. Indian Ayurvedic medical texts attribute etiology to misuse, abuse, and over- and under-use of the body. Both Chinese and Indian medical traditions focus on (in)appropriate timing of activity. Both employ metaphors of flow and blockage, of *qi* and *prana* (breath or life force). These provide alternative metaphors to understand disease, humans, and their relationships with others. In writing about the history of medicine and science in China and Africa, Helen Tilley uses the term "polyglot therapeutics" to refer to oscillations between conflicting and incommensurate epistemologies and ontologies. Tilley explains how "traditional medicine" undermines a positivist view of scientific progress toward a singular Truth by presenting communities who "occupy different 'conceptual realities' and bodily 'modes of existence' at one and the same time."[22] In other words, medical discourses are contested, and looking to Asia decenters Western narratives.[23]

Lessons for Educators

Asian perspectives provide different foundations for mythmaking. How would the narrative change if discourses of (dis)harmony and (im)balance replaced the mythological battle between forces of good and evil, which undergirds war metaphors? Would this help make explicit the complexity and complicity of policy decisions and increasing consumption as key contributors to COVID-19 and other epidemics?

The point is not to romanticize Asia as a radical or exalted other. The rhetoric of harmony can also be utilized to justify the status quo and oppress minority voices, but the ways harmony and balance are used and negotiated deserves consideration. Furthermore, the US is not the only place where public officials employ war metaphors against the virus, as the president of France, the prime ministers of the United Kingdom and Greece, other leaders in the European Union, and the Chinese Communist Party have also use them. Further analysis of Chinese officials' use of terms such as "wartime emergency mode" (*zhanshi zhuangtai* 战时状态) and the "People's War" (*renmin zhanzheng* 人民战争) against COVID-19 would be fruitful.[24]

Rather than accept the war metaphors employed by US public officials, educators can investigate the discourse on COVID-19 in parts of China, Japan, South Korea, India, and other areas of the world. What are their central metaphors? What are the mythmaking processes underlying other current and past narratives? Even if the answer is unclear at the moment as they are being contested and constructed, these are important directions to pursue.

Notes

[1] World Health Organization, "Naming the Coronavirus Disease (COVID-19) and the Virus That Causes It," https://www.who.int/emergencies/diseases/novel-coronavirus-2019/technical-guidance/naming-the-coronavirus-disease-(covid-2019)-and-the-virus-that-causes-it. My gratitude goes to an anonymous reviewer who suggested I more clearly distinguish "COVID-19" as the name of the disease from the name of the virus responsible for this disease. I follow the WHO in using "COVID-19 virus" due to the association of SARS-CoV-2 with Asia. I am also grateful for helpful feedback from the editor, two reviewers, and numerous colleagues who provided comments on earlier drafts.

[2] William Cummings, "'This Is Going to Be Our Pearl Harbor': Surgeon General Warns USA Faces Worst Week of Coronavirus Outbreak." *USA Today*, April 5, 2020, https://www.usatoday.com/story/news/politics/2020/04/05/surgeon-general-jerome-adams-coronavirus-rivals-pearl-harbor-9-11/2950230001/.

[3] Alexandre Christoyannopoulos, "Stop Calling Coronavirus Pandemic a 'War.'" *The Conversation*, April 7, 2020, http://theconversation.com/stop-calling-coronavirus-pandemic-a-war-135486.

[4] Wendy Doniger, *The Implied Spider: Politics and Theology in the Myth*, updated edition (New York: Columbia University Press, 2011). Doniger provides a political reading of the Indian epic, the *Bhagavad Gita*, and how it offers guidelines to follow ethical duty during war.

[5] Smithsonian Magazine, "Introducing Our Special Issue on America at War," January 2019, https://www.smithsonianmag.com/history/america-at-war-introduction-180971014/.

[6] Matt Reed, "War Metaphors and the Return to Campus," *Inside Higher Ed*, May 20, 2020, https://www.insidehighered.com/blogs/confessions-community-college-dean/war-metaphors-and-return-campus.

[7] Dahlia Lithwick, "The Problem with Being a Hero is You Stop Being a Human," *Slate Magazine*, April 20, 2020, https://slate.com/news-and-politics/2020/04/coronavirus-humans-vs-heroes.html. Lithwick explains how calling people heroes places the onus on individuals and allows policymakers to skirt responsibility and neglect systemic, long-term planning toward prevention. The majority (over three-fourths in New York City) of these "heroic" essential workers are underpaid racial minorities, indicating the hypocrisy in valorizing exploited marginalized populations. See Larry Neumeister and Marina Villeneuve. "Call for Virus Volunteers Yields Army of Health Care Workers." *AP News*, April 1, 2020, https://apnews.com/7fca3117e7fa0f394bc7b2dba9e26316.

[8] Marc N. Bacharach, "War Metaphors: How President's Use the Language of War to Sell Policy." PhD Dissertation. Miami University, 2006.

[9] David Davenport and Gordon Lloyd. *How Public Policy Became War* (Stanford, CA: Hoover Institution Press, 2019), 1–2.

[10] Kelly Denton-Borhaug, *U.S. War-Culture, Sacrifice and Salvation* (London: Routledge, 2014), 8.

[11] Kelly Denton-Borhaug, "War-Culture and Sacrifice," *Feminist Theology* 18, no. 2 (2010): 175–91, 186.

[12] Denton-Borhaug, "War-Culture and Sacrifice," 186.

[13] "War making, extraction, and capital accumulation interacted to shape European state making." Charles Tilly, "War Making and State Making as Organized Crime." In *Bringing the State Back In*, edited by Peter B. Evans, Dietrich Rueschemeyer, and Theda Skocpol (Cambridge: Cambridge University Press, 1985), 172. Referenced in Christoyannopoulos, "Stop Calling Coronavirus Pandemic a 'War.'"

[14] Four days after the president repeatedly used "Chinese virus," a non-Chinese Asian man and his two children were stabbed at a Texas supermarket. War metaphors contributed to the attacker's justification of the stabbing since the perpetrator believed the victims were Chinese and thus spreading the virus. See Melissa Borja, "The Wounds of Racism and the Pandemic of Anti-Asian Hatred." *Anxious Bench*, April 2, 2020, https://www.patheos.com/blogs/anxiousbench/2020/04/the-wounds-of-racism-and-the-pandemic-of-anti-asian-hatred/.

[15] Alfred W. Crosby, *America's Forgotten Pandemic: The Influenza of 1918*. Second Edition (Cambridge; New York: Cambridge University Press, 2003), 25.

[16] Sonia Shah, "Mass Consumption Is What Ails Us." *Foreign Affairs*, April 17, 2020, https://www.foreignaffairs.com/articles/world/2020-04-17/mass-consumption-what-ails-us.

[17] Michael Greger, "Their Bugs Are Worse than Their Bite: Emerging Infectious Disease and the Human-Animal Interface." In *The State of the Animals IV*, 2007, edited by Deborah J. Salem and Andrew N. Rowan (Washington, DC: Humane Society Press, 2007), 111–27.

[18] Shah, "Mass Consumption Is What Ails Us." Officials in China and around the world continue to push economic growth at the expense of animal welfare and environmental and food safety. The contribution of deforestation to zoonotic transmission of disease is often ignored. The increased demand for resources and the drive for economic growth is not criticized. Instead, the alien practices of using "wild" animals for Chinese medicine and the consumption of "exotic" animals are rebuked in and out of China, both after SARS and COVID-19. For more on the problems with these uninformed and ethnocentric criticisms, see Mei Zhan, "Civet Cats, Fried Grasshoppers, and David Beckham's Pajamas: Unruly Bodies after SARS," *American Anthropologist* 107, no. 1 (2005): 31–42, and Miranda Brown, "Don't Blame Chinese Medicine for the Coronavirus: A Response to the New York Times Op-Ed," *Chinese Food & History*, March 3, 2020, https://www.chinesefoodhistory.org/post/don-t-blame-chinese-medicine-for-the-coronavirus-a-response-to-the-new-york-times-op-ed.

[19] Mary P. Sutphen, "Not What, but Where: Bubonic Plague and the Reception of Germ Theories in Hong Kong and Calcutta, 1894–1897," *Journal of the History of Medicine and Allied Sciences* 52, no. 1 (1997): 84.

[20] For more on the differences between the *Shanghan* and *Wenbing* schools, especially in response to epidemics, including SARS, see Marta E. Hanson, *Speaking of Epidemics in Chinese Medicine: Disease and the Geographic Imagination in Late Imperial China* (Abingdon: Routledge, 2011).

[21] Sutphen, "Not What, but Where," 109.

[22] Helen Tilley, "How to Make Sense of 'Traditional (Chinese) Medicine' in a Time of Covid-19: Cold War Origin Stories and the WHO's Role in Making Space for Polyglot Therapeutics," *Somatosphere*, May 25, 2020, http://somatosphere.net/2020/tcm-covid-19.html/.

[23] Based on fieldwork in Indonesia and India, the medical anthropologist David Napier proposes alternatives to the warfare metaphor against disease. He offers metaphors of information assimilation by describing how the immune response is xenophilic—it seeks engagement with new information—rather than xenophobic. See, David A. Napier, "Epidemics and Xenophobia, or, Why Xenophilia Matters." *Social Research: An International Quarterly* 84, no. 1 (2017): 59–81.

[24] The good versus evil dichotomy rests on an Augustinian conception of sin, which does not apply to Chinese cosmology and views of human nature. See P. J. Ivanhoe, *Confucian Moral Self Cultivation* (Indianapolis: Hackett Publishing, 2000), 31–32. Chinese notions of goodness are to align properly with the flux of yin and yang. See Robin R. Wang, *Yinyang: The Way of Heaven and Earth in Chinese Thought and Culture* (Cambridge: Cambridge University Press, 2012), 109, 129.

7

Explaining the Impacts of the COVID-19 Pandemic on China-Africa Relations

Richard Aidoo

The COVID-19 pandemic, which started in Wuhan, China, in late 2019, entered Africa through Egypt, with the initial reported case in February 2020. A case was later found in Nigeria in sub-Saharan Africa, and the virus subsequently spread across the continent. Not surprisingly, the pandemic has affected relations between China and African countries, making an already complex relationship much more problematic to navigate in the face of a global health crisis that has shut down borders and boardrooms, impacting every aspect of human endeavor.

In the twenty-first century, China has expanded its diplomatic and economic engagements in Africa.[1] China's relationship with various African countries has elicited both celebration and concern.[2] The controversial parts of this relationship include the unequal economic partnerships between China and African countries; the debt burden of African economies as they continue to access Chinese loans; the exploitation of Africa's natural resources by a seemingly resource-hungry China; and China's apparent aloofness in encouraging democratic reforms among undemocratic African partners.[3] On the other hand, China-Africa relations feature expansive and beneficial trade among the economies; technology transfers that often accompany development aid and loans; security benefits that are hugely significant for some parts of Africa; and most visibly, the transformation of Africa's infrastructure landscape with Chinese finance and labor resources.[4]

So, for a rather multilayered and persistently scrutinized relationship, the global pandemic offers more avenues for dialogues about diplomatic distrust and economic exploitation. This has been particularly so, as COVID-19 has the potential to impact Africa's already frail economies, which would necessitate help from China, a global economic power with expanding influence on the continent. This pandemic raises further questions about an already unequal partnership. How has this particular global health crisis affected relations between China and Africa, and how can we teach our students these impacts with the nuance that is needed for understanding this important diplomatic relationship?

This chapter draws attention to some key factors to consider in evaluating and teaching about China's growing presence in Africa, particularly during this global health crisis. First, the chapter lays out the effect of the COVID-19 pandemic on the relationship between Africa and China, showing how this disorienting period has highlighted some significant debates about it. Next, it addresses issues to consider as we offer, teach, and engage explanations about China-Africa relations within the context of uncertainty resulting from the pandemic.

Impact of the COVID-19 Pandemic on China-Africa Relations

The COVID-19 pandemic affected every region of the world. Expectedly, like in most developing parts of the world, economies in Asia and Africa were considered to be susceptible to the destructive effects of the novel virus. As the origin of the virus, China has received global condemnation but has also served as a model for its mitigation measures. With the first reported case on February 14, countries in Africa have been commended for staving off the expected spread and effects of the pandemic but also cautioned by the World Health Organization (WHO) about the increasing number of COVID-19 cases. The International Monetary Fund (IMF) has warned African leaders of the potential destructive effects on economies on the continent.[5] Generally, the emergence and global spread of COVID-19 has intensified some ongoing debates that are presently impacting and will continue to shape the twenty-first-century character of China-Africa relations.

As the COVID-19 pandemic deepened in early 2020, the call for Chinese debt cancellation for African economies gained momentum and relevance. According to the American Enterprise Institute's (AEI) China Global Investment Tracker, the total value of Chinese investments and construction in Africa is close to $2 trillion since 2005.[6] A large portion of this is from loans and other forms of foreign assistance. Because of the pandemic, there was decreased demand in global markets for a wide range of African exports, disruption in global supply chains that deliver inputs from regions like Asia, Europe, and the Middle East, and reduced foreign direct investments (FDI) as economic partners from other continents redirected capital locally.[7] Amid such uncertainties, economic growth in Africa

Figure 1: The first China-Africa Economic and Trade Expo,
Changsha, Hunan, China, June 29, 2019.

is expected to shrink by an unprecedented 1.6 percent in 2020, according to the IMF.[8] Depending on predicted scenarios, Africa's economies could lose between $90 billion and $200 billion in 2020.[9] These figures bring to the fore the issue of debt cancellation, as countries across Africa have been accumulating debt through Chinese loans over the past two decades. As Africa's largest single state creditor, Chinese debt relief or forgiveness is considered a vital gesture to ensure a smooth post-COVID-19 economic recovery. France has called upon Beijing to consider debt relief to African countries, echoing the World Bank's call on G-20 leaders to render debt relief to the world's poorest countries.[10] China has reportedly granted some relief to its African debtors, though this does not constitute complete debt forgiveness but rather relief on zero-interest loans. In response to the issue of debt relief during this pandemic, the Chinese Foreign Ministry stated that "China supports the suspension of debt repayment by least developed countries and will make its necessary contributions to the consensus reached at G-20."[11] During a virtual conference in April 2020, the G-20 agreed to suspend the debt payments of the world's poorest (including African) countries based on a liquidity availability assessment by the World Bank and IMF, starting from May 2020 to the end of the year.[12] As this pandemic continues to negatively impact African economies, pressure will grow on China (in partnership with other developed economies) to provide greater debt cancellation.

Although the COVID-19 pandemic has spread slowly and unevenly across Africa, poor health care infrastructure and services means that more foreign assistance will be required if the pace of spread accelerates. This has opened up opportunities for the delivery of foreign assistance or humanitarian aid. To contain the pandemic, China's support is needed to provide ventilators and personal protective equipment (PPE) for African hospitals and health care workers.[13] Beijing has endeavored to step in and provide assistance to African countries, as have individual Chinese philanthropists, such as Jack Ma, whose donations have been widely reported. With a seeming competition between Western nations and China in Africa, the Chinese assistance during the COVID-19 pandemic has other global political implications. Such gestures echo sentiments of Asian-African allegiance from the 1955 Bandung Conference—rhetorical devices China has often capitalized on to strengthen its diplomatic and economic engagements in Africa. Chinese aid could be another manifestation of goodwill in China-Africa relations, particularly when China's assistance is often perceived as having undermined the development of African democratic freedoms.[14]

Expanded China-Africa relations have led to the rise of anti-Chinese sentiments in African countries and anti-African propaganda and clashes in China. The COVID-19 pandemic has extended existing tensions between locals and migrants, leading to the expression of deadly xenophobic sentiments in parts of both Africa and China. Within African communities, friction between the locals and Chinese migrants has intensified over the past two decades as Chinese capital and businesses have moved into these neighborhoods. The anger in these aggrieved constituencies is often exploited by political opponents who stoke anti-China rhetoric.[15] Locals in countries such as Kenya, Zambia, South Africa, and Ghana have expressed concern about living side by side with Chinese migrants, arguing that since COVID-19 originated in Wuhan, their migrant neighbors would spread the virus.[16] Anti-African violence also broke out in Guangzhou in April 2020, which saw maltreatment and discrimination toward African residents. These anti-African sentiments were founded on the unproven notion that African residents were spreading the coronavirus in their neighborhoods. Authorities responded by subjecting them to discriminatory forced quarantines, tests, evictions, and other forms of harassment. When such events are reported around the world, they create a positive feedback loop that thrives in this pandemic period of uncertainty and crisis. Vivid side-by-side portrayals of this subject matter are found in many news reports and documentaries such as *Laisuotuo*, a short film that explores the burdens of African and Chinese migrants in China and Lesotho respectively.

Explaining China-Africa Relations during the COVID-19 Pandemic

Over the past two decades, China-Africa diplomacy has been under scrutiny, especially by Western actors who often caution African countries about the effects of an unequal economic partnership with China. In short, accusations of neocolonialism have dogged this relationship. Not surprisingly, the pandemic is bound to complicate a seemingly uneven dynamic by offering more examples of inequity, with China as an exploitative global power and African economies as weak and incapable of responding to the unfair economic incursions of their dominant faux ally. For instance, Chinese PPE donations to Africa (like many of Beijing's diplomatic gestures), caricatured as *mask-diplomacy*, could be perceived as underhanded diplomatic overtures to curry economic favor from African regimes, particularly at a time when Africans are most in need of external support. Additionally, as COVID-19 leads to economic uncertainties, some African economies already indebted to China will likely need more resources from the global economic power, which will further deepen the debt problem for these countries. How do we use the pandemic to teach and discuss the multiple aspects of China-Africa relations? As educators, we must parse through China's diplomatic policies and encounters with African countries—most useful at an uncertain time when attention to detail may be overlooked.

First, to narrowly construct and interpret engagements between China and Africa (at any period) without a recognition of or reference to some of the main concepts and contexts that have served as bedrocks to China's current foreign policies toward Africa is to discount the needed nuance to objectively frame this twenty-first-century relationship. In Africa (and most parts of the developing world), China's appeal has been enhanced by the noninterference doctrine, in which China refuses to interfere in a partner's domestic affairs, even if the principle is untenable in other realms.[17] Some scholars have argued that precepts like the Five Principles of Peaceful Coexistence inform China's noninterference doctrine, as do traditional Chinese cultural concepts such as *weizheng yide* (rule by virtue), *renzhi* (rule of benevolence), and *guanxi* (networks).[18] Additionally, historical context matters in China-Africa relations. This relationship has been through anti-colonial struggles and the vicissitudes of the Cold War. Current Chinese engagements in Africa are grounded in their historical solidarity during anti-imperialist struggles in Angola, and China's encounters with Egypt, Ethiopia, Ghana, Libya, Sudan, and Liberia at the 1955 Bandung Conference in Indonesia. China's diplomatic rhetoric toward Africa often draws on its status as a noncolonizing power and a developing country that has an understanding of the economic plight of African countries, compared to the exploitative experience of Western colonizers in Africa. Even today, these partnerships still value the Asian-African fraternal links as embodied in the Forum on China-Africa Cooperation (FOCAC).[19] To understand and fully explain the impacts of the China-Africa debt burden, uneven trade, foreign aid dependency, and the surge in anti-China and anti-African sentiments, all of which have been impacted by the COVID-19 pandemic, we must recognize the principles and historical contexts that inform current China-Africa discourses.

Most research and discourse on China-Africa relations are often centered on state-to-state diplomacy, which means that the voices of political elites are often privileged above that of the masses. For instance, the oft-reported African acceptance of Chinese investments is mostly supported with statements from African government officials and political elites, not with the testimony of the popular masses who often experience the intended and unintended outcomes of these investments. There are variations among the voices of individual Africans—both within states and between various states. Research shows that there are different archetypes of China-Africa partnerships that depend on the economic nature and stature of each particular African country. For instance, Ethiopia and South Africa are considered to have well-developed partnerships with China relative to Côte d'Ivoire's nascent partnership.[20] These diverse relationships present different opportunities and challenges for the local dwellers, which might not necessarily match the intended objectives of the politicians and elites in power. Similar to other China-Africa issues, consideration of the wide-ranging impacts of the COVID-19 pandemic should account for voices of the political elites and, most essentially, the interests and concerns of the common people.[21]

Finally, when teaching about China-Africa relations during the COVID-19 pandemic, we must carefully scrutinize the many myths and memes that often impact the relationship. Over the past two decades, myths about China's unconditional lending to African countries, the lack of African agency in Chinese-funded projects, and the neocolonial relationship have eclipsed serious considerations of these matters in China-Africa relations.[22] As COVID-19 spreads across Africa, the myth that China has donated masks and medical equipment contaminated with the coronavirus to African countries has unnerved recipient populations.[23] Memes depicting African indebtedness to the Chinese generalize and trivialize the rather nuanced explanations of the issue and are circulated widely on the internet.[24] Periods of uncertainty heighten the production and use of such myths and memes, and the tendency to overlook them without adequate interrogation and investigation offers distorted explanations of China-Africa encounters. Short documentaries such as *The New Scramble for Africa* and *China's African Gold Rush* allow students to engage and analyze some of these myths and memes.[25]

In conclusion, the COVID-19 pandemic will certainly leave wide-ranging and lasting impacts on the twenty-first century. This era will also be defined by China's expansive reengagement of African countries—a feature of interest in global politics for the past two decades. The pandemic will most likely negatively impact the pace of economic development in the regions of Africa, while China will also continue to influence Africa's search for economic independence. COVID-19 presents possibilities, opportunities, and approaches for educators to present a balanced analysis of China-Africa relations in uncertain times.

Notes

[1] See Chris Alden, *China in Africa* (New York: Zed Books Ltd, 2007); and David H. Shinn and Joshua Eisenman, *China and Africa: A Century of Engagement* (Philadelphia: University of Pennsylvania Press, 2012).

[2] See Howard French, *China's Second Continent: How a Million Migrants Are Building a New Empire in Africa* (New York: First Vintage Books, 2014).

[3] See Ching Kwan Lee, *The Specter of Global China: Politics, Labor, and Foreign Investment in Africa* (Chicago and London: University of Chicago Press, 2017).

[4] Deborah Brautigam, *The Dragon's Gift: The Real Story of China in Africa* (Oxford: Oxford University Press, 2009).

[5] "Coronavirus: Africa Could Be Next Epicenter, WHO warns," BBC, April 17, 2020, https://www.bbc.com/news/world-africa-52323375 (accessed July 10, 2020); IMF, *Regional Economic Outlook: Sub-Saharan Africa: COVID-19: An Unprecedented Threat to Development* (Washington, DC: International Monetary Fund, 2020).

[6] See Jevans Nyabiage, "China's Trade with Africa Grows 2.2 percent in 2019 to US$208 Billion," *South China Morning Post*, January 18, 2020, https://www.scmp.com/news/china/diplomacy/article/3046621/chinas-trade-africa-grows-22-cent-2019-us208-billion (accessed July 9, 2020); Elliot Smith, "The US-China trade rivalry is Underway in Africa, and Washington is Playing Catch-Up" CNBC, October 9, 2019, https://www.cnbc.com/2019/10/09/the-us-china-trade-rivalry-is-underway-in-africa.html (accessed July 9, 2020).

[7] Kartik Jayaram, Acha Leke, Amandla Ooko-Ombaka, and Ying Suny Sun, *Tackling COVID-19 in Africa: An Unfolding Health and Economic Crisis that Demands Bold Action* (McKinsey & Company, 2020).

[8] IMF, *Regional Economic Outlook*.

[9] Kartik Jayaram, Acha Leke, Amandla Ooko-Ombaka, and Ying Suny Sun, 8.

[10] World Bank, "Remarks by World Bank Group President David Malpass on G20 Finance Ministers Conference Call on COVID-19," March 23, 2020, https://www.worldbank.org/en/news/speech/2020/03/23/remarks-by-world-bank-group-president-david-malpass-on-g20-finance-ministers-conference-call-on-covid-19 (accessed August 7, 2020).

[11] Yun Sun, "China and Africa's Debt: Yes to Relief, No to Blanket Forgiveness" *Brookings: Africa in Focus*, April 20, 2020, https://www.brookings.edu/blog/africa-in-focus/2020/04/20/china-and-africas-debt-yes-to-relief-no-to-blanket-forgiveness/?utm_campaign=Africa%20Growth%20Initiative&utm_source=hs_email&utm_medium=email&utm_content=87591010 (accessed July 11, 2020).

[12] "G-20 Agrees to Support Debt Relief for Poor Nations" *Kyodo News*, April 16, 2020, https://english.kyodonews.net/news/2020/04/b4d644947bd6-update2-g-20-agrees-to-support-debt-relief-for-poor-nations.html?phrase=postwords=&words= (accessed August 7, 2020).

[13] "Coronavirus Pandemic Helps China Expand Its Influence in Africa" *Deutsche Welle*, April 25, 2020, https://www.dw.com/en/coronavirus-pandemic-helps-china-expand-its-influence-in-africa/a-53241294 (accessed July 10, 2020).

[14] For a link between Chinese foreign assistance and African democratic development, see Steve Hess and Richard Aidoo, "Democratic Backsliding in Sub-Saharan Africa and the Role of China's Development Assistance," *Commonwealth & Comparative Politics*, Vol. 57, no. 4 (October 2019): 421–444.

[15] Richard Aidoo, "African Countries Have Started to Push Back against Chinese Development Aid. Here's Why," *The Washington Post*, October 16, 2018, https://www.washingtonpost.com/news/monkey-cage/wp/2018/10/16/african-countries-have-started-to-push-back-against-chinese-development-aid-heres-why/ (accessed September 4, 2020).

[16] Salem Solomon, "Coronavirus Brings 'Sinophobia' to Africa," *Voice of America*, March 4, 2020, https://www.voanews.com/science-health/coronavirus-outbreak/coronavirus-brings-sinophobia-africa (accessed July 12, 2020).

[17] For a detailed exposition on China's noninterference doctrine and its application in Africa, see Richard Aidoo and Steve Hess, "Non-Interference 2.0: China's Evolving Foreign Policy towards a Changing Africa," *Journal of Current Chinese Affairs*, 44, no. 1 (2015): 107–139; Steve Hess and Richard Aidoo, "Beyond the Rhetoric: Noninterference in China's African Policy," *African and Asian Studies* 9, no. 3 (2010): 356–383.

[18] See Steve Hess and Richard Aidoo, "Beyond the Rhetoric"; Stephen Chan (ed.), *The Morality of China in Africa: The Middle Kingdom and the Dark Continent* (New York: Zed Books Ltd, 2013).

[19] Read about the Forum on China-Africa Cooperation (FOCAC) from its webpage at https://www.focac.org/eng/ (accessed July 13, 2020).

[20] Irene Yuan Sun, Kartik Jayaram, and Omid Kassiri, *Dance of the Lions and Dragons: How Are Africa and China Engaging, and How Will the Partnership Evolve?* (San Francisco: McKinsey Global Institute, 2017).

[21] See, for instance, Howard French, *China's Second Continent: How a Million Migrants Are Building a New Empire in Africa* (New York: Knopf, 2014).

[22] Aubrey Hruby, "Dispelling the Dominant Myths of China in Africa," *Atlantic Council*, September 3, 2018, https://www.atlanticcouncil.org/blogs/new-atlanticist/dispelling-the-dominant-myths-of-china-in-africa (accessed July, 3, 2020).

[23] Kwasi Gyamfi Asiedu, "China Wants to Help Africa Fight Coronavirus but Not Everyone Is Welcoming," *Quartz Africa*, April 8, 2020, https://qz.com/africa/1834670/chinese-medical-aid-for-covid-19-in-africa-gets-mixed-support/ (accessed July 13, 2020).

[24] Deborah Brautigam, "A Critical Look at Chinese 'Debt-Trap Diplomacy': The Rise of a Meme," *Area Development and Policy*, 5, no. 1 (2020): 1–14.

[25] See "The New Scramble for Africa," *Al Jazeera*, July 27, 2014, https://www.youtube.com/watch?v=_KM06hTeRSY (accessed August 6, 2020); see also "China's African Gold Rush," *Al Jazeera*, December 15, 2016, https://www.aljazeera.com/programmes/101east/2016/12/china-african-gold-rush-161213120529920.html (accessed August 6, 2020).

8

INDIA'S PANDEMIC RESPONSE AS A MIRROR ON UNDERSTANDING INDIA'S COMPLEXITIES

Tinaz Pavri

This essay examines India's response to the coronavirus pandemic as a microcosm of understanding India itself in the new millennium. Prime Minister Narendra Modi's sudden lockdown of the country on March 25, 2020, took everyone by surprise. It allowed no time for preparation, cutting adrift millions of workers and migrants making up the core of India's informal workforce who were suddenly trapped without shelter in its major cities. The response has exacerbated religious tensions within the country, specifically with India's largest religious minority, Muslims. In general, it has laid bare many of India's long-standing challenges and dislocations, which the recent decades of economic development had obscured. The setback to India's economy and psyche from the pandemic and the pandemic response is expected to be deep, widespread, and long-lasting.

Beginning with post-independence India, I examine India's society, politics, and economy from the quasi-socialist eras of the first prime minister, Jawaharlal Nehru, and later, his daughter, Indira Gandhi. I move to a review of India's economic liberalization during the 1990s and the transformation of the country that it brought in its wake. I look at the sea change in politics that brought into power the current ruling party, the Bharatiya Janata Party (BJP), along with its charismatic but controversial prime minister, Narendra Modi, in the new millennium. I then turn to the pandemic and the government response, which has shone a spotlight on India's inequities and fault lines, and which above all allows us to understand modern India in all its complexity and challenge. It also serves as a case study of the tremendous and unprecedented trial that the pandemic has posed to the developing world.

Post-Independence India: Society, Economy, and Politics

After independence from the British in 1947, India's independence leaders embraced a quasi-socialist economy while maintaining a parliamentary democracy. Jawaharlal Nehru, India's first prime minister and a Cambridge-educated Fabian socialist himself, was convinced that the newly independent country—wounded by over a century of British rule, infrastructure-poor, and with a rising tide of population, illiteracy, and poverty—needed to protect its fledgling industries from foreign competition in order to strengthen them. His political party, the independence party of Mahatma Gandhi, the Indian National Congress (today, simply "the Congress"), maintained power in India through winning most of the national elections until the late 1990s. Indeed, India could be characterized as a single-party democracy in the decades after independence, so overwhelming was the support for the Congress, Nehru, and subsequent Congress party leaders. Soon after Nehru's death, his daughter, Indira Gandhi, was elected prime minister in 1966, and thereafter reelected like her father until she called for a national emergency in 1975, an extreme act permitted by the Indian Constitution under strictly limited circumstances. Citing domestic instability and foreign threat, although in reality goaded by her perception that the opposition was gaining ground, Gandhi suspended fundamental rights for the first time in independent India.[1] When she called for parliamentary elections again in 1977, the Congress lost for the first time, and the opposition Janata party came to power. This sea change in Indian politics, which repudiated the Nehru-Gandhi dynastic legacy, was widely hailed as evidence that Indian politics was finally coming into its own, a confirmation of the "democratic consolidation" of the former colony.[2]

Although Indira Gandhi was reelected in 1980, the era of single-party Congress rule in India had come to an end. After Indira Gandhi's death in 1984 (she was assassinated on the grounds of her home by Sikh bodyguards who were angered by her hard-line actions against Sikh separatists in Punjab and the sending in of troops into the Golden Temple), India entered a period of mostly coalition governments, in which the Congress was often a senior partner.

However, by the new millennium, a powerful new political force was forming across India, that of Hindutva, or the belief in Hindu strength and supremacy. Although an overwhelmingly Hindu country, India's constitution underlined a secular republic, and Nehru and the Congress party had always been strong advocates of India's minorities.[3] For the first time, the argument for a "Hindu

India" began to be openly articulated, and a political party, the BJP, took this on as its mantle. Steadily gaining ground in brief coalition governments, the BJP got voted into power in its own right in 1999. In the 2014 elections, with the polarizing Narendra Modi as its prime minister, the BJP was victorious again. It has since won an overwhelming majority in its reelection in 2019. While the economy has generally done well (until the pandemic, that is), the BJP has been condemned for fostering division within India's religious communities, particularly the Muslims, as well as promoting patriarchy and casteism (through its perceived favoritism of upper-caste Hindus).

At the beginning of 2020, India was looking back at nearly three decades of economic growth since the liberalization of India's economy in the 1990s. Privatization allowed hitherto state-held companies and sectors like infrastructure, insurance, and media to be partially owned by the private sector. As a result, Indian media went from a few nationalized television stations to hundreds of channels that brought the world into Indian homes. Foreign direct investment had been flowing into the country for decades, and a strong IT sector was now servicing the world. Economic growth ranging between 5 to 9 percent characterized many of the years during these decades, propelling hundreds of millions of Indians out of poverty and into the middle classes.[4]

Small businesses abounded, and the fruits of a technology revolution allowed even the poor to have access to a basic cell phone with which to conduct their business. Since much of the economy operates in the informal sphere, such access gave a powerful foothold for the relatively resourceless to become involved in the economic boom. Although, of course, problems of illiteracy, poverty, class and caste conflict, religious discrimination, and gender inequality certainly continued to be present and pervasive, the economic change was transformative. The "new India" was often heralded, and Prime Minister Modi enjoyed a wide approval despite some heavy-handed policies that backfired and ended up hurting India's poorest.[5]

Leading Up to the Pandemic Lockdown

Just weeks before the Western world, from Italy and Spain to the US, became convulsed with the spread of the coronavirus and scrambled to deal with the fallout, Modi had welcomed President Trump to India in a gigantic rally that underscored the friendship between these two world leaders. On February 24, 2020, in Ahmedabad, Modi's home state, a massive crowd of 125,000 people filled a stadium and offered a delirious welcome to Trump. In all, Trump, his wife Melania, Jared and Ivanka Trump, and their entourage only stayed three days, but the trip garnered enormous publicity in India and some deals were struck.[6] Little did either leader know at this point that the world's greatest economic and health calamity in a century would be devastating their countries just a few short weeks later.

In March, Europe, the US, and the rest of the world outside of East Asia began reeling from the spread of COVID-19. On March 25, Narendra Modi summarily ordered a complete lockdown with very little notice to the 1.3 billion Indians that it aimed to cover. The lockdown, with police patrolling India's major cities to ensure compliance, was one of the most restrictive in the world. People were not allowed on the roads, there were no gatherings in public spaces allowed, and public transportation was shut down. In cities like Mumbai, where millions lived in close quarters in vast slums, forcing everyone inside seemed cruel. The images of stranded migrant workers forced to walk hundreds of miles back to their villages were indelible, and they became symbolic of the callousness of the Modi government response. In addition, hundreds of thousands of Indian citizens were stranded overseas, especially in the Persian Gulf countries. Indian seamen were left without recourse on high seas as the government fumbled its response. Almost overnight, then, huge problems became evident that served to illustrate the enormous challenges that India faces in the social, economic, and political spheres.

After nearly eight weeks of lockdown, when the economy stood on the brink of collapse in many parts, India began partially opening up its remote villages (at that point mostly untouched by the pandemic), towns, and eventually all cities, even those like Mumbai, which were the worst hit. When Mumbai partly opened in early June after a strict lockdown, the pandemic was still ravaging through the city. Hospitals had run out of beds, and the private hospitals, which had been forced to open up for COVID-19 patients, were trying to circumvent the order. Health professionals, toiling without adequate protective equipment, were increasingly infected and dying. Initial testing was woefully inadequate, and dead bodies were piling up outside some hospitals. With the opening up of public spaces and transport, Indians cooped up indoors into small shared spaces came out in droves. The impact of this widespread opening amidst the raging pandemic is yet to be fully determined, but it is feared that the lack of social distancing while the pandemic is still ongoing could be disastrous, and parts of the country are periodically being forced to close down again. However, on the positive side, Mumbai's slums, feared to become super-spreaders, actually became models of effective containment. Testing has ramped up considerably. In mid-August, it hit a landmark of one million tests per day. The efficacy of these tests, especially rapid tests, remains in question, as does the veracity of the numbers of deaths, but as a percentage of the population, they are among the lowest in the world.

Figure 1: Workers scrambling to leave cities after public transportation was suspended nationwide during lockdown. Source: Wikimedia Commons.

Economic Impact

Despite the long strides India has made in the economic arena in the last few decades, a large percentage of the economy still consists of the informal sector, including independent street hawkers, unregulated domestic workers and construction crews, and migrant workers. In India's huge cities, many of these workers, living on wages that barely secure for them a meager existence in a slum or on the streets or on the grounds of the apartment buildings in which they work, suddenly found themselves unwelcome in the places that they had toiled in day after day. India's middle and upper classes, from the security of their own residences, and filled with initial anxiety and misinformation about how the virus spread, now banned their workers from sight, and many of them began a long, harsh, and tragic journey to villages that some had left years ago. Some of the initial misinformation surrounding the spread of the virus could be blamed on the government itself and its willingness to peddle false myths and "cures" surrounding the disease, which spread like wildfire on social media. With transportation cut off across India, especially the buses and trains that were the choice of the lower classes, these hapless Indians trekked hundreds of miles out of cities, some of them dying of hunger or exhaustion along the way. Horrifying visuals of thousands of hapless, displaced Indians being beaten by police batons in an effort to crowd control, or sprayed with disinfectant as they waited for transportation, became seared in the minds of the world.

In the precarious middle class, small shop and business owners were forced to close down and have now lost their livelihoods forever. Without a national social welfare safety net available, no substantial subsidies or salary replacement have been possible in India. Even a fund set up by the government to solicit donations and provide for poor Indians, the "PM Cares" fund, is mired in controversy and shrouded in secrecy as to its donors and amounts. Even though the government has belatedly announced some relief measures, they are few and far between and hard to apply for. There is widespread economic devastation, and the pandemic continues even after the lengthy lockdown has been lifted. In addition to the health crisis, India is now facing a hunger and poverty pandemic, the likes of which have not been seen in many decades and which has set growth back considerably.

Social Impact

The sudden economic devastation caused by the lockdown was mirrored by a concomitant social disaster. In the best of times, India is riven by class divisions that clearly delineate life for the upper-middle and upper classes from the large percentage of Indians still existing in poverty, with a precarious middle class in between. It is illustrative to note that according to the World Bank, India's per capita income in 2019 was $2,104, while its median income was just $600, which means that half of all Indians live on less than $600 per year.[7] Even more startling, in 2019, according to the Asian Development Bank, 10.7 percent of India's population lived on less than $1.90 per day.[8]

It is precisely these impoverished Indians who comprised many of the displaced workers, waiting for days and weeks to be able to leave the cities they worked in, which had now become hostile to them. Domestic workers were locked out of the homes they had cared for; drivers, couriers, security guards, and vendors were all reduced to a piteous existence where they begged for food from homeowners to stay alive in the streets, hiding to escape arbitrary police brutality. In a country which has historically adhered to a caste system that designated a hapless status to the lowest castes and "untouchables," this pandemic has brought to the fore the realization that the historical brutality of the caste system, combined with the vast inequalities in class, might have made it easier, even today, for those Indians of means to be numbed to the plight of their brethren. Of course, many did organize food, shelter, and transport to assist those without recourse, but it would be fair to say that the majority were in agreement with the government policy that cut off their workers' lifelines with little prior preparation, in return for the mirage of safely sheltering at home from the virus.

Figure 2: Municipal workers engaged in contact tracing and data collection in Tamil Nadu state. Source: Wikimedia Commons.

This terrible exodus has already ignited some soul-searching among Indians. There were some poignant posts on social media that asked fellow Indians to look deep within to try to understand how they could so easily accept the catastrophe that had befallen some of their fellow countrymen. How is it that these displaced Indians were looked upon as a problem to be solved, rather than the responsibility of all?

Religious Impact

In the last decade, India has truly become Modi's India. The prime minister enjoys extremely high approval ratings at upward of 60 percent. At certain times during the pandemic, his approval ratings hovered at 80 percent, although as the pandemic rages, he is being shown as someone out of his depth. Indeed, China, with whom India has had a border dispute for decades, has chosen this summer of weakness to breach the line of control on India's northeastern border, calculating that Modi was unable to respond forcefully or defend India robustly.

Modi's party, the BJP, was returned to power in 2019 with robust numbers. Since 2014, Modi's first term in office, it is fair to say that the relationship between majority Hindus and India's largest minority, Muslims, has significantly worsened. From the early years of independence, when the relationship among religions was more harmonious and India's secular nature was widely accepted, this relationship has turned tense in recent times. Just prior to the COVID-19 pandemic, the Modi government had undertaken two recent measures that had made Muslims feel even more oppressed in their own land.

First, soon after reelection in 2019, the government moved to revoke the constitution's special status accorded to Kashmir, India's only majority-Muslim state. Under article 370, Kashmiris have been given special rights and privileges, including job protections and land ownership, in the state.[9] With the revocation, many Kashmiri state legislators and other politicians were placed under a summary house arrest, and curfews, arbitrary arrests, and emergency rule blanketed the state. A majority of Indians supported the move, while Muslims felt further alienated. Then, in December 2019, the Citizenship Amendment Act (CAA) was passed by the BJP-led legislature, which aimed to benefit a number of religious minorities—those who had fled neighboring Pakistan, Bangladesh, or Afghanistan—by fast-tracking their Indian citizenship. Muslims were not included in the religions protected by the act, as the government said that the neighboring Muslim-majority countries were only oppressing other religions and so Muslims themselves did not need protection. This seemed exclusionary to the many Muslims who had fled countries like Bangladesh during war or famine and indeed to all Indian Muslims, especially those who, like millions of other Indians, do not always possess birth certificates or other government documents, and who viewed this as a veiled attack on their own citizenship status.

In March 2020, as the coronavirus started to make its terrible impact felt across the world, a Muslim missionary movement, the Tablighi Jamaat, held a large meeting in Delhi that was attended by Indian and foreign coreligionists. This meeting was found to be an early COVID-19 "super-spreader" event, and an effort was launched to track and test participants. Much blame was accorded to the community by frightened Indians, singling out Muslims as anti-nationalists, disease-spreaders, and rule-breakers. Hostile social media avenues openly blamed the community, and ugly rhetoric, including such terms as "COVID Jihad," was widespread. This became another wound in the heart of Muslims in contemporary India, which will continue to linger long after the realization by the country that the coronavirus would have spread throughout the country with or without this incident; no one talks about the Tablighi Jamaat anymore, but the harm has been done.

Post-Pandemic India

A few months into the COVID-19 pandemic finds an India that has, like many other countries, been set back many years in its development. The lifting of all boats through decades of economic development has been reversed. The lack of India's social welfare and health capabilities has been made glaringly clear. The hostility between religious communities has worsened and class conflict has deepened. The damage done will take decades to repair, and it is hoped that the repairing and rebuilding that will take place will not ignore these fault lines and cracks in Indian society that this pandemic has brought to the fore.

Notes

[1] Numerous books and articles have been written about Indira Gandhi and the Emergency. Among the reasons scholars have cited for Gandhi taking this step was her personality, with all its insecurities and the threats she felt from an emboldened opposition. Speculation about why she ended it and called national elections includes this conclusion: that despite her authoritarian bent, she was a democrat at heart who in the end believed in the democratic process.

[2] Political scientists employ this term to refer to countries that have maintained peaceful democratic transitions of power over time.

[3] Approximately 80 percent of India's population is Hindu. Muslims are the largest minority at around 14 percent, with Christians, Sikhs, Buddhists, Jains, Zoroastrians, and others rounding off the rest.

[4] Even though this robust rate of growth was lower compared to China's spectacular rates of growth over a longer period of time, India made steady progress.

[5] In addition to his general divisiveness, Modi has been criticized for a number of missteps that disproportionately affected and disenfranchised the poor, including demonetization and the revocation of Kashmir's special status.

[6] India purchased three billion dollars' worth of military equipment and helicopters, and it imported liquefied natural gas from Exxon Mobile. A more comprehensive trade deal was aimed at soon. See https://www.bbc.com/news/world-asia-india-51625503.

[7] GDP per capita (current $US)—India, The World Bank, 2020 available online at https://data.worldbank.org/indicator/NY.GDP.PCAP.CD?locations=IN (accessed August 31, 2020); Business Standard reporter, "India's Per Capita Income Lowest among BRICS: Gallup. New Delhi," *Business Standard*, December 17, 2013, https://www.business-standard.com/article/economy-policy/india-s-median-per-capita-income-lowest-among-brics-gallup-113121600968_1.html#:~:text=The%20yearly%20income%20earned%20by,99th%20position%20among%20131%20countries.

[8] Measured in Purchasing Power Parity, or PPP. See "Poverty Data: India," Asian Development Bank, 2020, available online at https://www.adb.org/countries/india/poverty (accessed August 31, 2020).

[9] These special privileges date back to 1947, when the first war between the newly independent India and Pakistan was fought over the status of Kashmir, the question concerning who Kashmir belonged to.

9

A Literature of Loss

Studying Narratives of Exile in Medieval Japan in the Context of COVID-19

Susan Spencer

The COVID-19 shutdown struck my undergraduate World Literature I survey class right before we entered the medieval period. We were about to begin our study of selections from *The Tale of Genji* and *The Tale of the Heike*. These two are the most famous of the *monogatari*, vernacular Japanese narratives that became popular during the late Heian and early Kamakura periods in the eleventh and twelfth centuries CE.

As we were forced to an entirely online format, which none of the students had chosen and several of the less technically motivated were apprehensive about, I found myself rethinking my approach to material I have taught for more than two decades. Since many of our students are from economically disadvantaged backgrounds and would have limited access to the Internet, I sought a form of delivery where they could access the material whenever they could and however they could. As some of my colleagues prepared to transition to synchronous video lectures modeled on the live classroom experience, we knew that some students would fall through the cracks if they were required to log in at a specific time. Even those with the necessary equipment and bandwidth were experiencing disruptions to their schedules. Many had family obligations or jobs that had been classified as "essential services," which often translated to irregular or even increased weekly hours.

With the campus computer labs closed, some students were limited to what they could receive on their phones, so I decided on a technologically retroactive direction: I composed new lessons, posting them to our learning management system[1] as plain HTML text with quick-to-load illustrations and, occasionally, links to short videos that wouldn't consume too much of their cell provider's allowance. But a text-based model would require more reading on top of a literature class that was already text-heavy, so I would have to be selective. I wanted to avoid simply replicating ideas that were available in our textbook's introductory material[2] or on the Internet. My resolution to start from scratch required me to contemplate carefully what I would include and to build my online "lectures" on a single theme that would hold everything together in a logical way and guide the students through a literary tradition they knew very little about.

I quickly discovered that there would be no need to reinvent the wheel by making an attempt to cover the basic frameworks of two long works in their entirety, as I would ordinarily do in an introductory lecture. Short explanatory videos, ranging between three and eight minutes, are freely available on the web; the Khan Academy, for instance, provides visually exciting introductions to the Heian Japanese court culture that pervades *The Tale of Genji* and to the lead-up and outcome of the Genpei War that dominates the Heike epic. For the benefit of visual learners, I linked to a couple of these and composed brief explanatory notes suggesting elements one might look for as especially relevant to the assigned passages in the stories themselves. I kept in mind that the videos needed to be provided as extra enrichment—but not as extra credit, which would not have been equitable, since students with significant bandwidth restrictions would be limited to their textbook's introductory material. I did, however, include a few screenshots from the videos alongside the text of my own web pages that followed, to provide continuity for those who had been able to get video access and to give a sense of visual context for those who had not. Additional illustrations that I provided to complement or clarify the background information, including *ukiyo-e* woodblock prints, were available through Google image search.

The task at hand, then, was to find a thread on which to hang the lessons. For the pandemic version of our Japanese literature unit I opted to concentrate on the themes of loss, sudden change, and a confrontation with the transitory nature of what one has taken for granted—life events that all of the students, regardless of background, were struggling with.

The *Genji* and *Heike* narratives are permeated with the Buddhist concept of impermanence. One particular geographical spot is especially associated with the themes that I wanted to emphasize: the coast of Suma, near today's city of

Kobe. Prince Genji's fall from grace in the capital and his subsequent exile to the Suma coast, combined with the added layer of tragedy after the pivotal Battle of Ichi-no-tani that occurred near the same spot some two hundred years later in the conflict recounted in *The Tale of the Heike*, is associated through centuries of Japanese literary history with nostalgia for a lost way of life. Genji was a fictional character invented by a Heian court lady over the course of several years at the dawn of the eleventh century; the battle that sealed the Heike clan's fate nearly two centuries later on March 20, 1184, was all too real. In both narratives, the episodes at Suma are significant dark intervals that occur within the context of complicated plotlines.

Once I had decided to build the unit primarily around a specific place, I made some changes to the syllabus. For *Genji*, I switched the assigned reading from my usual emphasis on the Shining Prince's early life in the capital city's palace to the events surrounding his exile, including an account that I had never assigned before of an impulsive affair with a woman from nearby Akashi, which had the resonance of a romance entered into at least partly on account of his sense of isolation—perhaps a cautionary tale, considering current circumstances.

The Tale of Genji tells us a lot about aristocratic values during an era when Japanese culture was at a peak, but it is not a very accessible book. Today, many of these values seem alien to modern readers. The intense emphasis on beauty in

Figure 1: This 1853 triptych woodblock print by the famous Edo *ukiyo-e* artist Utagawa Hiroshige depicts Prince Genji on the veranda of his home in exile at Suma. His impractically elegant clothing and hunched posture, turning his back on the prospect of Suma Bay, suggests his emotional rejection of the new world in which he has found himself. Rijksmuseum. Source: Wikimedia Commons: public domain.

all its forms, and the emotional intensity of Genji's many sexual conquests, make Lady Murasaki's protagonist very different from the action-oriented heroes we had studied in other long narratives such as *The Epic of Gilgamesh,* the Homeric poems, or even Valmiki's Hindu epic *Ramayana.* Yet it is possible to derive great joy from immersing oneself in this highly aestheticized bubble of a world, where there seems to be infinite time to devote to getting a poem just right or planning a future outing in a closed carriage to view the cherry blossoms in bloom. For those students who felt trapped in their homes, the ability to relate to this sense of infinite time was a new concept in their usually overcrowded schedules.

Like a darker echo of Genji's exile, the account of the Heike clan's flight from their family's palace complex at Fukuhara as they finally accept their refugee status is a touching account of a response to how a way of existence that they once accepted as natural is no longer possible for them. Unlike Genji, whose exile was temporary, they know that they can never return to the way things were before. They shelter amidst the decaying splendor of the palace buildings for one last night, then set it all on fire to keep their home from falling into enemy hands, a striking example of the stark difference between the beautiful bubble-world of Genji and this "new normal" of violence and destruction. Before the shutdown, we had studied the Fire Sermon of the Buddha, which explains that "everything is on fire" because the things of this world are transitory. I am not sure the students fully grasped the analogy until this point in the class.

When it came to deciding which elements to discard and which to keep in *The Tale of the Heike,* I chose to go deep rather than broad in the account of the war and focus more on the resonances of the Ichi-no-tani battle. Usually, my class looks at a chain of martial events in a cause-and-effect sequence, but the thematic focus enabled me to introduce them to adaptations of selected episodes in other traditional Japanese genres.

One of the most dramatic incidents amidst the fighting is a scene involving Atsumori, a doomed warrior of about sixteen, just a couple of years younger than some of the students themselves, who bravely takes a final stand on the beach in the face of certain death. The enemy soldier who has him cornered realizes that the youth reminds him of his own son, but with the battle lines advancing toward them he has no option but to offer Atsumori an honorable death.

The *Heike* text reports simply that the exchange so affected the soldier that he later gave up his arms and became a monk. About 200 years later, the Nō master Zeami Motokiyo composed one of his great masterpieces, *Atsumori,* which imagined an encounter between the soldier/monk and young Atsumori's ghost.[3] Unlike other Nō ghost dramas, which often feature a monk exorcising a hungry spirit whom he runs across in his travels, this one dives deeper since the monk was the actual instrument of the ghost's demise. The two exorcise each other; the

Figure 2: Another Hiroshige print, dated sometime between 1835 and 1839, portrays the final moments of the young Heike warrior Atsumori. Enemy warriors have overcome the Heike camp at Ichi-no-tani and can be seen advancing toward the beach in the upper left corner of the picture.
Minneapolis Institute of Art: public domain.

inability of Atsumori's spirit to rest is grounded in his inability to come to terms with the manner of his premature death, and the warrior-monk is haunted by a burden of guilt that keeps him from enlightenment. When forgiveness is reached, both of their spirits are released. The structure of mutual liberation echoes a similar exchange between two Buddhist nuns who enable each other to let go of worldly attachment in the opening chapter of *The Tale of the Heike*, "The Bells of Gion Monastery."

Although the period is outside the inclusive dates of our World Literature I survey, I also cited a haiku from the seventeenth-century Edo poet Bashō's *Backpack Notes*, as translated by Haruo Shirane: "Octopus traps— / fleeting dreams / under the summer moon." The summer moon, a traditional seasonal image, connotes the ephemerality associated with fleeting summer nights. The poem was composed while Bashō was lodging at Akashi; introducing the vernacular image of the octopus trap, he juxtaposes a seemingly peaceful modern scene with an implicit suggestion of the Heike warriors, caught between Suma Bay and a hostile army, who were massacred along the same shoreline half a millennium earlier. Just as the unwitting octopus crawls into a snug space that seems like a safe haven, the

Heike army's illusion of an unassailable position of security on a narrow stretch of land between a mountain and the open sea was overturned when their enemies discovered a pass on the mountainside and cut them off.[4]

Two more short works could be added seamlessly to the study of the *Genji* and *Heike* texts since the connections are obvious. For instance, Kamo no Chōmei wrote his moving *Hōjōki* (usually translated as "An Account of a Ten-Foot-Square Hut") in the year 1212, as the civil war described in *The Tale of the Heike* raged throughout Japan.[5] Although he does not directly address the fighting, the author reflects upon its impact as magnified by natural disasters: a citywide fire that devastated the capital in 1177, followed by a destructive whirlwind and a death-dealing earthquake, the sudden displacement as the capital was unexpectedly moved from its traditional center in Kyoto to Fukuhara, and widespread famine, events that combined to attract him to a hermit's life similar to that pursued by the women who retreat to a comparable hermitage in the *Heike* narrative's first episode. Akutagawa Ryūnosuke's brilliant short story "Rashōmon" (which bears little resemblance to Kurosawa's famous film, except in selected visual references), while written in 1915, is set in the same time period and echoes the details mentioned by Kamo no Chōmei as it imagines one man's moral crisis in the midst of society's breakdown.[6]

Hōjōki is only about fifteen pages in length and "Rashōmon" is less than ten. Both accounts contain exciting material that reads quickly and could promote further conversation about their underlying themes of impermanence and uprootedness and their use of common Buddhist symbolism to emphasize those themes.

The choice of central and supporting texts might have differed if I had not been working from an existing syllabus, a factor I might consider if circumstances suggest an iteration of the Japanese "literature of loss" unit. Many of Japan's canonical works are inclined toward this theme in the first place, so the instructor can choose which sources are most likely to appeal to a given group of students. Some to consider include the "love suicide" puppet plays of Chikamatsu Monzaemon, which provide an Edo-era contrast to the aristocratic monogatari with a concentration on working-class heroism undergirded by the rise of the more egalitarian faith of Pure Land Buddhism; many of Ichiyō Higuchi's Meiji-era short stories, especially if taught in combination with selections from her diary, which grounds her characters in precursors from episodes in *The Tale of Genji* or *The Tale of the Heike*; and Mishima Yukio's hauntingly tragic short story "Patriotism," based on events surrounding the failed coup d'état by a coalition of young army officers in 1936.[7] One might also examine human responses to crises peculiar to the modern era, such as Keiji Nakazawa's manga series (adapted as a film in 1976, with a more popular anime version following in 1983) *Barefoot Gen*, whose six-year-old protagonist survives the bombing of Hiroshima and its chaotic aftermath.

My reconfiguring of the World Literature I syllabus produced a different kind of story, certainly a darker story than previous years when I had emphasized more Confucian elements, such as the political world of the court and the clever ploys of the victorious generals. But it sustained student engagement in an otherwise distracting situation and, perhaps, was one that seemed a little less isolating in the face of this evidence that the sense of displacement we are all experiencing now is not unique to our own time and place.

Notes

[1] Our university's LMS is D2L ("Desire to Learn"). Other platforms, such as Blackboard or Canvas, would be equally suitable for this format.

[2] This semester, our class used the second edition of David Damrosch et al., ed., *The Longman Anthology of World Literature* (New York: Pearson Longman, 2009). The introductory essays and footnotes are excellent, and the selection of excerpts and entire works is well planned. I did, however, have to extend into some additional scanned pages from other editions of the two works we were studying so I could get exactly the passages I wanted to emphasize. I posted them to our D2L website along with the HTML pages I had composed to accompany them.

[3] Nō scripts are not very long, and this one is in our textbook, so I added Zeami's play along with an optional video clip of a scene in performance to demonstrate how *The Tale of the Heike* fired later imaginations.

[4] If I had wanted to dig yet deeper, I might have included an alternative version of the Atsumori episode from Namiki Sōsuke's 1751 puppet play, *Chronicle of the Battle of Ichinotani*, which can be found in Shirane's *Early Modern Japanese Literature* (New York: Columbia University Press, 2002), 410. That seemed a bridge too far for this particular class, so I merely mentioned it as a possibility for further exploration.

[5] Kamo no Chōmei's essay is not included in the *Longman Anthology*, which would have made it an easy add-on for my class. There is, however, an excellent annotated translation of it in the popular *Norton Anthology of World Literature* and several good translations of it can be readily found on the Internet and linked to.

[6] As a twentieth-century work, "Rashōmon" is found in the second volume of the *Longman Anthology*, which my students did not have, but this work too is readily available on the Internet. I teach this story regularly in the second semester of my World Literature survey, and it is one of the most popular things we read. I assign it early in the semester, generally within the first two weeks, and I've found it to be a reliable icebreaker for the students' first set of reading journals. Its moral ambiguity easily cuts through their initial reticence to open up in the first class discussions at the beginning of a new term. The protagonist, a samurai's servant who has just lost everything in the wake of his master's ruin, is a victim of circumstances beyond his control that have upended the comfortable assumptions he had lived by up to that point.

[7] The most famous of Chikamatsu's "love suicides" (*Shinju*) plays is his 1721 masterpiece, *The Love Suicides at Amijima*. I have had better luck teaching the less sophisticated *Love Suicides at Sonezaki* from 1703, a much shorter one-act play that can be easily read and comprehended in one sitting. Although it lacks the brilliance of the longer drama, it features the same star-crossed theme and has appeal as a ripped-from-the-headlines adaptation of a real incident that had occurred just a few months earlier. Both plays reflect sweeping cultural change in their approach to one's duty to society and to religion.

10

TEACHING THE EDGES OF EMPIRES

HONG KONG AND TAIWAN AMIDST THE COVID-19 PANDEMIC

Justin Wu

During a flight from Hong Kong to the United States in early January 2020, I noticed a number of staff members and passengers at the Hong Kong International Airport wearing face masks, which was not a common sight in ordinary circumstances. This was just days after the health authorities from Wuhan, the People's Republic of China (PRC), announced a pneumonia outbreak. While the world generally paid scant attention at the moment, one government did: beginning on December 31, 2019, Taiwan, or the Republic of China (ROC), started enforcing fever screenings on flight passengers arriving from Wuhan, followed by other inspection measures in subsequent weeks.

Amidst the global COVID-19 pandemic in 2020, Hong Kong and Taiwan have emerged as two largely "successful" cases of keeping the outbreak under control.[1] When other countries were still debating the merits of wearing face masks in early March, citizens of Hong Kong and Taiwan had already been stocking up. Such alertness can be attributed to two major factors: the experience gleaned from SARS in 2003 and recent geopolitical tensions with the PRC. The former instilled a sense of vigilance among the population regarding public health issues, and the latter demanded a higher level of conscientiousness in response to matters involving China.[2] The protests in Hong Kong since June 2019 further intensified Hongkongers' tension with their government and led many to question the "one country, two systems" model. The Taiwanese public have certainly been paying attention to developments in Hong Kong as well.

The COVID-19 pandemic presents an opportunity for instructors to pay more attention to Hong Kong and Taiwan in survey courses on China, East Asia, or the modern world. As "fragment of/f empires," to use the term coined by Wu Rwei-ren, both places, being situated on the edges of different empires, have been shaped by various forces such as colonialism, imperialism, and nationalism over the last few centuries.[3] Such experiences have contributed to the unique development patterns in both places. Drawing attention to them in the curriculum will enhance students' understanding of modern East Asia, an increasingly volatile region of growing economic and geopolitical significance. Furthermore, this will allow them to transcend the conventional nation-state framework by drawing attention to a special administrative region (Hong Kong) and the challenges it faces, along with a political entity (Taiwan), which is not officially recognized as an independent country by the United Nations and most countries across the globe.[4]

Two Societies, Both Alike in Dignity

Shortly after Hong Kong's transfer of sovereignty in 1997, a PRC official in Hong Kong famously remarked that Hong Kong was a difficult book to understand.[5] The same could be said for Taiwan. Both are predominantly Chinese-speaking societies influenced by a broadly defined Chinese culture. Yet, as exemplified by contemporary events, both also share complicated relationships with China and comparable notions of Chinese identity shaped by the historical development of both places.

For centuries, Taiwan was under the control of different powers, including the Dutch, the Spanish, the Zheng (Koxinga) regime, the Qing, the Japanese, and the ROC. After the First Sino-Japanese War (1894–1895), Taiwan became a Japanese colony until the end of World War II, when the ROC took over. Yet the ROC had a difficult time winning the support of the local population that resisted its authoritarian rule. The 228 Incident (1947), a civilian uprising against the ruling Nationalist Party (KMT), and the ROC's retreat from mainland China after the Chinese Civil War (1946–1949), led to the imposition of martial law in 1949. Those critical of the KMT regime and suspected of communist sympathy were arrested, tortured, or even executed. A number of dissidents went into exile and were "blacklisted" from returning to Taiwan after they made "critical" comments abroad.

Since the end of World War II, the ROC represented "China" at the UN and proclaimed itself to be "Free China," being an important ally of the US against "Red China." Yet the tide changed in 1971, as the PRC was recognized as the only legitimate representative of "China" in the UN, replacing the ROC. Since then, most countries have severed ties with the ROC and established diplomatic relations with the PRC instead. Domestically, within the ROC, calls for reforms

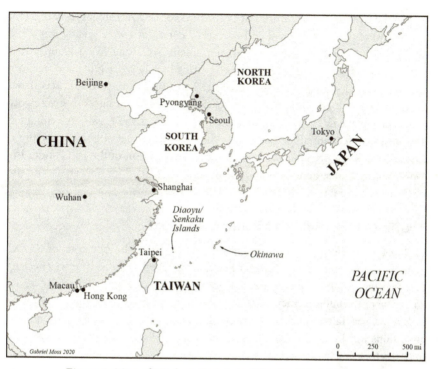

Figure 1: Map of Modern East Asia. Map by Gabriel Moss.

and democracy grew stronger over time, and martial law was finally lifted in 1987. In 1996, Taiwan had its first free presidential election, and in 2000, the Democratic Progressive Party (DPP) won the presidential election, marking the first time the KMT had lost power in Taiwan since 1945.[6]

Hong Kong, as is well-known, used to be a British colony. The British took parts of Hong Kong after the First Opium War (1839–1842) and occupied more territories in 1860 and 1898 respectively. Briefly occupied by the Japanese during World War II, Hong Kong, the "Berlin of the East," became an important frontier in the Cold War era. Both the CCP and the KMT engaged in ideological battles in the colony, exerting their influences through different channels such as newspapers, labor unions, and selected schools. Meanwhile, many Chinese who were fleeing from the Chinese Civil War or CCP rule escaped to Hong Kong. Hearing their stories about the great famine and political turmoil in mainland China, many Hongkongers became skeptical of CCP rule. Hence, despite a number of social problems in colonial Hong Kong at the time, including crowded housing, police corruption, and poor working conditions, in 1967, the local population largely supported the colonial government's suppression of the anti-colonial, pro-PRC riots, led by local pro-CCP leftists and inspired by the Cultural Revolution (1966–1976).

In the aftermath of the unrest of 1967, the colonial government reckoned that reforms were necessary. Social and economic conditions were greatly improved in the 1970s, and this helped strengthen a sense of Hong Kong identity that distinguished Hong Kong as "home," contrasting its relative stability and freedom with the turmoil and suppression in the PRC. Later, Britain and the PRC negotiated the Sino-British Joint Declaration (1984), determining the transfer of sovereignty would take place in 1997. The Tiananmen Square Massacre (1989) in Beijing led to widespread fear and uncertainty over the city's future, yet ultimately, on July 1, 1997, Hong Kong became a special administrative region of the PRC under the "one country, two systems" model, which is also intended for Taiwan should the PRC incorporate it in the future.[7]

The Trauma of SARS and Public Sentiment

In 2003, both Hong Kong and Taiwan suffered from the outbreak of SARS.[8] Then an unknown disease, it caught health officials off guard, adversely affecting everyday life and the economy. Certain governmental decisions were controversial and drew much public criticism, such as the Taipei City Government's decision to lock down the Taipei Municipal Hoping Hospital, which led to the worsening of conditions within it and the Hong Kong government's initial denial of an outbreak until doctors proclaimed otherwise.

The SARS experience proved to be a grave lesson for both places. Institutional reforms became necessary. In 2004, Taiwan established the Central Epidemic Command Center, responsible for coordinating with local authorities and implementing relevant measures in the event of a serious disease outbreak. Similarly, the SARS epidemic exposed a number of problems with the public health system in Hong Kong, including its deficient communication with the public (or even between officials) and risks posed to health care workers during a pandemic.[9] In 2004, Hong Kong set up the Centre for Health Protection, being primarily responsible for disease prevention and playing an important role in handling disease outbreak.

On a societal level, the SARS experience taught Taiwanese and Hongkongers much about public health precautions. Learning from the experience, the populations became vigilant and cautious in their everyday life and would react quickly upon a (potential) disease outbreak. One notable example is wearing face masks, especially when feeling unwell, to avoid spreading germs to others. Hence, while the outbreak of COVID-19 was yet to be taken seriously elsewhere, Hongkongers were already taking the initiative in wearing face masks, just as I observed in early January. The Taiwanese government also reacted promptly, restricting the export of face masks in late January and adopting a rationing system in early February to ensure citizens would have enough face masks for themselves.

Contemporary politics and activism in Hong Kong and Taiwan also help explain the response to the current pandemic. Hong Kong captured the world's attention in 2019 with the protests against a controversial extradition amendment bill and accusations of police brutality. Accompanied by years of debate over democratic reforms and government accountability, Hong Kong society has become extremely divided, especially concerning matters involving China. The public response to the COVID-19 pandemic reflected this dynamic, notably when medical workers led a five-day strike in early February to pressure the government into closing its border with China to prevent the spread of COVID-19 in the city.[10] The government later enacted a series of strict measures, but critics suggested they were less about public health safety and more about suppressing protest activities. The annual Tiananmen vigil, for instance, was banned for the first time, and dozens of pro-democracy activists were later charged for their participation.[11] With Beijing's imposition of a controversial national security law in Hong Kong in July 2020, the city enters a new stage of uncertainty with increasing degrees of governmental control and (self-)censorship.[12]

In contrast, the public in Taiwan held a favorable view of the government during the pandemic in the first half of 2020. As Taiwan followed Hong Kong's massive protests closely, President Tsai Ing-wen, who explicitly rejected applying the "one country, two systems" model to Taiwan, won reelection in the presidential race in January 2020 with a record number of votes, and the DPP also retained a majority in the legislature. This was a dramatic turn from two years ago, when the DPP lost tremendously in the local elections and Tsai's chances for reelection looked bleak. With such a strong mandate, the Tsai administration was able to swiftly implement precautionary and protective measures, working with private industry in the production of medical supplies. It also benefited from the coincidence that then Vice President Chen Chien-jen (who stepped down in May 2020 as he did not seek reelection) was an epidemiologist and served as Minister of Health during the SARS outbreak in 2003. The current Minister of Health, Chen Shih-chung, was widely praised for his informative daily briefings and bolstering of public confidence.[13] The level of trust in experts contributes to Taiwan's "success" in handling the pandemic, which is particularly significant considering Taiwan's exclusion from major international organizations such as the World Health organization (WHO). This presents an opportunity for the Taiwanese government to promote itself on the international stage.[14]

Contextualizing Hong Kong and Taiwan

In the twenty-first century, resistance against "mainlandization" in Hong Kong has grown stronger over time, and resistance against "Hongkongization" in Taiwan has increasingly rallied support.[15] As previously demonstrated, because of their unique developmental patterns, both Hong Kong and Taiwan share an uneasy relationship with China. Yet, such resistance has not always been the norm. Instead, instructors could draw on different examples to show the nuance of terms like "China" and "Chinese identity," and how people in both locales approach them in various ways.

One example that demonstrates the complicated relationship with "China" was the Baodiao Movement, or the "movement to protect the Diaoyu Islands." In the early 1970s, a territorial dispute between the PRC, the ROC, and Japan emerged concerning the Diaoyu/Senkaku Islands in the East China Sea.[16] Across the globe, and most prominently in the US, thousands of Hong Kong and Taiwanese students took to the streets to protest Japanese claims to the islands, chanting that they belonged to "China." Since the 1990s, some activists from Hong Kong and Taiwan, and also those from mainland China, have even tried to approach the Diaoyu/Senkaku Islands, demanding Japan recognize the sovereignty of "China" over these uninhabited islands. Whether this "China" meant the PRC, the ROC, or a broadly defined and depoliticized "China" depended on individual participants, but this case demonstrates that there have been moments when Hongkongers and Taiwanese actively declared their Chinese patriotism.

Even common classroom topics could be expanded to bring Hong Kong and Taiwan into discussion. During the Tiananmen Square Protests (1989), for instance, Hongkongers offered much support for protesters in Beijing. After the crackdown on June 4, there emerged a rescue mission called Operation Yellowbird, in which Hong Kong activists (with help from various sectors including politicians, celebrities, and even triad members) helped Tiananmen dissidents escape from China. The Tiananmen Protests became a collective moment for Hongkongers who grew incredibly concerned about the city's post-1997 future. In 1990, a year after Tiananmen, the Wild Lily Movement broke out in Taiwan, where student protesters demanded democratization after decades of authoritarian rule. Having paid attention to the movement in Beijing, protesters in Taiwan adapted their tactics, striving to avoid the same outcome.[17] Indeed, the movement ended with a promise of full democracy, leading to Taiwan's first free presidential election in 1996.

These two examples demonstrate how instructors can integrate Hong Kong and Taiwan in their teaching. The legacy of Tiananmen 1989, for example, did not only impact China, but it significantly influenced the subsequent development of Hong Kong and Taiwanese society as well. In other words, drawing on these examples allows instructors to transcend the conventional nation-state unit of analysis, demonstrating the broader impact of events beyond the nation-state and encouraging students to consider interactions between different political entities in the region. Similarly, Hong Kong and Taiwan's response to the COVID-19 pandemic should be considered in the context of their respective development but also in light of their relations with neighboring political entities, particularly the PRC. This approach would better explain why these two locales have emerged as "successful" cases in handling the pandemic.

Teaching the Edges of Empires

As scholars increasingly emphasize the importance of global connections, challenging students to "think globally" is essential. Drawing on different political entities, students can learn to conduct comparative analysis, situating historical events and figures in their respective contexts and assessing how the global circulation of various forces, including political ideas and rhetoric, shape historical development.[18] As educators, we can and should encourage our students to address and rethink the power dynamics of different political entities, including those that are not considered "nation-states" in the modern world.

In Hong Kong and Taiwan, we have two cases of different historical trajectories shaping their development and also their response to the current pandemic. These "fragments of/f empires" broaden our understanding of the dynamics within modern East Asia. They transcend the conceptualizations of nation-state boundaries, providing alternative frameworks within which to analyze intersocietal *modi operandi*, thereby complicating national narratives. Of course, this is not limited to Hong Kong and Taiwan; places like Okinawa and Macau, with their own unique histories, also have much to offer that could better students' understanding of contemporary history and geopolitics. Other political entities outside of East Asia, such as Palestine in the Middle East, Somaliland in Africa, or eastern Ukraine and Belarus in Europe, also offer similar lessons in understanding the complexity of regional and global histories and why they remain contentious today.

When teaching courses on China, East Asia, or the modern world, I find that students express much curiosity about Hong Kong and Taiwan. They frequently hear about these places in the news, most recently with the protests in Hong Kong and the controversy over Taiwan's WHO membership. Such contemporary events intrigue them, and these issues are worth exploring more in classrooms. The histories of Hong Kong and Taiwan force students to reconsider the conditions of the modern world, be it the different forms of colonialism, economic progress after World War II, the complex question of identity formation, or the divergent trajectories in pursuit of democracy. The COVID-19 pandemic provides a valuable opportunity for these types of discussions.

Notes

[1] As of August 14, 2020, Hong Kong has 4,361 cases of COVID-19 and sixty-seven deaths, while Taiwan has 481 cases and seven deaths. Since July, Hong Kong has witnessed a significant increase in reported cases; for comparison, by July 13, it had 1,522 reported cases and eight deaths.

[2] Kin-man Wan, Lawrence Ka-ki Ho, Natalie W. M. Wong, and Andy Chiu, "Fighting COVID-19 in Hong Kong: The Effects of Community and Social Mobilization," *World Development* 134 (October 2020), https://doi.org/10.1016/j.worlddev.2020.105055 (accessed July 2, 2020).

[3] Wu Rwei-ren, *Shoukunde xisiang: Taiwan chongfanshijie [Prometheus Unbound: When Formosa Reclaims the World]* (New Taipei: AcroPolis, 2016).

[4] As of August 2020, the ROC has full diplomatic relations with only fifteen countries in the world, including the Vatican.

[5] "'Xianggangshiben nandongdeshu': duoshizhiqiuchongwen Jiang Enzhu jiuhua ["'Hong Kong Is a Difficult Book to Understand': Revisiting Jiang Enzhu's Words in a Turbulent Time,"] *Hong Kong Economic Times*, October 7, 2019, https://china.hket.com/article/24451 77/%E3%80%90%E4%BF%AE%E4%BE%8B%E9%A2%A8%E6%B3%A2%E3%80%91%E3 %80%8C%E9%A6%99%E6%B8%AF%E6%98%AF%E6%9C%AC%E9%9B%A3%E6%87% 82%E7%9A%84%E6%9B%B8%E3%80%8D%20%E5%A4%9A%E4%BA%8B%E4%B9%8B %E7%A7%8B%E9%87%8D%E6%BA%AB%E5%A7%9C%E6%81%A9%E6%9F%B1%E8% 88%8A%E8%A9%B1 (accessed August 9, 2020).

[6] For more on modern Taiwanese history, see Shelley Rigger, *Why Taiwan Matters: Small Island, Global Powerhouse* (Lanham: Rowman & Littlefield, 2011).

[7] For more on modern Hong Kong history, see John Carroll, *A Concise History of Hong Kong* (Lanham: Rowman & Littlefield, 2007).

[8] Hong Kong had 1,755 cases of SARS and 299 deaths, while Taiwan had 346 cases and seventy-three deaths.

[9] Lee Shiu-hung, "The SARS Epidemic in Hong Kong: What Lessons Have We Learned?" *Journal of the Royal Society of Medicine* 96, no. 8 (2003): 374–378.

[10] Sarah Wu, "Coronavirus Widens Hong Kong Anger at Government, China," *Reuters*, February 20, 2020, https://www.reuters.com/article/us-china-health-hongkong-protests-insigh/coronavirus-widens-hong-kong-anger-at-government-china-idUSKBN20F0E3 (accessed June 18, 2020).

[11] Elson Tong, "Explainer: After Months of Protests, Is Hong Kong Selectively Enforcing Covid-19 Laws?" *Hong Kong Free Press*, April 17, 2020, https://hongkongfp.com/2020/04/17/explainer-after-months-of-protests-is-hong-kong-selectively-enforcing-covid-19-laws/ (accessed May 8, 2020); Elaine Yu, "Dozens Charged in Hong Kong for Taking Part in Tiananmen Protest," *The New York Times*, August 6, 2020, https://www.nytimes.com/2020/08/06/world/asia/hong-kong-tiananmen-protest.html (accessed August 8, 2020).

[12] Gina Anne Tam and Jeffrey Wasserstrom, "The Future of Hong Kong," *Dissent*, June 30, 2020, https://www.dissentmagazine.org/online_articles/the-future-of-hong-kong (accessed June 30, 2020). The AAS released a statement expressing deep concern over the national security law, especially on its possible infringement on academic freedom. "AAS Statement on the 2020 Hong Kong National Security Law," Association of Asian Studies, July 10, 2020, https://www.asianstudies.org/aas-statement-on-the-2020-hong-kong-national-security-law/ (accessed July 11, 2020).

[13] Brian Hioe, "'Asia's Orphan' During the COVID-19 Pandemic," *The Asia-Pacific Journal* 18, issue 14, no. 8, July 15, 2020, https://apjjf.org/2020/14/Hioe.html (accessed August 9, 2020).

[14] Sung Wen-ti, "Taiwan's COVID-19 Diplomacy and WHO Participation: Losing the Battle but Winning the War?" *The Diplomat*, June 2, 2020, https://thediplomat.com/2020/06/taiwans-covid-19-diplomacy-and-who-participation-losing-the-battle-but-winning-the-war/ (accessed June 23, 2020).

[15] Ho Ming-sho, *Challenging Beijing's Mandate of Heaven: Taiwan's Sunflower Movement and Hong Kong's Umbrella Movement* (Philadelphia: Temple University Press, 2019).

[16] For an overview of the territorial dispute, see Kimie Hara, "Okinawa, Taiwan, and the Senkaku/Diaoyu Islands in United States-Japan-China Relations," *The Asia-Pacific Journal* 13, issue 28, no. 2, July 13, 2015, https://apjjf.org/2015/13/28/Kimie-Hara/4341.html (accessed July 8, 2020).

[17] Mark Wenyi Lai, "Two Student Movements, One Learning from the Other," *Taiwan Insight*, June 5, 2019, https://taiwaninsight.org/2019/06/05/two-student-movements-one-learning-from-the-other/ (accessed June 21, 2020).

[18] Sebastian Conrad, *What Is Global History?* (Princeton: Princeton University Press, 2016).

Section 2

Pedagogical Tools and Methods for a Pandemic

11

ZOOMING TO INDONESIA: CULTURAL EXCHANGE WITHOUT STUDY ABROAD

Gareth Barkin

At the end of a challenging semester in which the COVID-19 pandemic forced the cancellation of my summer study abroad program in Indonesia, I was gratified to hear a student reflect in class on the results of an online collaboration I had hastily developed to stand in the place of travel. She noted that, although she was extremely disappointed she could not go to Indonesia, she had nonetheless accomplished "more of what study abroad is really about" through our online exchange than when she actually studied abroad in Europe the previous year. She described her time there as "very much like you're in a museum, and you're walking around as a spectator . . . you trap yourself in a bubble and don't even talk to locals, [coming] back with evidence of travel, not immersion." In this online exchange, she instead spent hours on Zoom delving into personal, cultural, and academic topics with Indonesian peers from diverse backgrounds. Based on their reflection work, she and others—both in the US class and in Indonesia—had come away with a deeper understanding of differences and commonalities between national and regional culture both at home and abroad.

How were we able to achieve these outcomes, given that the abroad portion of the program was canceled? This chapter focuses on two related goals: first, discussing the development of a series of online cultural exchange assignments completed by a class of students at the University of Puget Sound (UPS) and a distributed group of Indonesian students from the Young Southeast Asian Leaders

Figure 1: Balinese participant Lisa Purwanti
introduces herself in a short video posted to the
program's social media group.

Initiative (YSEALI) who were to have participated jointly in the abroad portion of this embedded cultural exchange program. Second, it discusses the pedagogical philosophy behind the assignments, their relationship to the historical use of ethnographic methods as an avenue toward experiential learning in study abroad, and what exercises like this mean for post-pandemic study abroad, particularly in Asia.[1] The assignments discussed, their autoethnographic framework, and the surrounding pedagogical approach may be of use to any college or high school instructor with connections to facilitate the involvement of Asian peers in an online cultural exchange program.

Background

Every year or two, I conduct short-term study abroad programs in Indonesia, mobilizing what I call the "extended semester" model of embedding the time abroad within the rigors of semester-long, on-campus preparation and post-travel reflection.[2] As part of my research into American study abroad practice and a growing awareness of the ways international education can re/produce colonial power relations, I have worked to shift the balance of pedagogical authority on the programs, chiefly through involving Indonesian students and academics.[3] Thanks to partnerships with the Henry Luce Foundation and the US Embassy in Jakarta (who administer the YSEALI program), my last two programs have focused on providing a forum for Indonesian and American students to work collaboratively, focusing on cross-cultural dialogue and relationship-building, and with a goal of providing similar benefits for all involved. I have been able to identify and enroll Indonesian students from across that diverse country and bring them into conversation with UPS students, in and around Atma-Jaya University in Yogyakarta. To foster fluent communication, and because Indonesian language study at UPS has been limited, we have prioritized English language skills in our recruiting of Indonesian participants, alongside regional and ethnic diversity and low-income applicants. This is a less than ideal solution to a difficult problem, as I have discussed elsewhere,[4] but it is the best we have been able to devise given our financial and institutional constraints.

In Yogyakarta, YSEALI and UPS students share rooms and attend the same class sessions but spend most of their time in small groups conducting ethnographic activities that encourage them to work together, exploring anthropological ideas from the classroom through real-world engagements, observations, interviews, and service. The program is built around best practices in experiential learning abroad, which draw on Kolb's four stage model,[5] as well as the interventions highlighted in Bennett and Hammer's work on intercultural competence.[6] At the same time, I argue that these approaches are fixed on a mid-century vision of anthropology, borrowing much of its ethnographic tool kit while largely avoiding the lessons of the "crisis of representation" that reshaped the discipline in the 1980s.[7] At that time, anthropologists (largely from wealthy, Western countries) began to reflect on their own authority to represent the Global South. Among other things, this led to a shift toward collaborative ethnography, through which "culture" is posited as a product of interaction rather than a repository of information prime for extraction.[8] In this spirit, I have developed my abroad programs to focus on cultural exchange and collaboration between UPS and YSEALI students, using assignments intended to be equally beneficial for all involved.

As a result of the COVID-19 pandemic, my 2020 program was canceled halfway through its spring semester preparatory course. Students were disappointed, as one would expect, and many have expressed hope that, despite differing schedules, we might still conduct some postponed version of the program—a sentiment echoed by the Indonesian partners with whom I develop these programs. Other partners,

Figure 2: Participants in the "Power and Politics" group continued their discussions informally, long after the required topics had been covered.

such as the US Embassy in Jakarta, were eager to investigate ways to take advantage of the relationships we had already built with the Indonesian students who had been admitted into the program. Embassy YSEALI staff had helped to develop, publicize, and run the recruitment for Indonesian students, fielding hundreds of applications and helping to interview scores of applicants. My UPS students had already begun communicating with this group through videos and messages posted to an online forum and were preparing to shift toward collaboratively developing visual research projects in the second half of the semester.

Abroad Online: Reassessing Goals

As it became clear the travel portion of the program would be canceled, I began thinking through ways we could all still make something of these connections we had worked hard to establish. I spent spring break researching online collaboration work between distant partners and developing an "online abroad program" that would ideally achieve some of the same goals I had for the trip itself while being sensitive to students' various constraints. The goals were built around investigating five cultural themes we focused on throughout the course—gender/sexuality, religion, ethnicity/race, human ecology/environment, and power/politics—with the goal of broadly increasing intercultural competence for all participants. These themes were chosen specifically to highlight areas of cultural difference and similarity between (and within) Indonesian and North American[9] program participants, and were reflected in course materials, readings, and discussions. The assignments I developed were built around a series of structured, small-group conversations, a collaborative curation of reading and viewing materials, and a shared personal reflection.

In my recent work, I critically explore discourse and practice surrounding short-term study abroad culture in the US and argue for a broad refocusing on pedagogical outcomes. The coronavirus experience compelled me to approach the same discussion from a juxtaposed perspective, concentrating on which pedagogical goals associated with study abroad might be achieved (or at least approached) through other means—means that remain available without travel.

My programs have focused on bringing people from varied backgrounds together to explore trenchant cultural issues collaboratively and in social context. The challenge of this moment has been in rapidly crafting interventions that do not rely on the exploration of social contexts, and that can work within the narrow confines of online communications technology (as well as inequal access to it). To do this, I turned to the idea of *autoethnography*, in which participants reflect not just on their own lives, but on how those personal experiences intersect with broader cultural patterns and processes.[10]

Online Autoethnography

Principles

The assignment structure for this program was built around several principles. First, UPS and YSEALI participants should have the same workload and responsibilities—the program should not position Indonesian participants as repositories of cultural knowledge, but should instead provide an egalitarian forum for cultural exchange and dialogue. Second, participants should be working toward a common, collaborative goal. Although I also included an individual reflection, the program was built around an assignment that compelled participants to peer-review one another's representations of their work together, incentivizing them to draw one another out and foster investment.[11] Third, though conversations between participants needed to include personal, autoethnographic reflection, they were built around an academic agenda. While developing rapport and drawing on personal experience are essential to an effective exchange, the focus of that exchange must be structured around key topical themes to foster a productive forum for intercultural learning. Finally, reflecting Kolb's stages of experiential learning, all participants needed to be given agency in shaping the foci of those discussions to reflect their own interests and backgrounds. What follows is a brief description of each assignment.

Overview

The Online Collaboration Assignment consisted of two to four videoconferences between teams of four (two UPS students and two YSEALI students), and a collaboratively written piece addressing questions surrounding each team's cultural theme, to which all team members had to contribute. For UPS students, this assignment informed other coursework such as their research papers; however, reflecting principle 1 (above), it was an independent assignment focused on egalitarian collaboration between UPS and YSEALI partners. Because we could not conduct ethnographic field assignments together, participants were encouraged to turn the ethnographic lens on themselves. Collaborations across cultural themes focused on students' own experiences and backgrounds, as well as our reading and research into the themes (which were made available to YSEALI participants via a shared Google Drive folder). Because of this, participants were encouraged to choose a theme they were comfortable discussing in relation to their own personal experience.

Assignment: First Conversations

Before work on this project began, all participants were assigned to topical, four-person teams reflecting the course themes and their own preferences (smaller teams served to keep scheduling and technology challenges manageable). UPS students had completed coursework and an annotated bibliography, developing some background knowledge on their theme in the Indonesian context. Teams then communicated to schedule online conversations using Zoom or similar software. Participants were encouraged to take notes during or after the conversations.

Instructions for the conversations were very specific, including a numbered agenda outlining an order of events, with the expectation that students could lean on this structure when their discussions did not flow naturally. This first conversation's instructions focused on students getting to know one another and discovering what drew each team member to the group's theme. In addition to building rapport, the goal of this conversation was for students to develop a better understanding of how each member defined, conceived of, or framed the cultural theme, what they associated with it, and how those associations grew from their background. The secondary goal was to better understand the similarities and differences between these framings and their relationships to other themes such as class, gender, or ethnicity. Students were instructed to prepare five-minute autobiographies for these first conversations, as well as a story or anecdote from their own lives that exemplified why they were drawn to the team's particular theme. They were also encouraged to prepare and pose a question to the group connected to the theme, such as (for the religion team) how religious identity was expressed publicly in the regions where everyone had grown up.

Assignment: Discussing Readings

While the initial conversations (which lasted for one to two hours) were designed to allow students to get to know one another and broach topics related to their

Figure 3: "Human Ecology and Environment" group members discussed intersections between environmental activism and religion.

cultural theme, the remaining conversations were intended to refocus groups' attention on concrete case studies related to those themes. They also allowed for a degree of agency through students' choice of sources and discussion-leading.

For the second and subsequent conversations (students could use their own judgment as to how many would be required), the focus shifted to these shared case studies drawn from scholarship and popular media. Team members chose and shared theme-related articles, news reports, and videos with one another, and then met online to discuss each of them as a group. These media sources had to relate to the team's theme as it intersected with either Indonesia, North America, or both. The goal of these conversations was to explore how academics, journalists, and others have investigated topics related to each group's theme in ways that resonated with students' academic and personal interests, and to explore how those works highlighted cultural similarity and difference. Along with their sources, each student wrote and distributed three open-ended discussion questions to the rest of their team, and in their Zoom conversations, the student who had chosen the source also lead the discussion.

Assignments: Collaboration and Reflection

After these conversations concluded, teams were asked to discuss their takeaways and develop a plan to address the assignment's comprehensive essay prompt in a collaborative fashion involving all members. Students were encouraged to write in a way that reflected their collective rather than personal perspectives, summarizing shared themes from the conversations, and reserving their individual perspectives for a separate reflection video. I chose to grade the collaborative essay as a group project (a practice I normally avoid) as a way of encouraging students to actively involve their peers and promote interdependency. The prompt itself asked students to explore their shifts in understanding surrounding the group's theme and its manifestation, both internationally and domestically, linking the shifts to shared literature and autoethnographic insights. It further asked students to reflect on how their own cultural backgrounds had been cast into relief through the cultural patterning revealed in their online discussions.

Finally, all students were asked to complete a personal reflection video, shared on the final day of class, when we attempted (with a degree of success) to bring together all the YSEALI and UPS participants in one Zoom meeting. Students were asked to reflect on what insights they gained regarding similarity and difference between and within Indonesia and North America, as well as what they learned about their theme through the collaboration that they likely would not have otherwise.

Disambiguating Outcomes

Based on students' collaborative written work and oral presentations, the program was successful in cultivating the sorts of insights, relativism, empathy, and perspective-shifting associated with intercultural competence.[12] Among the themes that emerged across the teams, differences in the role of religion in daily life proved highly fertile ground for discussion, as did commonalities in colorism and the construction of racial categories. I would argue this success derives from mobilizing not just experiential learning theory, but also twenty-first-century ethnographic approaches to collaboration and dialogue. When I am able to bring students to Indonesia again, this experience will inform the focus of assignments, and among other things, it has revealed to me the value in allowing students from UPS and Indonesia greater agency in shaping conversations toward their own experiences, backgrounds, and personal interests.

At the same time, the program was not without its challenges. Scheduling online discussions across twelve- or thirteen-hour time differences proved challenging, particularly in the month of Ramadan. Whereas UPS students were completing the assignments as part of a course, the YSEALI students were no longer as directly incentivized to invest in the program and were themselves contending with shifting university schedules and coronavirus-related challenges. Nevertheless, all participated in the online conversations, and many reported staying up for hours, chatting about their lives, popular culture, academics, the pandemic, and more. Although students continued to express disappointment that the travel portion of the program could not take place as planned, the experience was enough of a success that it generated discussion around the ubiquity of study abroad as the de facto framework for approaching these outcomes.

Indeed, crafting interventions like these compels us to think through what "learning outcomes" mean in the context of short-term study abroad: how much of what we are doing as international educators is fixed in the exoticism and novelty of touring and the commodified culture it so readily affords? Reflecting on the diverse and layered social contexts we encounter traveling abroad, how well are our students equipped to genuinely engage and apprehend them? Are students consistently given the background needed to effectively draw sophisticated insights from time spent in culturally novel settings? How much of our collective project is instead about demystifying faraway places or "lighting a spark" that may lead students toward more fulsome engagements in the future? If that is a central goal, to what extent are we in these programs, consciously or not, leveraging the very Orientalist dogmas we otherwise seek to deconstruct in the project of nudging students toward an imagined global citizenship? These are the questions I have struggled with in (re)imagining what "study abroad" might look like without actually going abroad.

The coronavirus pandemic has compelled many international education advocates to consider alternative approaches to achieving desired outcomes, but at the time of this writing, it is difficult to apprehend the extent to which this experience might broadly reframe faculty and staff attitudes in relation to study abroad. Such a reassessment could well resonate with the shift I have been advocating in my recent work: reframing study abroad as a pedagogical framework that—while it opens a range of experiential interventions that are largely impossible otherwise—is not itself a pedagogical outcome.[13] It is a shift, in other words, that would disambiguate travel from learning and critically center the power-inflected touring narratives that have undergirded study abroad since its inception.[14] While I would be pleased to witness such a shift and have found myself pushed further toward it by the pandemic, I am not optimistic such changes are likely, given the role short-term study abroad has come to play in the neoliberal university.

An *outcomes-centered approach* to international pedagogy frames time spent abroad as a forum for rich and unique pedagogy, including cross-cultural collaboration, but in this chapter I have argued that there are other ways to approach some of the same outcomes without travel. In my research and university administration work, I have been disappointed to see how uncommon the prioritization of pedagogical outcomes such as intercultural competence remains. I would argue this reflects the historically *travel-centered approach* to international education that frames all program benefits as coming from students being, to quote Bennett, "in the vicinity of events."[15] While few would dismiss the extraordinary range of experiential learning opportunities opened up by international travel, to the extent that studying abroad in Asia remains difficult in the wake of the pandemic, exploring alternate ways to achieve some of study abroad's core goals has become imperative. Even when global health is no longer a concern, the challenges of conducting short-term programs in Asia, including the sometimes-exclusionary expense and hefty carbon footprint, mean international education advocates should always weigh the benefits of online exchange programs such as the one described here against international travel.

Notes

[1] Stephen Ceccoli, Gao Jiayong ,and Han Li, "Experiencing China through a 'Wide-Angle Lens," *Education about ASIA* 22, no. 3 (2017); Jane Jackson, "Ethnographic Pedagogy and Evaluation in Short-Term Study Abroad," *Languages for Intercultural Communication and Education* 12 (2006), 134.

[2] Gareth Barkin, "In the Absence of Language: Modeling a Transformative, Short-Term Abroad Experience," *Teaching Anthropology* 4, no. 1 (2015).

[3] Neriko Musha Doerr, "Do 'Global Citizens' Need the Parochial Cultural Other? Discourse of Immersion in Study Abroad and Learning-by-Doing," *Compare: A Journal of Comparative and International Education*, no. ahead-of-print (2012), 1–20.; Talya Zemach-Bersin, "Global Citizenship and Study Abroad: It's All about US," *Critical Literacy: Theories and Practices* 1, no. 2 (2007), 16–28.

[4] Ibid.

[5] David A. Kolb, *Experiential Learning: Experience as the Source of Learning and Development* (Pearson Education, 2014).

[6] Milton J. Bennett, "Paradigmatic Assumptions and a Developmental Approach to Intercultural Learning," in *Student Learning Abroad: What our Students are Learning, What They're Not, and What We Can Do about It*, eds. Michael Vande Berg, R. Michael Paige and Kris Hemming Lou (Sterling, VA: Stylus, 2012), 90–114.

[7] George E. Marcus, "Beyond Malinowski and After *Writing Culture*: On the Future of Cultural Anthropology and the Predicament of Ethnography," *The Australian Journal of Anthropology* 13, no. 2 (2002), 191–199.

[8] LukeEric Lassiter et al., "Collaborative Ethnography and Public Anthropology," *Current Anthropology* 46, no. 1 (2005), 83–106.

[9] Not all of the UPS students in the program were native English speakers nor were they from the United States.

[10] Tony E. Adams, Stacy Linn Holman Jones, and Carolyn Ellis, *Autoethnography: Understanding Qualitative Research* (New York: Oxford University Press, 2015).

[11] The assignment structure drew inspiration from the classic "jigsaw classroom" concept developed by Aronson (Elliot Aronson, *The Jigsaw Classroom* (Sage, 1978)).

[12] Mitchell R. Hammer, "The Intercultural Development Inventory: A New Frontier in Assessment and Development of Intercultural Competence," in *Student Learning Abroad: What Our Students Are Learning, What They're Not, and What We Can Do about It*, eds. Michael Vande Berg, R. Michael Paige and Kris Hemming Lou (Sterling, VA: Stylus, 2012), 115–136.

[13] Gareth Barkin, "Either Here or There: Short-Term Study Abroad and the Discourse of Going," *Anthropology & Education Quarterly* 49, no. 3 (2018); Gareth Barkin, "The Imperative of Access in Short-Term Study Abroad: Provider Agencies, Liminality, and the Mediation of Cultural Difference," in *Study Abroad: Service, Student Travel and the Quest for an Anti-Tourism Experience*, eds. Michael A. Di Giovine and John Bodinger de Uriarte (Lanham, MD: Lexington Books, 2020).

[14] William Hoffa and Stephen C. DePaul, *A History of US Study Abroad: 1965–Present* (Carlisle, PA: Forum on Education Abroad, 2010), 511; Zemach-Bersin, "Global Citizenship and Study Abroad: It's All about US," 16–28.

[15] Bennett, "Paradigmatic Assumptions and a Developmental Approach to Intercultural Learning," 110.

12

SOMATIC APPROACHES TO TEACHING ASIA ONLINE

A CASE STUDY OF TAIJIQUAN TRAINING FOR ACTORS

Adam D. Frank

In the time of pandemic, many of us find ourselves caught between the choices of either teaching our subject online or not at all. In this essay, drawing upon the example of a college-level theatre course called Tai Chi for Actors, I will make the case that somatic pedagogies offer useful alternatives to traditional lecture and discussion formats for teaching about Asia online.[1] While my focus in the chapter is on a college-level course, I conclude with several modifications for teaching younger students.

Somatics: Definitions

The term "somatics," originally coined by philosopher Thomas Hanna,[2] generally refers to psychophysical practices that enhance awareness of the body from a first-person, or insider, viewpoint. As Hanna wrote in 1986:

> Somatics is the field which studies the soma: namely, the body as perceived from within by first-person perception. When a human being is observed from the outside—i.e., from a third-person viewpoint—the phenomenon of a human *body is* perceived. But, when this same

human being is observed from the first-person viewpoint of his own proprioceptive senses, a categorically different phenomenon is perceived: the human soma.

Hanna explains this proprioceptive element—i.e., stimuli perceived internally—in terms of the relationship between the "sensorium" (the sensory apparatus as a whole) and "motorium" (the parts of the organism concerned with movement, as opposed to sensation). He notes, "It is not possible to have a distinct sensory perception of any external objective situation without having a distinct motor response already established."[3] This process, he postulates, is a selective one whereby the internal awareness one places on, for example, a knee requires relaxation of the motor neurons around the knee while inhibiting the other neural areas of the body. Thus, consciousness "is not a static 'faculty of the mind' nor a 'fixed' sensory-motor pattern. To the contrary, it is a learned sensory-motor function. And the range of this learning determines 1) how much we can be conscious of, and 2) how many things we can voluntarily do."[4]

Somatic Pedagogies in the Arts and Humanities

As a broad conceptual approach that associates practiced, first-person understandings of bodily experience with movement, somatics has become particularly well-known in three areas: healing arts, performance arts, and social sciences, chief among them somatic psychology, of which there are at least half a dozen doctoral-level programs in the United States. A brief discussion about each of these areas will provide a pedagogical context for the more recent trend of applying somatic methods to traditional liberal arts and humanities subjects.[5]

In his lifelong work on somatics and healing, Hanna took a particular interest in the body awareness and healing methods of Moshe Feldenkrais.[6] Along the way, he also brought attention to the deep tissue massage method known as Rolfing; to the Alexander Technique, a nineteenth-century body retraining method initially developed to address actor vocal issues; and, as Mullan notes, he indirectly brought attention to Pilates and other methods steeped in the German physical culture tradition.[7]

In the realm of the performing arts, dance has been the focal point for somatic training methods, though music, theatre, and opera have all taken up the somatics banner in one form or another.[8] Dance and somatic therapist Martha Eddy, writing at a fairly early stage of the somatic dance training movement, noted, "In the past decade 'somatics' has burst onto the dance scene. With the recent proliferation of practices, somatics has become an accepted mode of dance learning. However, despite the recent popularity of the term and its growing practices, somatics is not a monolith."[9] In the past two decades, writing and research about somatics and the application of somatics to dance have indeed proliferated, covering such topics as "somatics as radical pedagogy"[10] and "ecosomatic" pedagogy in dance training.[11]

In the social sciences, humanities, and other fields, somatic pedagogies have also generated substantial interest. Summarizing the results of an interdisciplinary symposium on somatic pedagogies, Belmar decries the classroom as "a site of 'from the neck up' processing, where the body fades into the background of all that mental labour."[12] Rigg applies Buddhist mindfulness techniques to management training.[13] And Shusterman, writing about the application of "somaesthetics" to the humanities, argues "that because the body is an essential and valuable dimension of our humanity, it should be recognized as a crucial topic of humanistic study and experiential learning."[14]

"Taijiquan for Actors": A Case Study in Somatic Pedagogy

Taijiquan (aka "tai chi") is a Chinese martial art most commonly taught for health, meditation, and self-defense.[15] It has also gained some traction as an actor training method, and several college and university theatre programs in North America offer taijiquan courses or incorporate taijiquan into movement training for actors.[16] In spring 2020, I taught Tai Chi for Actors for the first time as a one-credit elective for theatre and film majors at the University of Central Arkansas.[17] The class met twice weekly from early January through mid-March, when it went entirely online due to COVID-19. As of this writing, Tai Chi for Actors will be offered as an entirely online, asynchronous course during the fall 2020 semester. I begin with a summary of the spring 2020 course and a discussion of how the obstacles encountered in that course (both related to and aside from the pandemic) led to a course design that more firmly integrated Chinese philosophy, medical theory, poetry, and painting. I then describe the plan for the fall 2020 revision of the course.

Tai Chi for Actors: Spring 2020 Version

The initial objective for Tai Chi for Actors was for students to learn about a third of the 108-move Wu (Jianquan) style of taijiquan by the end of the sixteen-week term.[18] The first several weeks of the semester focused on taijiquan movement principles, such as holding one's head erect as if suspended by a string, relaxing the shoulders, dropping the tailbone, and clearly differentiating between the weighted and unweighted foot. Students also learned the opening move of the Wu style solo slow form, "raise hands." Reference to basic movement principles opened a door for discussion about the name "taijiquan" and the Daoist principles the name evoked. Most of the students were already familiar with the *taijitu* ("diagram of the supreme ultimate," or, colloquially, "the yin-yang symbol"), and we were able to use the symbol as a common reference point to understand movement principles like "empty vs. full," "soft vs. hard," and "energized vs. collapsed."

As the semester progressed, we developed a system of repetition that allowed us to emphasize movement principles and internal body awareness. Key to this approach was the requirement for students to keep a notebook, turned in weekly, where they could describe technical problems (such as forgetting a move), as well as somatic experiences (e.g., warmth or tingling flowing throughout the body during practice).

In mid-March, the university moved entirely to online classes. For a movement-based class, this presented unique challenges. Not only did students have to struggle with varying degrees of internet access and camera quality, they also had to contend with the confusion and depression that immediately hit so many of us during that period. At the same time, it became clear that online delivery entailed pedagogical and safety challenges that I had not previously considered. To at least partly address those concerns, I enrolled in a remote seminar on teaching movement arts online conducted by Jeremy Williams of Convergences Collective. A number of other companies also offered online trainings and workshops to assist faculty suddenly thrown into the deep end of the COVID-19 swimming pool. Following training, the focus moved away from learning Wu style taijiquan and toward learning some much simpler, easier to remember energy development and deep relaxation forms (*qigong*, or "vital energy work"). Aside from simply acknowledging the technical difficulties of teaching taijiquan online, I also felt compelled to teach the students exercises that would reduce, rather than exacerbate, their stress and that might conceivably build their resistance to illness. Recording and sharing the short qigong sets in advance, I was able to teach these both asynchronously and synchronously, and students learned a basic set of about eight movements by the end of the term.

Tai Chi for Actors: Fall 2020 Version

For fall 2020, I have both flipped and enhanced the course content so that students are introduced to basic conceptual frameworks concurrently with their movement practice. The course is now divided into four three-week units that can be taught online, are largely asynchronous, and involve at least two hours of independent work outside of class each week. Each unit has specific movement objectives and accompanying Asian Studies objectives. Each also includes a specific, asynchronous online component. The units include the following:

1. Somatic Toolkits, Ancient and Modern

Movement Learning Objective: For students to acquire a habit of attention regarding where their body is located in space. The practices of *waigong* (basic warm-ups and stretches) and *zhan zhuang* (literally, "standing like a stake"; standing meditation) are emphasized during the first three weeks. Students are asked to practice at least two times per week outside of class and to briefly respond to journal prompts. Journal prompts ask students to differentiate between third-person viewpoints of their bodies (for example, by using a mirror to describe their standing posture) and first-person viewpoints (for example, describing specific areas of tightness or pain, odd sensations of electricity or warmth, etc.).

Asian Studies Learning Objective: To provide historical context for Chinese martial arts and to introduce basic cosmological principles, e.g., *wuji* (devoid of extreme; "beforeness"), *taiji* (the extreme of the extreme), yin-yang theory, *qi* (air, energy), *yi* (mind-intent), and *xin* (heart-mind). In journal entries and group discussion, students interpolate their somatic understandings of these concepts with dictionary definitions and historical-cultural contexts. The idea of taijiquan and qigong as "invented traditions" is also introduced.[19]

Online Obstacles/Solutions: Based on a two-unit class, students meet online synchronously once every two weeks for experience-sharing drawn from their journals (at my university, using BlackBoard or Zoom). Twenty-minute movement lessons are recorded in advance, viewed by each student asynchronously, and taught individually once per week online in twenty-minute sessions. Students may also join a synchronous group practice. In addition, students are asked weekly to draw upon and briefly write about short YouTube videos dealing either with movement concepts or Daoist concepts introduced during the unit.

2. Poetry and Painting in Motion

Movement Learning Objective: The emphasis for this three-week unit is "moving naturally." We explore what "natural" and "nature" (*ziran*) mean from a Daoist standpoint and continue practice of basic taijiquan and qigong movement principles in light of those ideas. Students continue with zhan zhuang and new qigong postures are introduced.

Asian Studies Learning Objective: The Tang-period poetry of Du Fu and Li Bai is introduced as well as nature-inspired painting from various periods. Students are also introduced to calligraphy and begin to connect the movement of taijiquan and qigong with the movement of the calligraphy brush.

Online Obstacles/Solutions. Students continue with their online learning and meeting schedule. In response to a journal prompt, students write a "Daoist" nature poem based on a personal memory or experience. An experienced calligrapher joins the group discussion and teaches an online calligraphy lesson. Students share their poems and discuss how poetry and calligraphy inform and comprise their internal bodily experience.

3. Kung Fu Philosophy

Movement Learning Objective: Understanding stillness in movement vs. movement in stillness. Through continued standing meditation and qigong practice, we focus on the function of intention in movement and how the somatic experience of stillness informs the quality of movement for the actor. Introduction of the first three movements of a six-move, abbreviated version of Wu style taijiquan. During one-on-one sessions, in addition to reviewing new movements, students will be asked to perform a one-minute monologue, attending to the movement principles they have been exposed to thus far.

Asian Studies Learning Objective: A deeper look at Chinese Buddhism, as well as religious vs. philosophical Daoism (*Daojiao* vs. *Daojia*) and the intellectual history of how these concepts were introduced to the West through popular culture forms like kung fu movies and TV shows.[20] Through journal prompts, students are asked to identify and discuss their own preconceptions about Chinese philosophy and religion.

Online Obstacles/Solutions: One-on-one lessons continue. Students will also asynchronously watch excerpts from King Hu's *A Touch of Zen* as well as Stephen Chow's *Shaolin Soccer*. Synchronous group discussion will focus on the films.

4. Traditional Chinese Medicine and the Energy Body

Movement Learning Objective: Our focus in this unit is on further, gentle opening of the joints, relaxing the hips, and understanding how the various "bows" of the body act like springs or rubber bands as we move. No new postures are introduced. In one-on-one sessions, students will perform monologues through exercises that emphasize elasticity and energized movement. (These exercises are particular to the course and serve as the explicit bridge between taijiquan movement principles and the actor's art.)

Asian Studies Learning Objective: Students will be introduced to basic Chinese medical theory and the concept of qi from a medical standpoint. They will learn about acupuncture, moxibustion, and qigong in the context of healing. They will also learn about the *qigong re* (qigong fever) of the late 1990s in China that resulted in mass arrests of qigong practitioners. In journal prompts, students will be asked to make connections between somatic concepts (e.g., proprioception) and traditional Chinese medical terminology.

Online Obstacles/Solutions. Students will be assigned short videos on Traditional Chinese Medicine (TCM) to be watched asynchronously. We will also be joined during one group by a local TCM practitioner for a question and answer session.

5. Review and Final Exam

The final three weeks of the course are devoted to review. The final exam will be a performance of the one-minute monologue in three different ways, each incorporating a different movement principle or Asian Studies concept introduced in the course.

Adapting Somatic Methods to Varying Age Groups and Curricula

At the risk of waxing Pollyannaish about the rich opportunities that disease and economic destruction lay at our feet, the pandemic has indeed forced teachers of Asian Studies content at every level to reassess how we are to deliver our subject. For many teachers and students, Zoom and other online platforms have become little hells to which we are condemned for hours a day, draining the lifeblood and passion out of teaching and learning. Through careful course design, somatic pedagogies can reinject life into the online teaching of Asian Studies. These may be as simple as asking students to stand up and stretch during class or may be as complex as teaching taijiquan to actors. Tai Chi for Actors offers but one model for incorporating somatic methodologies into teaching Chinese humanities. Whatever the emphasis or combination of subject matter, the key to the successful use of somatic pedagogies is providing checkpoints throughout the course where students can reflect on somatic experience and connect lecture and reading to bodily experience.

Finally, while Tai Chi for Actors as described here is a college-level course, components and principles noted in this essay are adaptable to any age group. Over the years, I have frequently been invited to teach taijiquan to elementary and middle school students, and as long as the emphasis is on playing, stimulating the imagination, and creating a safe atmosphere for discovering movement, somatic methods will be successful with younger students. For a middle school teacher introducing a China unit as part of an online world history class, asking students to pick up a pen and experiment with Chinese characters can be rewarding for both teacher and student. Without anyone looking over their shoulder and without peers making fun of them, many students will take more chances online than they might otherwise in the classroom. While I am not advocating for the abolition of in-person teaching in favor of Zoom hell, there is something to be said for carving out space for the shy or insecure young person to fully express themselves and fully engage their senses without judgment.

Notes

1 For more on teaching Asian Studies through experiential methods, see Adam D. Frank, "Taijiquan: Teaching Daoism through Experiential Arts Learning." *Education about Asia* 15, no. 2 (2010), 31–34; Adam D. Frank, "Re-thinking Asian Studies in the Interdisciplinary Honors Setting," *Honors in Practice* 7 (2011), 71–85; and Adam D. Frank, "Shadow 'R & J' and 'The Girl Who Flew': Introducing Asia through Theatre in an Interdisciplinary Honors Program," *Education about Asia* 21, no. 1 (2016), https://www.asianstudies.org/publications/eaa/archives/shadow-r-j-and-the-girl-who-flew-introducing-asia-through-theater-in-an-interdisciplinary-honors-program/ (accessed July 12, 2020).

2 Thomas Hanna, "What is Somatics?" *Somatics Magazine: Journal of the Bodily Arts and Sciences,* 1986, https://somatics.org/library/htl-wis1; Kelly Mullan, "The Art and Science of Somatics: Theory, History, and Scientific Foundations," MA thesis, Skidmore College, 2012.

3 Thomas Hanna, "What is Somatics?"

4 Thomas Hanna, "What is Somatics?" For more on the principles and history of somatics, see Martha Eddy, *Mindful Movement: The Evolution of the Somatic Arts and Conscious Action* (Chicago: Intellect, Ltd., 2016); and Kelly Mullan, "The Art and Science of Somatics: Theory, History, and Scientific Foundations."

5 The terms "somatics" or "somatic pedagogy" may include a wide variety of experiential learning methods but generally refer here to bodily practices specifically intended to enhance body consciousness or bodywork techniques that promote healing.

6 Thomas Hanna, "What is Somatics?"

7 Kelly Mullan, "The Art and Science of Somatics: Theory, History, and Scientific Foundations."

8 Andrea L. Kleesattel, "Applications of Somatic Practices to Cello Playing and Pedagogy," PhD diss., University of Wisconsin-Madison, 2012; Heather J. Buchanan, "Body Mapping: Enhancing Voice Performance through Somatic Pedagogy," in *Teaching Singing in the 21st Century,* edited by Scott Harrison and Jessica O'Bryan (Dorcrecht, Netherlands: Springer Netherlands, 2014), 143–174; Christina Kapadocha, "Toward Witnessed Thirdness in Actor Training and Performance," *Theatre, Dance, and Performance Training* 9, no. 2, 203–216.

9 Martha Eddy, "Somatic Practices and Dance: Global Influences." *Dance Research Journal* 34, no. 2, 2002, 46–62. https://www.continuummovement.com/docs/articles/somatics-and-dance.htm; see also Martha Eddy, *Mindful Movement: The Evolution of the Somatic Arts and Conscious Action.*

10 Sara Reed, "Dance Somatics as Radical Pedagogy: Reflections on Somatic-Dance Practice within UK Dance Higher Education and Training," in *Practising Dance: A Somatic Orientation,* edited by Jenny Coogan (Berlin: Logos-Verlag, 2016), 176–180; Donna Dragon, "Creating Cultures of Teaching and Learning: Conveying Dance and Somatic Education Pedagogy," *Journal of Dance Education* 15, no. 1, 2015,

https://www.researchgate.net/publication/273914422_Creating_Cultures_of_Teaching_and_Learning_Conveying_Dance_and_Somatic_Education_Pedagogy.

[11] Rebeca Enghauser, "The Quest for an Ecosomatic Approach to Dance Pedagogy," *Journal of Dance Education* 7, no. 3, 2007, 80–90.

[12] Sima Belmar, "Somatic Approaches to Academic Pedagogy: Notes from Somatics, Scholarship, Somatic Scholarship: Materiality and Metaphor,'" *Performance Matters* 2, no.1, 2016, 92–98.

[13] Claire Rigg, "Somatic Learning: Bringing the Body into Critical Reflection." *Management Learning* 49, no. 2, 2017, 150–167.

[14] Richard Shusterman, "Thinking through the Body, Educating for the Humanities: A Plea for Somaesthetics," *The Journal of Aesthetic Education* 40, no. 1, 2006, 1–21.

[15] Adam Frank, *Taijiquan and the Search for the Little Old Chinese Man* (New York: Palgrave, 2006); Peter A. Lorge, *Chinese Martial Arts: From Antiquity to the Twenty-First Century* (Cambridge: Cambridge Univ. Press, 2012). In general, I employ the pinyin system of romanizing Mandarin Chinese. Exceptions occur when a word or name has come down to me with a different style of romanization, or I have treated a term as a borrowed word and opted for the more popular usage (e.g. using "tai chi" in place of "taijiquan" in a course name).

[16] A sampling of North American theatre or dance programs that incorporate taijiquan or other Chinese internal martial arts practices into their actor training curriculum include Chapman University (Tai Chi for Theatre), Tufts University (Tai Chi: An Experience of Time and Tempo), University of Hawaii (Taiji for Actors), and the University of Ottawa (various, under Daniel Mroz).

[17] My own background in taijiquan includes more than forty years of practice in the United States and China and over twenty years teaching the art.

[18] It quickly became apparent that the goal was overly ambitious. The revised syllabus instead emphasizes *qigong, waigong* (basic stretches), standing meditation forms, and a half dozen movements from the Wu style taijiquan. In order to learn the complete form, a minimum one-year program would be required.

[19] Eric Hobsbawm and Terrence Ranger, eds. *The Invention of Tradition* (Cambridge: Cambridge University Press, 2012).

[20] "Kung Fu" is the common English romanization of the mandarin *gongfu* 功夫, a term that generally refers to "skill" or "skill acquired through hard work," but it has also come to be used (in both Chinese and English) as a catchall term for Chinese martial arts. "Kung Fu philosophy" is a term used by respondents in previous fieldwork (see Adam Frank, *Taijiquan and the Search for the Little Old Chinese Man*) to describe a frequent encounter, starting in the late 1960s, between Chinese immigrant martial arts teachers in the US and non-Chinese students who equated martial arts with traditional Chinese philosophy. The course uses *wuxiapian* (knight errant films) and *wudapian* (contemporary stories involving modern renditions of martial skills) to underscore the social and cultural origins of basic assumptions American students bring to the study of Chinese martial arts.

13

PODCASTING DURING THE PANDEMIC AND BEYOND

Tristan R. Grunow

The coronavirus pandemic has had an undeniable impact on higher education. Many schools have quickly pivoted to online teaching as a way to prevent the spread of the virus through vulnerable student populations, forcing educators to adapt their courses to unfamiliar online teaching platforms and techniques, sometimes with limited institutional infrastructure or support. The results have not been entirely encouraging. At the same time, many academics have found it impossible to stay productive during the pandemic, overwhelmed by demands of adjusting to new teaching environments, increased caregiving responsibilities at home, and the heightened stress and anxiety of a deadly global virus. With so many more pressing issues—caring for sick relatives; social distancing; having enough toilet paper, food, or prescription medications—teaching and staying productive naturally took a back seat. To make things worse, the closure of primary and secondary schools has placed new burdens on parents, especially mothers. Statistics from journal editors have borne out the labor inequities many have long suspected: even as the number of overall manuscript submissions increased during the pandemic, submissions by women decreased precipitously. In many ways, the pandemic has highlighted and intensified long-existing inequalities in higher education, from differing levels of reliable access to high-speed internet, to gender imbalances in labor demands.

Yet, we should not too quickly assume that systemic shortcomings within academia will go away once the pandemic is over. Even after medical experts develop a vaccine for COVID-19, scholars will still need to address the lack of adequate training in digital skills or online teaching resources that has made the transition to distance learning so difficult, along with rigid tenure and promotion guidelines that do not accommodate the unique personal circumstances that have affected both teaching and scholarly productivity. In other words, the current pandemic has exacerbated a number of crises that already beset Asian Studies and are still in need of collective responses. As educators and scholars consider best practices for teaching about Asia in this moment, we should be mindful that our ideas and solutions do not simply address the pandemic, but also tackle more deep-seated problems within the field and lay the groundwork for improving our larger academic environment.

With this in mind, one digital tool scholars can use to maintain rigorous learning environments, whether during a time of global pandemic or not, is podcasting. I have actively employed podcasting both inside and outside my classroom since 2017: assigning podcast episodes as substitutes for course readings, giving students opportunities to produce their own episodes as alternatives to written work, and producing multiple podcast series as platforms for presenting new research in Japanese Studies to both specialists and the broader public around the world. In this chapter, I offer preliminary thoughts on the benefits of incorporating scholarly podcasting into our pedagogy, suggesting that podcasts can offer highly accessible conduits for asynchronous online learning and unique exercises for students to explore new methods of scholarly creativity. In this way, podcasting not only allows scholars to remain active and engaged during moments of crisis, but also to learn new digital skills that will enhance their teaching and research beyond the pandemic.

The popularity of podcasts as a media form has exploded in recent years. As of April 2020, the Apple podcast store boasted over one million individual podcast series, with the total number of available podcast episodes surpassing twenty-nine million. For comparison, just two years ago, there were only 550,000 active podcasts on Apple podcasts. Likewise, the percentage of the US population who has listened to at least one podcast has more than doubled in the last ten years, reaching 55 percent this year. Today, not only has 37 percent of the population reported listening to podcasts within the last month, but the average podcast consumer regularly listens to as many as six different podcasts each week. And podcasts are most popular amongst the student-aged population, with nearly half (49 percent) of twelve to thirty-four-year-olds reporting in 2020 that they had listened to a podcast within the last month.[1]

With so many of our students already consuming podcasts on a regular basis, scholars should make the most of this previously untapped pedagogical resource in our classrooms. This is especially important when considering how

Photo courtesy of the author.

we as educators can maintain rigorous learning environments when teaching asynchronously or from a distance. Writing for the Podcast Host website in 2017, professional podcaster and podcasting advisor Colin Gray outlined a number of pedagogical benefits to incorporating podcasts into the classroom, noting that students will listen longer than they will read and can use podcasts for lecture review or to make up missed classes. First and foremost among the benefits, according to Gray, is the "flexible availability" of podcasts: students can choose to listen to lessons when it is convenient for them, and they have the extra level of autonomy that comes from being able to stop and rewind when necessary for review.[2] Writing for *Education about Asia* in the same year, Jared Hall added that podcasts might serve as "a jumping-off point for further individual exploration" by students pursuing new research topics.[3] But these are only the beginning of the benefits of incorporating podcasts and podcasting into the virtual classroom.

In my own courses before the pandemic, podcasts were most effective when used as (1) substitutes for traditional print-based reading assignments, and (2) as flexible, virtual alternatives to written assessments. Teaching for several years at a major urban R1 institution with only a small percentage of on-campus residents, I quickly learned that many of my students commuted long distances to school by car, bus, subway, or some combination of private and public transit—as long as one-and-a-half hours or more each way for some students! What's more, because of unprecedented extracurricular demands on students' time in the form of jobs, caregiving, athletics, and other activities, students had very tight commuting and class schedules. Indeed, more than one student sheepishly confessed to me that they took one of my classes simply because it was the most intriguing option that fit into their narrow window of availability. Such demands greatly limited the amount of time students could devote to scrutinizing assigned readings or meeting in person with classmates for collaborative projects.

Needless to say, the ongoing coronavirus pandemic has only exacerbated these demands and presented new challenges in online teaching and learning for both educators and students. Now students are spread across different time zones, attending lectures asynchronously, finding time to review lecture recordings and assigned materials while navigating unfamiliar routines. How can we as educators make our lecture content and course materials more flexible and mobile to fit students' new daily schedules? How can we assign collaborative work for students living in different parts of the city or the country? How can students complete assigned readings or review lectures while they are in their car, doing daily household chores, or walking around their neighborhood? Or, how can they contribute to group projects virtually using a medium they are already familiar with and excited about? Podcasting fits the bill on all accounts.

To be sure, substituting podcast episodes for traditional print readings entails some challenges. First is the availability of relevant episodes. As a Japanese historian, I have been lucky. Not only are there several expertly produced and well-documented, lecture-based podcasts about Japanese history, such as Isaac Meyer's *History of Japan Podcast*, but there are also several interview-based series covering a wide range of topics, including the *Japan Forum* and *Michigan Talks Japan* podcast series. My own *Meiji at 150 Podcast* includes 120 episodes of interviews with scholars of Japanese Studies discussing their recent publications, ongoing research projects, and teaching methods. In other words, there is no shortage of relevant content to choose from for Japanese Studies, while the *New Books in East Asian Studies*, *East Asia for All*, and *East Asia Now* podcasts are just a few series that will be useful for those outside Japanese Studies (See Appendix 1 for a partial list of Asian Studies podcast series). A second challenge concerns how much students engage with and retain the podcast content. However, this is no different than any assigned reading, and podcasts are most effective as learning resources when educators directly address the content in classroom lectures, discussions, and exercises.

I also brought podcasting into my classroom even before the pandemic by offering students the opportunity to produce their own episodes as an alternative to written assessments. In this regard, I have experimented with a number of student podcast formats, listed in order of the time commitment and student-teaching interaction required: (1) one-on-one interviews about pop culture topics of the students' own choosing, such as J-Pop, horror movies, and video games;

(2) thematic podcasts covering current events, including homelessness in Tokyo, the Japanese Self-Defense Forces, or ongoing territorial disputes in East Asia, which I assigned to individual groups and published on *Japan on the Record*; and finally (3) individual episodes groups produced under my direction for a longer documentary-style series about the 1907 Anti-Asian Riots in Vancouver that we published as *The Wildest Night in Vancouver*. Each format requires different amounts of coordination, from agreeing on questions beforehand for one-on-one pop culture interviews to revising episode scripts multiple times for documentary episodes. While I was present in the university sound studio to facilitate the recording, students were responsible for conducting their own research, writing and revising scripts, recording the audio, doing the sound editing, and producing the final episodes.

Without question, the pandemic has changed how such collaborative podcast production exercises will work. For one, students will no longer have access to professional-quality recording studios or equipment on campus, nor will they be able to work in groups during class time to author and revise scripts. Still, students will be able to work together to draft and revise narrative scripts using Zoom and Google Docs from a distance on their own time. They can then record audio clips using their phones or built-in computer microphones and share files with groupmates online using cloud-based services like Google Drive or Dropbox. Meanwhile, free VOIP recording websites like Zencastr make remote interview recording simple, while free audio editing software like Audacity allows students to efficiently produce high-quality podcast episodes with zero associated costs. In short, because of its digital nature, collaborative podcasting is an exercise that can be easily adapted to asynchronous online completion.

As with any nontraditional exercise, using podcasts as an alternative to written work raises questions about the pedagogical value and learning outcomes of such assignments. Below, I outline six pedagogical benefits of introducing podcasting exercises into the classroom based on my own experiences and on feedback from students:

1. Because the "nuts and bolts" are the same when writing either an essay or narrative podcast script, podcasting builds research skills in a way no different than conducting research for a written essay. Students analyze primary and secondary sources to construct an original argument and then marshal evidence to support their arguments.

2. Listening to podcasts reminds students to think critically about source material and media credibility, offering opportunities for classroom reflection on how to assess the reliability of provided evidence and arguments.

3. In writing their own podcast scripts, the spoken format allows students to practice verbalizing their arguments cogently and concisely in a more conversational tone. This enhances writing skills by encouraging students to consider their audience and how to most powerfully organize and convey their arguments.

4. In a related way, producing a scholarly podcast episode encourages students to reflect on different modes of scholarly production and how different forms of scholarship target different audiences.

5. Producing a podcast episode provides students an opportunity to learn new digital skills, or to apply skills they already have, that they might not expect to experience in a classroom. In this way, podcasting not only engages students' interests, but also builds new skills applicable outside the humanities classroom.

6. Finally, because of the public-facing nature of podcasts, students can take ownership and pride in a memorable finished product that they can immediately share with friends around the world in a way they might not feel compelled to with a traditional written report.

Assigning podcast exercises also requires the articulation of a detailed rubric for evaluating the finished product. Because students will be unfamiliar with nontraditional assessments such as podcasts, the absence of such a rubric will cause unnecessary confusion and anxiety, particularly around grading. Much like traditional assessments, podcasting exercise rubrics should prioritize the originality and strength of the argument, along with the effectiveness of the delivery. Yet, where podcasting rubrics differ is that delivery will be evaluated not on writing style, but on the organization and "listenability" of the episode in terms of sound quality, sound editing, and other factors (see Appendix 2 for a rubric template for podcasting exercises).

Now that the pandemic has brought to light the systemic challenges scholars and educators of Asian Studies at all stages and career levels have faced in recent years and forced many of us around the world to "go virtual," podcasts are even more vital as pedagogical resources. Not only do podcasts allow for asynchronous instruction in the form of recorded lectures, but they also afford students a new level of flexibility in their learning. Because of their digital format, moreover, podcasts can be quickly integrated into the virtual classroom, both as required listening for group discussion and as collaborative exercises students can contribute to remotely. Engaging with podcasting also encourages the acquisition of new digital skills that will allow us as scholars and educators of Asian Studies the agility to respond to the ever-evolving circumstances and expectations of higher education and to alleviate some of the long-standing inequities afflicting the profession. As we confront a new academic environment, one where distance learning, social distancing, and self-quarantine are regular parts of our academic identities, I urge scholars of Asian Studies to consider podcasting as a tool to maintain their rigorous classroom learning environments and active research portfolios, both now and beyond the pandemic.

Acknowledgments

The author would like to sincerely thank Paula R. Curtis and Jooyeon Hahm for helpful comments on an earlier draft of this chapter.

Notes

[1] The Podcast Host, "Podcast Stats in 2020: Latest Industry Growth & Listening Trends," https://www.thepodcasthost.com/listening/podcast-industry-stats (accessed July 14, 2020).

[2] The Podcast Host, "Podcasting in Education: What Are the Benefits?" https://www.thepodcasthost.com/niche-case-study/podcasting-in-education (accessed July 14, 2020).

[3] Jared Hall, "Podcasting Asia," *Education about Asia* 22:3 (Winter, 2017), https://www.asianstudies.org/publications/eaa/archives/podcasting-asia (accessed September 7, 2020).

Appendix 1: Partial List of Asian Studies Podcasts

Inter-Regional

New Books in East Asian Studies
https://newbooksnetwork.com/category/east-asian-studies

East Asia for All
https://www.eastasiaforall.com

East Asia Now
https://eastasia.wisc.edu/podcast

East Asia Hotspots
https://nrc.elliott.gwu.edu/east-asia-hotspots-podcast

Postcards from Asia
http://ceas.ku.edu/postcards-asia

New Books in Central Asian Studies
https://newbooksnetwork.com/category/peoples-places/central-asian-studies

New Books in South Asian Studies
https://newbooksnetwork.com/category/peoples-places/south-asian-studies

Southeast Asia Crossroads Podcast
https://soundcloud.com/seacrossroads

Center for Advanced Study of India Podcast
https://casi.sas.upenn.edu/podcasts

University of Chicago East Asian Studies Podcast
https://podcasts.apple.com/us/podcast/east-asian-studies/id391209825

China

Harvard on China Podcast
soundcloud.com/fairbank-center

UPenn Center for the Study of Contemporary China Podcast
https://cscc.sas.upenn.edu/podcasts

Chinese Literature Podcast
https://www.chineseliteraturepodcast.com

Japan

The Meiji at 150 Podcast
https://meijiat150.podbean.com

Japan on the Record
https://jotr.transistor.fm

Hokkaido 150
https://hokkaido150.transistor.fm

Michigan Talks Japan
https://ii.umich.edu/cjs/podcast.html

Japan Forum
https://soundcloud.com/soas-university-of-london/sets/japan-forum

History of Japan Podcast
http://isaacmeyer.net/category/podcasts/history-of-japan-podcast

Appendix 2: Podcast Exercise Grading Rubric Sample

30% **Research and Argument**

The episode presents an original argument supported by sufficient evidence drawn from primary and secondary sources. Contains a balance of analysis and a citation of sources.

20% **Presentation**

The episode is compellingly organized, content is cogently presented, and the episode contains all required elements (introduction, content, "sign-off").

20% **Listenability**

Is the podcast well edited, removing gaps, extraneous noises/sounds, avoiding blips, etc.? Does the episode use background music and sound effects to punctuate topics? Are the music/sounds relevant to the content?

15% **Groupwork**

Did each group member contribute to the episode in some way (research, scripting, editing)? This score may change depending on individual contributions.

15% **Referencing**

Does the podcast write-up correctly list consulted sources and provide citations for quoted materials? Have appropriate sources been consulted?

14

Designing and Implementing a Tandem Language Learning (TLL) Program for Learners of Chinese and English Using the Social Media App QQ

Jeffrey Gil, Han Lin and Gwendolyn Campbell

In this chapter, we discuss our experiences designing and implementing an online Tandem Language Learning (TLL) program for university undergraduate-level learners of Chinese and English. Our TLL program, called the Chinese Corner/ English Corner, involved native English-speaker learners of Chinese in Australia and native Chinese-speaker learners of English in China interacting via the social media app QQ to learn each other's languages. We first explain the rationale for establishing a TLL program for these two groups of language learners, then describe the learning activities we designed and the principles which informed them. Following this, we discuss the benefits for students of the Chinese Corner/ English Corner; namely, active engagement, substantial use of the target language, sustained participation, increased knowledge and understanding of the target language culture, and flexibility of access.

We offer our experience in the hope it will benefit language teachers who need to shift their teaching activities online in the wake of the COVID-19 pandemic, where learning cannot take place in physical space. Our experience is relevant here because the Chinese Corner/English Corner had originally run in face-to-face mode but had to be shifted to online mode because of a decrease in enrollments of English-language learners of Chinese background at Flinders University. QQ was a suitable solution because it allowed an international collaboration in which Flinders University's Chinese language learners could interact with English language learners at the University of Jinan without the need for students to be physically present in the same location.

The Rationale for TLL

Research suggests there are a number of ingredients that are either essential to, or contribute significantly toward, successful second language acquisition (SLA). These are: exposure to the language; opportunities to use the language in meaningful, communicative interactions; explicit attention to language forms; and feedback on learning.[1] Successful SLA is determined by the amount, type, and quality of these ingredients available within the context in which SLA takes place, and the use learners make of them.

A distinction is often drawn between second language (SL) contexts and foreign language (FL) contexts. An SL context is a situation in which the target language is widely used in the community outside of the language classroom. An FL context, on the other hand, is a situation in which the target language is not often, or usually, used in the community outside the language classroom.[2] In reality, SL and FL contexts are not absolutes but form a continuum, "ranging from high-visibility, ready access to the target language outside the language classroom to little access beyond the classroom door."[3] With this caveat in mind, it is reasonable to say Chinese language learners in Australia and English language learners in China are both in an FL context. The nature of this context poses challenges to their learning.

While the language classroom does provide explicit attention to language forms and feedback on learning, exposure to the target language and opportunities to use it in meaningful, communicative interactions are typically limited. The classroom cannot expose learners to the target language for all purposes or functions, and the interaction that takes place in the classroom is not always meaningful or communicative (for example, the repetition of a new vocabulary item or grammar structure). In addition, contact is usually only a small number of hours per week, and the teacher is often the only proficient speaker with whom learners have regular contact.[4] In our teaching experience, this applies to learners of Chinese in Australia and learners of English in China.

We saw TLL as a way to address this challenge. According to O'Rourke, TLL is "an arrangement in which two native speakers of different languages communicate regularly with one another, each with the purpose of learning the other's language."[5]

We called our TLL program the Chinese Corner/English Corner, an adaptation of the English Corner commonly found in China. An English Corner is a gathering of English language learners in a park, square, or university campus to practice speaking English together; it also sometimes involves native speakers of English. We hoped this would be a familiar practice to Chinese learners of English and also Australian learners of Chinese who had gained some knowledge of China through their studies.

Designing the Online Chinese Corner/English Corner

We chose the social media app QQ as the platform for our TLL program and designed a series of connected information exchange tasks to guide interactions between the two groups of learners involved.

The Social Media App QQ

QQ was developed by the Chinese technology company Tencent. It was originally an instant messaging service, then expanded to provide services such as games, shopping, microblogging, and group and voice chat. It is now one of the most widely used social media apps in China and is also available internationally. It can be used on a PC, iPad, or mobile phone.

We established an online conversation space on QQ, in which students met and had weekly conversations using the voice live interaction and messaging functions. First, students were asked to resister a QQ account if they did not already have one. We established a QQ group called "Flinders University-University of Jinan Chinese Corner/English Corner," and students were notified of the group name and required to join by searching for the group name on QQ. Twenty-three English language learners from the University of Jinan and six Chinese language learners from Flinders University joined the group. The Chinese language learners were second- and third-year undergraduates who had not studied Chinese prior to commencing university. The English language learners were second-year undergraduates who had previously studied English in primary and high school. Due to the difference in learner numbers, we further divided them into six subgroups, each containing one Chinese language learner and three or four English language learners. Each of these groups had a separate subgroup within the larger QQ group. The Flinders University Chinese language tutor (one of the authors) was the manager of all groups, monitored their interactions, and provided feedback and suggestions for improvement.

There were some minor technical and organizational issues because some learners at both universities had difficulty locating and logging into the QQ group. These were resolved relatively easily through communication between Flinders and University of Jinan staff, and the technology functioned well for the duration of the Chinese Corner/English Corner.

We chose QQ because of its availability in both China and Australia, and because Chinese university students were already familiar with it. However, this arrangement could be replicated on other social media platforms, providing they have voice live interaction and messaging functions. Another option for running a TLL with students in China is WeChat. If the TLL was to be run with Chinese and English learners outside of China, possibilities would include WhatsApp and Facebook Messenger. It could also be replicated through online teaching platforms such as Collaborate or Zoom.

Materials Design

We designed a series of tasks to guide interactions between learners. Tasks that require learners to exchange information about a topic are an effective means of producing exposure to the language and meaningful, communicative interactions.[6] We therefore developed tasks around topics relevant to students' lives and experiences, and which would generate discussion about similarities and differences between China and Australia. Each learner would have information about the topic from their own perspective and experience and would need to use their target language to communicate this to their partners, as well as to learn about their partner's perspective and experience on the topic.

As we were aware that Chinese language learners would have a lower level of proficiency in their target language than their English language learner counterparts, we aimed the tasks at different levels of complexity. The tasks for Chinese language learners were "Self-Introduction," "Age, Chinese Zodiac, and Western Star Signs," "My Family and My Country," "Shopping and Online Shopping," and "Travels and Wishes." The English language learners were given the tasks of introducing themselves, explaining significant birthdays in Chinese culture, discussing forms of identification and licenses in China, comparing shopping centers in China to those in Australia, and explaining the procedures for seeing a doctor in China. Each task was intended to build on the previous one by expanding from the individual learner to the broader world.

We included model conversations in Chinese and English which highlighted new and important words and phrases that would be useful for the conversations. Learners could then use similar sentences to conduct their conversations with their partners. We also included useful words and phrases for arranging a time to conduct the conversation, as well as ones for canceling and rearranging a time. We did this because research demonstrates that planning can have a positive effect on successful task completion and fluency of language use during the task.[7] There were five tasks altogether, each of which followed the same structure. An example task worksheet is included in the appendix.

All participants were required to use Chinese when the Chinese language learners were performing their task, and all participants were likewise required to use English when the English language learners were performing their task. The Flinders University Chinese language tutor monitored language use to ensure both groups of learners had the same opportunities to use their target language.

Implementing the Chinese Corner/English Corner

Five sessions of the online Chinese Corner/English Corner took place over as many weeks. TLL programs are usually evaluated by learners' perceptions of their learning and improvements in their language proficiency.[8] However, determining whether participation in the Chinese Corner/English Corner improved language proficiency was complicated because the tasks were focused primarily on the expression of meaning, and the peer-to-peer conversations involved a more fluid way of learning than a usual classroom situation. In light of this, we focus here on learners' perceptions of the benefits of participation and our own perceptions as their tutors and course coordinator. We draw on our observations of learners' conversations, learners' comments to us, and our own reflections to discuss the benefits of the Chinese Corner/English Corner.

There were several benefits to learners. First, they were very interested in the task content, and because of this, they engaged actively in the Chinese Corner/English Corner. This is demonstrated by the fact that the conversations in all groups lasted much longer than we expected, each taking around thirty minutes. Learners would often go beyond the set task and discuss related topics. For example, in session 2, learners not only identified their own Chinese and Western horoscope sign, but also asked questions about their partners'. English language learners who knew more about the Chinese horoscope explained the characteristics of its twelve animals to their partners in English, while those Chinese language learners with higher levels of Chinese proficiency were able to explain a little about the personality traits associated with their Chinese star sign.[9]

Another example of learners' desire to continue the conversations with their partners occurred in session 5. One Chinese language learner explained the process of seeing a physician in Australia in Chinese to his English language learner partners. One such learner responded, "I didn't know it's so troublesome to see a doctor in Australia. In China, you can just walk into a hospital. There is a board in the entry hall with all doctors' photos and what they specialize in. You can pick one and pay a registration/admission fee. Then the doctor will see you."[10] It was encouraging to see this level of participation still occurring in the final session of the Chinese Corner/English Corner. Even during the exam period, there were two groups who continued with the set tasks and also talked about how they performed during the exam and how difficult the essay questions were.

Students also expressed they had learned much about the target language culture from the model conversations and the conversations carried out with their partners. For example, in session 3, "My Family and Country," the English model conversation featured an Australian university student who addressed his father as "John" and his lecturer as "Maggie." In the Chinese model conversation, on the other hand, a Chinese university student addressed her professor as "Li Jiaoshou" (李教授 Professor Li) and her friend's father as "Wang Shushu" (王叔叔 Uncle Wang). Many English language learners were surprised by the model conversation and asked their partner if it was true that one can call their father by his given name at home in Australia.[11] Similar content, such as model conversations of appropriate and inappropriate compliments and questions in Chinese and English, all generated great discussions.

Learners also felt that the online Chinese Corner/English Corner offered them flexibility because there was no set time for the groups to conduct their conversations. As long as they completed the tasks within the week, they could do it at any time that was convenient for them.[12] Group members could negotiate with each other to set a time to conduct their conversations, and this negotiation was an opportunity to practice their target language. Similarly, learners felt the online tasks were focused and easy to follow. One Chinese language learner said, "the online material is much easier to follow," and added, "our partners will explain [the meaning] of the new words if I have trouble [understanding them]."[13]

The Chinese Corner/English Corner's provision of exposure to the target language and opportunities to use it in meaningful, communicative interactions clearly benefited learners.

Conclusion

Designing and implementing a TLL program for learners of Chinese and English led to positive results in terms of learner engagement, use of the target language, sustained participation, and increased knowledge and understanding of the target language culture. The online format also provided learners with flexibility. Our Chinese Corner/English Corner experience can be useful in a wide variety of learning environments, especially where such a pedagogical approach is necessitated by COVID-19.

We see three possible applications of this to teaching during the COVID-19 pandemic. First, teachers could use the Chinese Corner/English Corner as a supplement to their existing curriculum. Native English-speaker learners of Chinese and native Chinese-speaker learners of English could be recruited internationally or locally, depending on circumstances. In either case, the Chinese Corner/English Corner could operate as we have described in this chapter. A second possibility is that teachers incorporate the Chinese Corner/English Corner into their curriculum. This could be done by designing tasks around the content of their curriculum (i.e., tasks that cover the subject matter, vocabulary, grammar, and cultural content of the curriculum), then requiring learners to undertake them at set times during the course. Opportunities for learners to reflect on their performance of and learning from tasks could also be given during regular classes. Third, teachers who do not want or are unable to establish a TLL program could still use QQ (or another platform) and the task structure we described here to teach their existing curriculum online. This would involve creating information exchange tasks based on the content of their curriculum and requiring their learners to perform them online. The process of setting up an online conversation space and designing the tasks we outlined will be useful for those who choose to pursue this option. All three applications provide opportunities for language learning and teaching to continue in the context of a global pandemic.

Notes

[1] H. Douglas Brown, *Principles of Language Learning and Teaching: A Course in Second Language Acquisition* (6th ed.) (White Plains: Pearson Longman, 2014), chapter 10; Rod Ellis, *The Study of Second Language Acquisition* (2nd ed.) (Oxford: Oxford University Press, 2008), chapters 6–8; Patsy M. Lightbown and Nina Spada, *How Languages Are Learned* (4th ed.) (Oxford: Oxford University Press, 2013), chapter 4.

[2] Muriel Saville-Troike, *Introducing Second Language Acquisition* (2nd ed.) (Cambridge: Cambridge University Press, 2012), 4.

[3] H. Douglas Brown and Heekyeong Lee, *Teaching by Principles: An Interactive Approach to Language Pedagogy* (4th ed.) (White Plains: Pearson Longman, 2015), 161.

[4] Lightbown and Spada, *How Languages are Learned*, chapter 5.

[5] Breffni O'Rourke, "Form-Focused Interaction in Online Tandem Learning," *CALICO Journal* 22, no. 3 (2005): 433–466, 434.

[6] David Nunan, *Task-Based Language Teaching* (Revised ed.) (Cambridge: Cambridge University Press, 2004), chapter 4.

[7] Nunan, *Task-Based Language Teaching* (Revised ed.), chapter 6.

[8] David Little and Ema Ushioda, "Designing, Implementing and Evaluating a Project in Tandem Language Learning Via Email," *ReCALL* 10, no. 1 (1998): 95–101, 99.

[9] Learners' conversation, session 2.

[10] Learners' conversation, session 5.

[11] Learners' conversation, session 3.

[12] Comment to Chinese language tutor.

[13] Comment to Chinese language tutor.

Appendix: Example Task Sheet

Teacher's Notes: The goal of this task is for students to conduct a conversation about their personal experiences with shopping and/or online shopping. Students will learn words and phrases related to shopping in context. Students will also learn about different ways of shopping and shopping habits in Australia and China.

Session Four: Shopping and Online Shopping

四：购物与网购

gòuwù yǔ wǎnggòu

[note: 购物 general shopping, a more formal expression compared with 买东西；网 net, Internet; 网购 online shopping, can be used as a noun or verb, e.g.: 我喜欢网购。我网购了一本书]

Task in Chinese: *Show and tell your partner something you bought recently or a long time ago. Describe the thing you bought, how much you spent, where you bought it, and recommend your partner some good places for shopping online or at actual shops. The conversation can be carried out like this. You can of course change the time and the object.*

XX, 我前天买了一本书。(XX, I bought a book the day before yesterday.)
什么名？(What's the name [of the book]?)

liángshānbó yǔ zhùyīngtái
梁山伯与祝英台. (Liang Shanbo and Zhu Yingtai).
wà
哇！你也喜欢这本书啊?! (Wow! You also like this book?!) [note: 哇 a particle to express that you are surprised.]

       tuījiàn
是啊，我们中文老师推荐的。(Yeah, our Chinese teacher recommended it.)
[note: 推荐 to recommend].

     gānggāng   luómìōu zhūlìyè
好巧啊！我们英语老师也刚刚推荐了罗密欧与朱丽叶。(What a coincidence! Our English teacher also just recommended *Romeo and Juliet*.)
[note: 刚刚 just]

   bùtóng wénhuà què jiǎngshù   xiāngsìde àiqínggùshì
两本书，<u>不同的文化</u>，<u>却</u> <u>讲述了</u> <u>相似的</u> <u>爱情故事</u>。(Two books, different cultures, but told similar love stories.) [note: 不同的 different；却 but；讲述 to tell；相似的 similar；爱情 love；故事 story]

　　　　tǐng　　　　　　huā
是啊，挺有意思的。对了，你花了多少钱？在哪儿买的？(Exactly, that's quite interesting. By the way, how much did you spend? Where did you buy it?) [note: 挺quite; 花 spent; 在哪儿买的is a simple way of saying, "Where did you buy this book?"]

　　　　piányìba　　　　　　　　　　　yàmǎxùn　　　wǎnggòu
十五块。便宜吧！我在网上买的 or 我上网买的，亚马逊。你喜欢网购吗？
(15 yuan. Isn't it cheap! I bought it online, amazon.com. Do you like shopping online?)[note: 便宜 cheap; 吧 here indicates the speaker wants to get agreement on his/her statement; it can also be used when you want to show off something. Eg: 漂亮吧！Isn't it beautiful!; 在网上 on internet; 上网 go online, same meaning; or you can say: 我在亚马逊网购的。网购 here is a verb.]

　　　　　　dehuà　　yìbān　dāngdāngwǎng
喜欢啊！买书的话，我一般上当当网。　(I do! If buying a book, I normally go to dangdang.com)
[note: … 的话 if…; 一般 usually, normally; 当当网a popular online bookstore in China; Pay attention that you use the verb '上'for going online.]

　　　　　　táobǎowǎng　　　　　　xìngjiàbǐgāo
买衣服的话，我一般上淘宝网，　　性价比高。(If buying clothes, I usually go to taobao.com, good value for money.) [note: 淘宝网 taobao.com which is a bit like ebay.com; 性价比高good value for money]

　　huàzhuāngpǐn　　　　　jiǎhuò
但是化妆品我一般去大商场，淘宝假货太多。(But for cosmetics, I usually go to big department stores, taobao fake products are too many.) [note: 化妆品 cosmetics, makeup; 假货fake products, unauthentic products].

　　　　　　jīngcháng　　wǎnggòu
你们澳大利亚人也经常　　　网购吗？(Are you Australians also often shopping online?) [note:经常 often]

　　　　　　fāngbiàn　chāoshì　dōngxī　　　dànshì　bāoyóu
是啊，经常。网购很方便。超市的　东西也可以网购，但是　不包邮。
(Yes, often. Online shopping is very convenient. Supermarket products can be also bought online, but postage is not included.) [note: 方便convenient; 超市 supermarket; 东西 things, products; 但是 but; 包邮 include postage]

Task in English: Ask your partner about grocery shopping in China, big supermarket chains, shops, restaurants, department stores, and trading hours on weekdays and public holidays. Also tell your partner something about Australian retailers such as Woolworths, Coles, Foodland, Westfield Shopping Centre, Myer, David Jones, Priceline, Harvey Norman, etc.

15

DIGITAL INVESTIGATIONS

USING VIRTUAL FIELDWORK IN THE CLASSROOM

Byron Haast and Phillip O'Brien

There is a well-known phrase, often attributed to the Chinese philosopher Xunzi: "I hear and I forget. I see and I remember. I do and I understand." Having students *see* and *do* provides for significantly more meaningful learning experiences and has long been a staple of the geography classroom. That said, getting out and seeing the world is subject to many variables at a school and personal level, and it has been further complicated by the COVID-19 pandemic. This therefore necessitates new pathways for fieldwork, giving rise to the use of research, virtual reality, and satellite technology and imaging in the learning arena. This provides exciting opportunities to find ways of integrating often preexisting student skill sets in digital literacy, developed through their own exploration of satellite programs like Google Earth and games like *Minecraft*. Furthermore, the use of the digital medium has been shown to improve engagement, interest, focus, and permanent learning.[1] From *Carmen Sandiego* to *GeoGuessr*, the use of digital geography and gaming to enhance and support the learning of our world is not a new phenomenon per se—Kirriemuir and McFarlane suggested that the use of simulations and virtual immersive worlds are increasingly being used to supplement traditional teaching—but the use of a digital medium for geographic fieldwork is a growing and exciting area.[2]

Lockdowns, quarantines, and social distancing have created a need for teachers to explore new ways to bring the world into their classrooms; this resource essay aims to shine a light on the myriad possibilities that exist, as well as an in-depth look at how one can "take" students to visit Fukushima, Japan. One of the joys of virtual fieldwork is the ability to visit locations that cannot physically be accessed (such as Fukushima or Chernobyl) or that would otherwise be unsafe (conflict zones); no paperwork, permission, visas, or vaccinations required.

Getting Started

Geographic fieldwork is generally mandated by most curricula, such as the International Baccalaureate, British, American, Canadian, and Australian Curriculum. Virtual fieldwork has an invaluable role to play in meeting these requirements. Better still, it can broaden horizons in terms of where and when students investigate, with broad applicability well beyond the geography classroom. Perhaps students of ancient history would like to visit renowned archaeological locations and museums in the Near East or the Mediterranean? Art classes could walk the halls of some of the world's most well-known galleries, or students of literature and languages can dive firsthand into streets and sites to illuminate their learning. In a crowded curriculum—in addition to demographic change and institutional pressures—the use of a digital "virtual" medium provides real opportunity for increasing fieldwork opportunities.[3] In terms of planning, one need only consider the core knowledge or concept to be covered and from there, simply visualize a suitable location to "see" it in action. For example, if one were looking at coastal landforms, a virtual visit to Australia's Great Ocean Road may be in order; if the topic was deforestation, one could "take" the students to Borneo or the Brazilian Amazon. With a concept in mind, there are a broad range of straightforward options for conducting the virtual visit, but perhaps the best and broadest is Google Earth (www.google.com/earth). Satellite imagery, once primarily the domain of the military and meteorology, is now an increasingly integral part of our lives; tapping into skills with which students have some degree of familiarity both accelerates and excites the learning process.[4]

With no equipment required other than a computer and a connection to the Internet, one can readily begin to develop familiarity with digital visits. Within Google Earth, one can use Google Street View to zoom down to street level, a wonderful tool for exploring human geography in particular. An excellent starting point for the beginner is Google Earth Outreach (https://www.google.com/earth/outreach/learn/), which provides a series of short, guided visual modules for professional development and skill acquisition. As one develops familiarity, there are a range of other options available to begin to customize content, including:

- Google Tour Creator: https://arvr.google.com/tourcreator/

- Google My Maps: www.google.com.au/maps

- Google Maps Treks: https://www.google.com.au/maps/about/treks

Here one can begin to establish clear tours for students to follow. For schools with access to Augmented Reality or Virtual Reality equipment and software, the possibilities grow even further:

- Google Expeditions: https://edu.google.com/products/vr-ar/expeditions/

- VR Glaciers: https://vrglaciers.wp.worc.ac.uk/wordpress/

Many of the aforementioned sites have ready-made sample tours and examples that can inspire and guide teachers as they develop their own ideas and expand them into their units. When supporting fieldwork with further opportunities for digital investigation by accessing rich quantified data sources such as the United Nations, World Bank, NASA, and national or state census records, teachers can prepare rich learning units for their students.

- UN Data: https://data.un.org/

- World Bank Open Data: https://data.worldbank.org/

- NASA Open Data: https://nasa.github.io/data-nasa-gov-frontpage/

- CIA World Factbook: https://www.cia.gov/library/publications/the-world-factbook/

In addition to the excitement of global learning opportunities, one can also use virtual fieldwork in a local context. The Victorian Certificate of Education—the senior high school award for the Australian state of Victoria—mandates fieldwork as a core element of the geography curriculum three times across the two-year course in the differing contexts of hazards and disasters, tourism, and land use change and management. In the case of investigating the potential for sea level rise to create issues on a local scale as part of the hazards and disasters unit, students at McKinnon Secondary College investigate the preparedness of the local bayside suburbs to deal with this hazard and to explore existing flood mitigation strategies in place. With a blanket ban on excursions in place as a result of the COVID-19 pandemic, students have used the tour feature on Google Earth and Google Street View to explore the area remotely, capturing images of key features and noting the geographic characteristics of the region. Supplementing this with data available online via the local government authorities and comparing it to national averages via the Australian census, students were able to build a profile and gain sufficient data to discuss the topic at length. For the teacher, this involved preparing the tour beforehand and flagging key sites of note; however, student feedback emphasized the ease with which they were not only able to collect data, but also to revisit and expand their knowledge using skills they had, in many cases, developed independently.

Using Virtual Fieldwork to Drive a Unit of Learning: Fukushima, Japan

A unit of learning centered on disaster provides an excellent point of study for students to consider the origins and impacts of hazards. In the Australian state of Victoria, the study of hazards forms a core component of the senior geography curriculum. In other curriculum contexts, there is broad applicability to consider hazards and disasters within a range of different units of study at different levels. Virtual fieldwork in these locations also allows students to gain a sense of scale and empathy for the people involved in these phenomena and empowers students to consider how disasters can be managed and mitigated in the future. Furthermore, Hupy demonstrated that students working with geospatial data sources reported far greater clarity with the content than beforehand, overcoming previous uncertainty with the material. Indeed, the presentation of conceptual content in actual settings proved of great support for student understanding.[5] Ultimately, virtual fieldwork allows students to access places that would otherwise be off-limits, like the exclusion zone surrounding Fukushima Daiichi Nuclear Power Plant in Okuma, Japan, which suffered a catastrophic meltdown in the aftermath of the 2011 Tohoku earthquake and tsunami. This investigation fits within both the International Baccalaureate "Geophysical Hazard" component and Key Stage 3 of the National Curriculum in England: "Human and Physical Geography."

Before considering the impact of this event on places and people, students will need to consider the wider context of the Daiichi power plant's position within its surrounding coastal landscape and its location in one of the most geologically active regions on earth. The island of Honshu, located at the edge of the Pacific Ring of Fire, exists as the meeting place for the Eurasian, Pacific, and Philippine tectonic plates. This is an important point where students will need to consider tectonic plates on a global scale and a great opportunity to add some academic and scientific rigor before delving into a regional- and local-scale investigation of the 2011 earthquake and tsunami. Here, students can dissect top-quality publications, like the report from the UK Geological Society (The Geological Society of London—Tohoku Earthquake, Japan, 2020) on the Tohoku Earthquake from the "Plate Tectonic Stories" section of their website, which explains the plate movements at the heart of the event.[6] This could be digested after a wider introduction to global plate movements.

On a local scale, students could then focus on the coastal landscape of northern Honshu, which bore the brunt of the resulting tsunami. This is where

Figure 1: IAEA experts depart Unit 4 of TEPCO's Fukushima Daiichi Nuclear Power Station on 17 April 2013 as part of a mission to review Japan's plans to decommission the facility. Photo Credit: Greg Webb / IAEA.
Source: Wikimedia Commons.

students begin to consider the impacts of geomorphological hazards in the context of the destruction that occurred in the Tohoku region, including the meltdown of Fukushima Daiichi. Fukushima Beach is an interesting case study of a coastal landscape interconnected with human uses of this landscape. Coastal landforms can be taught to students; they can consider a Google Maps scavenger hunt using coordinates for various coastal landscapes in the area before considering the potential effects of longshore drift on nuclear power plants located in coastal environments like Dungeness Nuclear Power Plant in the UK. Digesting the causes of this event and considering how erosion interacts with human uses of coastal landscapes, students can now begin to investigate the destruction wrought by the event itself.

- Preparation: Impacts: https://www.theatlantic.com/photo/2012/02/japan-earthquake-before-and-after/100251/

- Conducting fieldwork—the *Guardian* walk-through: https://www.theguardian.com/environment/ng-interactive/2018/mar/12/fukushima-360-walk-through-a-ghost-town-in-the-nuclear-disaster-zone-video

More than nine years after the event, a number of great quality visual media exists to facilitate virtual fieldwork activity that adequately investigates the

Figure 2: A map of the instant radioactivity of the
Fukushima reactor area, as measured from the air.
Source: Wikimedia Commons.

aftermath of both the tsunami and the meltdown. *The Atlantic*'s "5 Years Since the
2011 Great East Japan Earthquake" allows for an in-depth list of the short-term
impacts through captivating photos, which can be discussed and written about at
length. The primary fieldwork tool involves the *Guardian*'s "Fukushima 360: Walk
Through a Ghost Town in the Nuclear Disaster Zone." This tool allows users to
return to the evacuation zone with a former resident. Users can rotate the camera,
view current radiation readings, and consider how places change as a result of
disasters. For teachers of other disciplines like science, this resource is a great
tool for teaching about nuclear radiation, sieverts, or microsieverts, or for a wider
study about the human body responding to its external environment.

At this point, students may be beginning to grow weary of hazards and the
toll they take on people, places, and environments. This is a pertinent opportunity

Figure 3: Satellite picture of the Himalaya Mountain ranges and the Tibetan Plateau. Source: Wikimedia Commons.

to begin investigating the Japanese government's response to the disaster by empowering students to apply their investigative skills. Having investigated the causes and impacts of the disaster, spatial technology can now take center stage as students apply their understanding. Spatial technology is an important point of difference for geography as a discipline as students learn to interpret the data generated by these tools and use the tools themselves. Students should be given a solid understanding of the various costs and benefits of using spatial technology in aiding responses to problems and understanding phenomena before undertaking this task.

Google My Maps is a custom mapmaking tool that allows users to add polygons, pins, descriptions, and media to a location of their choice around the world. For the purpose of this unit, My Maps can be used to create an overview of the disaster. A pin can be placed on the epicenter of the earthquake, off the coast of Japan, and a description can be added outlining how events unfolded on the day of the earthquake and tsunami. Pins and polygons can then be added to the coastline, indicating immediate impacts and the eventual exclusion zone surrounding Fukushima Daiichi Nuclear Power Plant. For assessment purposes, students will have already built a sound understanding of these events through their classroom work, so the assessment allows students to recap what they have learned and to really start to refine their writing as they will be revisiting phenomena they have already written about. Students can be assessed on their ability to describe, explain, and analyze causes as they relate to tectonic plate movements. They can also be assessed on their ability to analyze the government's response and evaluate this response by referring to agreed criteria such as whether or not citizens have been allowed to return to the area or whether or not the exclusion zone is still in effect. Another avenue could involve students mapping the route they took while using the *Guardian's* "Fukushima 360" fieldwork tool referred to earlier in this piece.

In terms of supporting students with learning needs, using My Maps as an assessment tool provides a number of benefits. First, it is easily turned into a nondigital equivalent if required. For example, a teacher could easily provide a printout with assigned squares in which the student could write. This allows graphic organizers to take the place of digital tools, which could allow for "virtual" fieldwork to be carried out in cases where there is no available internet connection. Alternatively, the teacher can provide sentence starters in a teacher-created map, which can then be shared with the student. Finally, the assessment requires a summary of the content covered throughout the unit so the student is scaffolded throughout the process, and this can be made explicit to the learner perhaps through a portfolio in which they save their work, ready to compile it for the assessment.

Virtual fieldwork has a viable place in the classroom, particularly in geography. In addition to the acquisition and development of new skills, students also enjoy opportunities to be effective digital citizens and more confident online learners. In terms of engagement, studies indicate that the use of virtual mediums certainly supports increased participation and excitement. Getchell et al. reported that "a wave of excitement and activity rolled over . . . as the other groups, spurred on by the outcome, began to try to complete the stage with renewed interest."[7] "Hooking" students is key to developing deeper engagement; virtual fieldwork certainly has a key role to play and provides exciting possibilities to continue and expand programs regardless of the current public health climate.

Further Sites to Explore

There are myriad possibilities for virtual fieldwork and opportunities for taking students "out" of the classroom. Some curated highlights include:

- CyArk: https://cyark.org/
- Ib Digital Geography: http://ibgeography.digital/

- Geography.org: https://www.geography.org.uk/Virtual-fieldwork
- Mt. Everest 3D: http://www.everest3d.de/
- Joseph Kerski: https://www.josephkerski.com/
- ArcGIS Storymaps: https://storymaps.arcgis.com/
- Esri Storymaps: https://storymaps-classic.arcgis.com/en/
- Digital Geography: https://digital-geography.com/
- Swiss Topography: https://www.swisstopo.admin.ch/
- Palestine Open Maps: https://palopenmaps.org/
- All Global Cities: https://globalcities-koptiuch.jimdofree.com/
- Chernobyl Walkthrough: https://www.cbc.ca/news2/interactives/360-chernobyl/chernobyl-full.html
- Virtual Museums and Monuments: https://www.historyextra.com/magazine/virtual-remote-museum-exhibition-tours-how-explore-history-from-home/
- Archaeological Institute of America—Virtual Field Trips: https://www.archaeological.org/programs/educators/media/virtual-field-trips/

Notes

[1] Mustafa Girgin, "Use of Games in Education: Geoguessr in Geography Course," *International Technology and Education Journal* 1, no. 1 (2017), https://files.eric.ed.gov/fulltext/ED581261.pdf (accessed May 31, 2020).

[2] John Kirriemuir and Angela McFarlane, "Use of Computer and Video Games in the Classroom." *Proceedings of the Level Up Digital Games Research Conference*, Universiteit Utrecht, Netherlands, 2003.

[3] Robert Rundstrom and Martin Kenzer, *The Decline of Fieldwork in Human Geography, The Professional Geographer* 41, no. 3 (1989), 294–303.

[4] Aaron Rothman, Mishka Henner, Danile Leivick, Clement Valla, "Beyond Google Earth," *Places Journal*, May 2015. Maps also provide unique opportunities to discuss issues of cultural power dynamics and inherent bias as manifest in place names, points of interest, orientation, and projection (Mercator or Peters, for example).

[5] Joseph P. Hupy, "Teaching Geographic Concepts Through Fieldwork and Competition," *Journal of Geography* 110, no. 3, 2011, https://www.tandfonline.com/doi/abs/10.1080/00221341.2011.532229 (accessed May 29, 2020).

[6] Geolsoc.org.uk, The Geological Society of London—Tohoku Earthquake, Japan. Available at: https://www.geolsoc.org.uk/Policy-and-Media/Outreach/Plate-Tectonic-Stories/Outer-Isles-Pseudotachylytes/Tohoku-Earthquake (accessed May 28, 2020).

[7] Kristoffer Getchell, Alan Miller, Ross Nicoll, Rebecca Sweetman, Colin Allison, "Games Methodologies and Immersive Environments for Virtual Fieldwork," *IEEE Transactions on Learning Technologies* 3, no. 4, 2020, https://ieeexplore.ieee.org/stamp/stamp.jsp?arnumber=5557838 (accessed June 1, 2020).

16

Blogging as Digital Citizens in an Online Course

Nabaparna Ghosh

Faced with a global pandemic in March 2020, schools in North America and many other countries moved their courses online. The midsemester pivot from in-person to online course delivery opened a floodgate of questions on pedagogy: Would an online course delivery alter the course objectives? How would students and faculty recreate a flipped classroom in a virtual setting? What would synchronous class discussions mean for students living in different time zones or in spaces not conducive to a nurturing education environment? As the Fall 2020 semester began, the pandemic was still surging in the United States. It is imperative for educators to reflect on how online courses can best facilitate student learning as an integral part of education under COVID-19 and in the post COVID-19 future.

An online course cannot replace the vibrant physical setting of an in-person classroom, and the absence of human contact can easily frustrate students. Even with these challenges, an online course can develop unique skill sets that an in-person course cannot. For instance, online courses can equip students with proficiencies like digital awareness or utilizing technology in responsible ways in an increasingly interconnected world. An online Asian history course, done correctly, can effectively weave together global and digital awareness, transforming students into responsible digital citizens who are aware of global cultures and are trained to use social media in sensible ways.

In Spring 2020, the South Asian History course I was teaching pivoted online. I revised the course assignments to emphasize a new course goal: training students to be responsible digital citizens. To that end, I canceled the midterm paper—in its place, I designed two blog assignments. These blogs required students to read the book *I Am Malala* and carry out online research on the book's central characters. Blogging prepared students to use their readings to retrieve factual information from online platforms. Students also had a chance to comment on each other's work, engage in virtual dialogue, and learn as a community.

I Am Malala is a fascinating account of activist Malala Yousafzai's relentless struggle to secure education for women in Pakistan.[1] Cowritten with Christina Lamb, the autobiographical work is a glimpse into the world of Pashtuns who live in the picturesque hills of Swat Valley. High school and undergraduate students find the autobiography a captivating read for the vivid details it provides of lively Pashtun customs and festivals that Taliban invaders muzzled in the 1990s. What is specifically noteworthy about *I Am Malala* is the way in which the book provokes discussions on global inequalities while revealing the power of young people as changemakers.

The first of the two blogs I assigned was a think-through character blog. Students had to understand the perspective of any one character in the book and review a current social or political event from that character's point of view. The blog required students to step outside their own frames of reference as they analysed various social, economic, and cultural factors. Additionally, students carried out online research and listed hyperlinks that they thought would be of interest to that character. The second blog, a courage activism blog, required students to connect the text with the world in which they live. The blog made students reflect on social injustices in their immediate world—racism, gun violence, climate change, immigration curbs, and so on—and weigh in on their role as potential changemakers.

Blogs and Gen Z Learners

A recent study carried out by Meghan Grace and Corey Seemiller on Gen Z learners offers crucial insights on how Gen Z learns in the classroom.[2] The book argues that our pedagogical practices are not in sync with the needs of Gen Z learners. Most classroom pedagogy is tailored for millennials; Gen Z learners have a whole new set of attributes and learning skills that remain unaddressed in the classroom. For example, millennials value lectures, but Gen Z prefers flipped classrooms. There are also significant differences in their approach to social media. The authors describe social media as a double-edged sword. Social media can provide a wealth of information for educators to stay relevant. At the same time, Gen Z views certain platforms, such as Twitter, as a safe space away from the scrutiny and judgment of authority figures where they can freely express their views. It is important that instructors respect students' sense of safety and use social media in responsible ways.

Figure 1: Malala Yousafzai is a campaigner who in 2012 was shot for her activist work. As part of WOW 2014, she talks about the systemic nature of gender inequality and bringing about change. Source: Wikimedia Commons.

Further, Gen Z regards higher education as a worthwhile experience, but they are also concerned about the cost of education. Students naturally have very high and specific demands for their college or university experiences. They question whether higher education can sufficiently prepare them for a professional career. They want more experiential or problem-based learning that yields real-life experience.

A blog can meaningfully connect classroom instruction with real-world experiences. When blogging, students get a chance to connect the readings with their own lives and also connect dots between the past and the present. While making connections between their own world and the reading, students can choose to keep their personal space intact—they have the power to decide on ways to engage with social media that are within their comfort zone. Blogging is an excellent option for those who want to remain anonymous even when engaging with social media. Students can decide whether their blog will be public or anonymous, moderating their interactions accordingly. For instance, they can create a username that only the teacher knows (so that the teacher can give credit for participation) but others in the class do not know. This anonymity builds a virtual space where students who are generally quiet or who hold alternative or minority perspectives feel more comfortable articulating their views.[3]

Finally, blogs benefit students who do not have the physical space conducive to participating in synchronous discussions. Intrusive parents, sick family members, or another sibling attending a class in the same room can curtail their participation. Blogs can generate asynchronous dialogue between creators and visitors, including those in different time zones. They reply to their followers' feedback and comments when they want to do so. Besides, blogging is a fun and innovative process where students can creatively express their views. In addition to regular writing, blogs enable students to think creatively and develop unique and original content through new themes, headers, layouts, designs, and images.

Think-Through Character Blog: Becoming Digital Citizens

One of the key pedagogical goals in reading a book together is building community. While some students are familiar with the geography and traditions of South Asia, others are learning about these for the first time. As a community, students can assist each other to deepen their knowledge of South Asia. In a face-to-face class, community building is easier as students interact in person. In an online course, building community can be tricky. Technical malfunctions and the lack of human contact can make it difficult to shape community consciousness.

Blogs are asynchronous conversation boards that allow students to engage in dialogue with each other. These conversations do not happen in real time, but they shape a meaningful discourse on course topics. Student conversations become even more instructive when they are asked to represent a perspective different from their own: a think-through character analysis blog does exactly this. It requires students to identify any one character from the book and use that character's perspective to create a blog.

In my spring 2020 course, students used the websites Wix and Squarespace to create their blogs. Both websites offer an easy interface to integrate texts with images. Students wrote at least 300 words for this blog. To guide them through the initial steps in writing the blog, I provided a note-taking assignment. Several platforms like Google Docs, Notejoy, and NoteLedge can make online note-taking easy and fun. With Google Docs, one student started the document and shared it with the class. In the document, the students drafted preliminary notes on characters in the book. Some notes were simple descriptions of a character, including who they interacted with and how their character grew through the story. Some provided critical analysis of what was missing in the book, strengths and weaknesses of characters, and comparisons between them. Other students then added additional notes in tables designated for each character. The table guided students as they developed good note-taking strategies. Other students used NoteLedge, which gives students many nontextual note-taking options, including drawing and mapping. Students were able to record audio when taking notes, and

Figure 2: Go Big Read Display for "I Am Malala." Source: Wikimedia Commons.

a web clipper option allowed them to add elements from the web to the notes (video clips or animation). Still other students worked with PDFs, highlighting and annotating and linking important facts from multiple PDFs and organizing them in their notes.

In addition to promoting critical thinking skills, blogging hones skills like digital communication, curation, critical evaluation, and visual literacy. Reading and writing online is not linear. Students in my class threaded together information that was fragmentary and hyperlinked, like pieces in a puzzle, sharpening their analytical abilities and improving problem-solving skills.

The spring 2020 blog assignment required outside research to facilitate critical thinking. Students were asked to include a sidebar with at least three links grouped around a theme of interest to that character. The blog required them to find a photo of the character with a brief description of his or her role, relationships, goals, location, and other characteristics. These tasks pushed students to reflect on ways to navigate the extensive information available online to find the most trustworthy facts. In addition, a retweet sidebar assisted students to further hone their critical thinking skills. For the retweet option, students were asked to read about current social and political tweets and suggest what the character they represented would retweet and what additional comments they would include in that retweet.

One Twitter account my students followed was the South Asia Center of the Atlantic Council.[4] Many of these tweets link to published opinion pieces. I invited my students to reflect on each publication by asking a series of questions: Who is the author? Can there be biases? Is there anything missing in the opinion? Students were asked to think about what comments Malala might post if she retweeted this, or what her mother would retweet and why. A think-through character analysis blog allows students to comprehend, empathize with, and demonstrate a nuanced understanding of divergent worldviews.

Commenting on each other's blogs, students were able to replicate the in-person discussions of the physical classroom. At the same time, online learning provided opportunities for interaction, participation, and collaboration. Retweeting perspectives empowered them to recognize how ideas, events, and actions in one location have consequences elsewhere. Retweets with comments assisted students in understanding power inequities among different cultures, societies, countries, and regions in both historical and contemporary contexts.

Courage Activism Blog

Students grasp readings best when they collectively live the text. Students who identify with the protagonists of a story are transported to countries and cultures different from their own. Furthermore, sensory details and relatable vulnerabilities make students more invested in matters of global justice. In an online course, where instructors only see the virtual students, it is difficult to determine whether students make an emotional connection with the reading. This connection is absolutely necessary to make students reflect on their identity and understand their role in the community and the wider world. For instance, students reading *I Am Malala* often assume that they cannot be global changemakers. Many students point out that they lack the courage to fight the Taliban like Malala did; others say that they want to fight injustice but do not know how.

The second blog assignment I used in spring 2020 was a courage activism blog, helping students become aware of their power to initiate change. A courage activism blog has two steps. In the first step, students were placed in small groups where they brainstormed ideas. Both WebEx and Zoom have "breakout group" options. Students were then asked to reflect on school and community-based political issues—such as the need for new facilities or gender-neutral spaces on campus—or wider issues like climate change or gun violence. After selecting one specific issue to address, they carried out online research to find one news article on the topic. When deciding which article to select, I encouraged students to reflect on a few questions: What kind of digital news forum is this? What is the author's background in this subject? Who is the intended audience? Is the author being objective or subjective? Is the author stating fact or opinion? How well are the author's opinions supported? Does the tone of the writing suggest that the author may be biased?

The class later reconvened and each group had five minutes to summarize their findings. Following this, students were asked to carry out a similar activity on their own and write a blog on a social justice issue that they felt required immediate attention. Their blog had to reference a web article that best explained the issue. They had to think critically and explain why they selected this issue over others and why they picked a certain web article. A carefully selected image at the center of the blog attracted the reader's attention to the topic. Next, the blog laid out an action plan for justice. In the blog that I assigned, students were asked to reflect on resources to which they have access (owing to nationality, class, gender, and so on) that Malala did not have and, through this difference, review their identity and place in society.[5]

Critics often claim that social media activism is a tool for mobilizing protesters for an immediate cause but that it fails to build long-term relationships. Platforms like Facebook and Twitter spread and receive information, but conversations on those forums are brisk. Clearly, these fora favor broadcasting over deep conversations. However, as professor Clay Shirky argues, social media can be utilized for long-term goals of strengthening civil society and the public sphere.[6] The courage activism blog can inspire students interested in social media activism to remain engaged beyond the semester. By introducing students to resources such as Affinity.works, which facilitate the organization of social movements online, educators can help students' long-term relations with other activists.

Conclusion

The COVID-19 pandemic brought a paradigm shift in the way students learn at a time of anxiety and loss. Instructors acclimated to face-to-face instruction are quickly encountering the challenges of online teaching. Their communications with students across continents and time zones are complicated by technological glitches and government censorship. Yet, the use of technology to facilitate learning can be effectively woven into course goals. Blogs can be one of the many tools to help students become digital global citizens as they navigate through our socially distanced world.

Notes

[1] Malala Yousafzai, *I Am Malala: The Girl Who Stood Up for Education and Was Shot by the Taliban* (United States: Little, Brown, 2013).

[2] Meghan Grace and Corey Seemiller, *Generation Z Goes to College.* (Germany: Wiley, 2015).

[3] A. F. Pearson, "Real Problems, Virtual Solutions: Engaging Students Online," *Teaching Sociology* 38, no. 3, 2010, 207–214.

[4] https://twitter.com/acsouthasia?lang=en.

[5] Both blogs were graded on form (use of headings, subheadings, images, font, takeaway points, and so on), content (analysis of topics, personal views, fact-based examples, critical thinking, questioning web-based materials), and originality (What new topics did their blogs add to the course themes?).

[6] Clay Shirky, *Planning for Web Services Obstacles and Opportunities* (Sebastopol, CA: O'Reilly, 2002).

17

TEACHING ASIA

ONLINE HARKNESS DISCUSSIONS

Jared Hall

Like many teachers this past spring, the responsibility of teaching online for the first time required significant and unique instructional changes. What follows is a reflection on my experiences making Harkness-informed pedagogy applicable to online Asian Studies. This entails a further explanation of Harkness and an articulation of how key elements of an online Chinese history course for upper-secondary-school students can mesh with meaningful discussion habits, the cultivation of cultural competence, and the realities of course assessment.

Why Harkness?

Those inspired by the Harkness method eschew lectures, summaries, and the traditional scaffolding of textbooks and worksheets. While we have goals for our courses, units, and each class session, we recognize that the vitality of the learning process allows conversation to remain fundamentally open-ended, even when it takes a different shape than we might have imagined when beginning a class. Why implement Harkness in person, let alone in an online environment where teachers sacrifice much structure and control over the learning process? Bill Jordan, a history teacher at Phillips Exeter Academy, gives a simple and compelling response: "I could be wrong." This "epistemic humility" is valuable modeling of what Harkness instructors hope to inspire in their students.[1]

Harkness refocuses instructors from being knowledge purveyors to being facilitators of knowledge creation. Harkness requires teachers who believe in critical thinking to trust students to do the cognitive heavy lifting through presenting their own ideas in classroom interactions. This means teaching students how to frame questions and draw their own connections and supporting them in presenting arguments. In person, the Harkness approach is represented by the teacher sitting alongside their students at an oval seminar table.

We have a lot to learn from our students, and it is important for our students to realize that they have much to learn from one another. As Flower Darby, the author of *Small Teaching Online*, explains, "We may understand complicated concepts differently as a result of someone else explaining it to us in a way that makes more sense than the teacher's explanation had."[2]

Purpose and Connection

For active, collaborative learning to occur online, learners need to have a clear sense of why they are gathered, who is present, and how group interactions can enhance learning. A small in-person class with motivated students can develop momentum organically and feel successful, even if these structural matters are not made visible to students. Virtual learning simply requires a bit more intentionality for learning and interconnection to feel meaningful.

When I ask, "Why are we gathered?" I am not simply repeating the backward design principles from *Understanding by Design*.[3] Of course, good unit design is key to successful online learning delivery, but I have something more elemental in mind. When students look back in five or ten years, what will they remember about my course other than it was about China? On the first day of class I set out that frame:

- Demonstrate fearless, independent thinking;
- trust and engage one another in community; and
- adopt the mindset of a historian and a cosmopolitan.

These are not just the course goals I share with my students on the first day of class; they also serve as touchstones I am explicit about referencing throughout the course. These exhortations need not be directly tied to specific lessons, though my students have found direct relevance to passages in *The Analects*: "When Confucius says, 'The gentleman is not a vessel,'" one student asked, "does he mean we should think for ourselves?"

It is also crucial that my students feel seen as individuals and are prepared to connect with one another. Learning online can be isolating and distant. One exercise I find useful for building that connection is drawn from SEED (Seeking

Figure 1: A Harkness table being used at the College Preparatory School in Oakland, CA. Source: Wikimedia Commons.

Educational Equity and Diversity). The exercise involves everyone in the class creating a name placard that tells the story of the name—or names—they go by. All students have a moment to share name rationales, and the class practices each student's name. This process illustrates that something as simple as a name can be constructed in many ways and can draw on a variety of inspirations. The exercise is especially useful for students from China or of East Asian descent who might be sharing the meanings of their given names for the first time in an English-speaking context. Face to face, I might facilitate this activity by showing up with colored pencils and cardstock. Online, the exercise is reconfigured, completed asynchronously, and posted on Canvas, our learning management platform.

Connections are ongoing and a simple question like "How are you feeling?" can be useful. The Harkness method recognizes that learning is both social and emotional. If a student indicates they are having a tough day, it is a good opportunity to follow up individually or avoid putting them on the spot. In addition to asking students how they are doing, it is important to keep an eye out for patterns that might suggest disengagement. Liz Katz, who directs student support at the online school One Schoolhouse, explains, "When you're online, you have to use data in a different way, and your data is different." While in an in-person context, we might wait weeks before following up with a parent or advisor, Katz encourages her colleagues to follow up "if a student is missing more than two assignments . . . [or] isn't responding to messages. One of the things that we know about students working in an online space is that when students have a hard time, they go downhill pretty quickly."[4]

Building Strong Discussion Habits

In *The Discussion Book*, authors Stephen Brookfield and Stephen Preskill admit they "both used to have faith in the spontaneous group process. . . . If the right people came together there would be a joyful combustion of energetic brainstorming with everyone involved." It is not that "this never happens, but it's the Bigfoot of classroom, organizational, and community life—secretive, rarely seen." Instead, they propose an idea that riffs on the concept of *wuwei* 無為 ("effortless action"): "you have to plan for spontaneity."[5]

Harkness works best when participants have a shared set of agreements or expectations, sometimes called a "class charter." In my own classes, I find it helpful to offer a few initial suggestions (using names when referring to others, committing to democratic use of time, etc.) and then open the process up for additions, edits, and tweaks. When introducing histories and cultures far removed from my students' own experiences, I add in a few other norms: for example, we make time to examine what is "weird" or "strange," and after some reflection commit to describing, rather than judging, practices that are unfamiliar. In an online environment, it is important to establish additional norms for how students might like to use chat features and the trade-offs that come with other windows, notifications, or second screens. While I am comfortable declaring my own list of expectations, I prefer to invite students to participate in this process as a way to increase buy-in and demonstrate that I care what they think.

I recognize that class charters involving students are often aspirational and may take several rounds of initial individual and collective reflection to impact classroom habits. One tool that can help translate those aspirations to concrete feedback is Equity Maps, an iPad app (currently in development for other platforms) that provides detailed data on who is speaking, how long they are speaking, and the patterns of interaction in either a physical or virtual classroom.[6] Tracking discussions can help me address commitments like democratic use of time in ways that rebalance the focus from those who might be perceived as too "quiet" to those who might be taking up too much air time.

"The Original Flipped Classroom"

Seminar discussions can be understood as the original "flipped classroom." Effective Harkness discussions are supported by thoughtfully selected assignments that reflect an awareness on the part of the instructor not just of a sequence of topics, but of a clearly defined set of learning objectives. Instructors can further prepare students for productive in-class discussions by making those goals explicit in the assignment description and by asking questions or providing tips that guide the students from understanding to application and creativity.

With good preparation, the next step is balancing predictability with novelty. Predictability comes in a couple of forms. The first is the familiar skills we touched on early—the clearly articulated habits introduced early and returned to throughout the course. The second is the establishment of predictable classroom routines. My students know, for example, that on a given class day, we almost always conduct some sort of quick check-in, followed by a low-stakes check-for-understanding, which is a multiple-choice quiz powered by Kahoot! or Google Forms (the lower the stakes, the less inclined students are to misrepresent what they know). We then dedicate most of the time to engaging together around a text.

A variety of approaches is important for seminar viability. As Brookfield and Preskill suggest, "Even the most energizing discussion protocol becomes routine if it's overused. You need to make people feel that they're not quite sure what's going to happen in the class. . . . It's a kind of pleasurable uncertainty."[7] For that to be possible, though, it is crucial to think about the materials that are framing the discussion. Rather than just rely on historical writing for a history class, consider bringing in a short story; or, perhaps share a recorded lecture, podcast, or a portion of a documentary or movie. Sometimes even appending a short clip to a reading can help it come alive; for example, rare footage of Sun Yat-sen calling on the Chinese people to "wake up!" in a thick Cantonese accent as captured in *China: A Century of Revolution*.[8] Another option that has become more accessible with the sudden move to online learning is organizing a "field trip" to a museum online. The Peabody Essex Museum, for example, has recently expanded their virtual tours, and portions of both the "Asian export" and "maritime" exhibits present materials that can be used in discussing nineteenth-century trade ties between Asia and the United States.[9]

In digital seminars, possibilities are as rich as face-to-face encounters. Zoom breakout groups are useful for allowing more opportunity for individual expression and for playing out activities that involve "expert groups" and debates. Even when everyone is present on the same screen, it is possible to designate certain speakers to participate in a "fishbowl" and have others either pose questions or simply take notes and take the mic at the end to reflect on what they heard. One exercise that fits this model well is the "May Fourth Roundtable," which invites students to work with a partner to prepare for discussion involving a diverse array of figures engaged in dialogue around prepared questions: students in this scenario might be asked to take up the role of Cai Yuanpei, Ding Yingchao, He Zhen, Hu Shi, Li Dazhao, Lu Xun, or Mao Zedong. At times, I assign roles to students—for example, a facilitator, a notetaker, a questioner, or a devil's advocate. And at other times,

I might take a more active facilitating role to delineate moments when we are reading supportively or critically, a frame that is especially useful when examining claims that might still be viewed as controversial within the context of our class, including most commentary on Sino-US relations.

Other strategies that promote interactive student engagement include digital polls as well as "silent discussion" together on a shared Google Doc. This strategy is useful both to engage in close reading and to reflect on the variety (and frequency) of voices expressed in this format versus the usual classroom space. One of the most common asynchronous approaches that approximates Harkness-style engagement is a discussion board. Readers who have taken an online course themselves know discussion boards can be rich opportunities to exchange ideas when managed well or tedious and exhausting when not. I generally divide students into smaller groups and forgo more than a minimal fixed requirement to respond to a certain number of posts and instead ask students to share a certain number of "original ideas."[10] Releasing some measure of control is both consistent with the Harkness ideal and also may put students at ease when discussing more emotionally difficult content.[11] Likewise, I have found that it is important to actively monitor and participate in these discussions, both to be present for my students and also, as Darby suggests, to "carefully monitor online discussions for culturally sensitive language and behaviors, such as a student making a derogatory comment, or students simply neglecting to reply to some students."[12]

Inclusion and Cultural Competency

When all students feel welcome online—both "silent" and asynchronous discussions provide opportunities to introverts that may not be available around an in-person Harkness table. One challenge I face teaching Chinese history in the United States is knowing that what may feel like an academic exercise for me may be highly personal for those with direct ties to the places and events being studied. In *The Political Classroom*, Diana Hess and Paula McAvoy identify two potential responses for educators who encounter potentially sensitive material: avoidance and deliberation.[13] While avoidance has an unmistakable negative ring to it, there are certainly moments where it is worth considering. A parent of one of my mainland Chinese students once told me that her son would not be participating in discussions about Chinese history for the period after 1949. He indeed remained silent in full-class discussions, though he participated cautiously in smaller groups where he felt more comfortable expressing his reactions to the readings and the statements made by his classmates. Moreover, the Black Lives Matter movement has helped me reflect on what kind of role-playing simulations are appropriate for the classroom. Moving forward, I have committed not to ask students to ever playact roles that involve dehumanizing others, meaning I will have to substantially rethink the dramatic reenactment I have students do of land reform scenes from Ding Ling's *The Sun Shines over Sanggan River*.

Hess and McAvoy also describe a deliberative approach marked by "exemplary materials, strong pedagogy, and enforced norms for civil discourse."[14] During both synchronous and asynchronous encounters, this means stepping in to support students who might be vulnerable and helping students who are speaking insensitively to reframe their arguments. Knowing when to do so puts a high premium on my engagement or "presence" as an instructor, and it requires some intentional information gathering in the form of anonymous surveys to probe the ideological commitments and identities of my students. It also means staging my course so controversial topics are placed later in the syllabus and leaning on my expertise to identify and defuse potential minefields. Finally, I recognize that I may not understand all the salient factors that shape how a student will respond, particularly in an online environment where students could be logging in from vastly different settings. To keep an ear out for what my students are encountering, I collect feedback anonymously throughout the course using a simple Google Form modeled on Stephen Brookfield's critical incident questionnaire.[15]

Assessment

The final piece of the online Harkness puzzle is assessment. Before constructing one's assessment structure, it is important to consider *why* assessment matters in our courses. I tend to weigh preparation and discussion heavily (at least 20 percent) because reading and engaging together are critical components of the learning objectives of the course. Reflecting on Jesse Strommel's four-word pedagogy, "Start by trusting students," I aim never to play "gotcha" with students and always to focus on growth and build in opportunities for grace.[16]

As noted, low-stakes "checks for understanding" help me understand what students have read and what they have understood from that reading. I use a six-question multiple choice format, with the final question related to an earlier reading from the course. This provides me an instant read on how quickly we can press forward to higher order questions and takes a cue from James Lang's *Small Teaching* to support memory recall.[17]

The most important standard I use for assessing discussion is the charter we agree on together at the outset of class. I aim to engage students in self-assessment in monthly intervals and then compare their responses to my notes and impressions. I focus my comments on concrete suggestions, and when the results are divergent, I invite a brief conversation to try to work with the student to understand the source of the disconnect, leaving open the possibility that it might be me that needs to engage in more focused observations of that student to adjust my impressions or that the class as a whole may need to adjust by providing more space for that student. Ideally, my students and I begin to align our own assessment of their discussion long before progress reports are submitted.

Conclusion

Like many teachers plunged suddenly into online teaching this past spring, I am looking forward to the possibility that additional time for reflection and preparation might produce a better experience for my students in the months ahead. In pursuing this template of purpose, connection, shared commitments, discussion, and assessment, I hope that even when online learning is "weird," it will still be "weirdly normal" (to cite my own students' reflections) and that a core part of that sense of normalcy will be the feeling that learners in my classroom feel empowered to help guide their individual learning process and that of our class. That, for me, is the essence of the Harkness method.

Notes

[1] "The Exeter Difference: Bill Jordan," Phillips Exeter Academy. https://www.exeter.edu/people/bill-jordan. To access a number of Mr. Jordan's valuable resources, see his personal website: https://sites.google.com/site/billjordanhistory/for-teachers.

[2] Flower Darby, *Small Teaching Online* (San Francisco: Jossey-Bass, 2019), 76.

[3] Here I have in mind Grant Wiggins and Jay McTighe, *Understanding by Design*, 2nd ed. (Alexandria, VA: Association for Supervision and Curriculum Development, 2005).

[4] "Student Support for Distance Learning," One Schoolhouse, April 10, 2020, https://www.oneschoolhouse.org/learning-innovation-blog/student-support-for-distance-learning.

[5] Stephen D. Brookfield and Stephen Preskill, *The Discussion Book: 50 Great Ways to Get People Talking* (San Francisco: Jossey-Bass, 2016), 4.

[6] Equity Maps, https://equitymaps.com/.

[7] Brookfield and Preskill, *The Discussion Book*, 5.

[8] *China: A Century of Revolution*, "Part One: China in Revolution, 1911–1949 (PBS, 1989). https://zeitgeistfilms.com/film/chinaacenturyofrevolution.

[9] Peabody Essex Museum, "Virtual Tours," https://www.pem.org/virtual-tours.

[10] John Orlando, "What Research Tells Us about Online Discussion," *Faculty Focus*, March 16, 2017, https://www.facultyfocus.com/articles/online-education/research-tells-us-online-discussion/, cited in Darby, *Small Teaching Online*, 234.

[11] For instance, I have occasionally used Hu Jie's 2006 documentary on the murder by students of a vice principal at a Beijing secondary school in *Though I Am Gone*, which predictably evokes strong emotions in students.

[12] Darby, *Small Teaching Online*, 94.

[13] Diana E. Hess and Paula McAvoy, *The Political Classroom: Evidence and Ethics in Democratic Education* (New York: Routledge, 2015).

[14] Hess and McAvoy, *The Political Classroom,* 176.

[15] Brookfield asks his students the following questions: "At what moment in class this week did you feel most engaged with what was happening? At what moment in class this week were you most distanced from what was happening? What action that anyone (teacher or student) took this week did you find most affirming or helpful? What action that anyone took this week did you find most puzzling or confusing? What about the class this week surprised you the most?" Stephen D. Brookfield, *The Skillful Teacher: On Technique, Trust, and Responsiveness in the Classroom*, 3rd ed. (San Francisco: Jossey-Bass, 2015), 34.

[16] The phrase first appeared in a tweet by Jesse Strommel on April 30, 2016, https://twitter.com/Jessifer/status/726424167420145664. He created the hashtag #4wordpedagogy to invite others to create their own condensed pedagogy: https://twitter.com/hashtag/4wordpedagogy.

[17] James M. Lang, *Small Teaching: Everyday Lessons from the Science of Learning* (San Francisco: Jossey-Bass, 2016), 76.

18

WHAT'S IN A WET MARKET?

ANTHROPOLOGY OF FOOD AND ASIA DURING THE COVID-19 PANDEMIC

Sarah G. Grant

When my university closed the door to face-to-face instruction in March 2020, my upper-division Global Ethnographies of Food class had already discussed the ramped-up xenophobia at Chinese restaurants across the United States. In fact, we had been discussing the novel coronavirus, COVID-19, since January. Although the pandemic felt distant at the time, thousands of miles away in East and Southeast Asia, my students had pressing questions about the pandemic and how it related to food and zoonosis. Before too long, the questions I always dread in discussions of food, fieldwork, and cultural difference came up: Have you ever eaten bat, rat, or dog? Or, what is the weirdest thing you have consumed in Asia? Primed by travel shows, the intrigue of cultural difference, or simply the Western gaze, students who ask these questions have likely not thought sincerely about what we *all* eat every day and how we procure it.[1] I felt obligated to position emergent media about food and COVID-19 within a larger critical food studies framework. Given our frequent encounters with the media spectacle of "bat soup," wet markets, and "wild" or "bush" meat, there was a sense of urgency to unpack these matters with requisite cultural relativism and thoughtfulness. Pandemic or not, I wanted my students to leave the course furnished with an understanding of Orientalism, equipped with a toolbox to critique the exoticizing and often reductionist representations of food in Asia. I also wanted to leave my students with a curiosity about the politics of representation in Asia. Guided by my experience conducting ethnographic research in Southeast Asia, I found that teaching Asia during a pandemic harkens back to fundamental questions about the language, culture, and history of place.

This essay elucidates why it is important to unpack the cultural significance and context of "wet markets" in Asia. Tamara Giles-Vernick's essay, "Should Wild Meat Markets Be Shut Down?" points out the ubiquitous use of the "wet market" across social media platforms and in discourse about the origin and spread of COVID-19 in China. This essay furthers this dialogue by encouraging students to think about a deceptively big question—What is a wet market?—and position it in a larger, empirically informed understanding of the wet market itself.[2] Part ethnographic narrative, part teaching resource essay, it outlines why teaching about the pandemic *through* the anthropology of food and Asia will help develop critical thinkers and holistically trained students via classroom activities. It also offers recommendations on how to avoid exoticizing Asian wet markets and perpetuating racist tropes while recognizing the significance of cultural difference—perceived or otherwise. Even the long-addressed question of zoonotic transfer in wild animal meat markets requires careful empirical study before blanket bans are issued to the primary food sources for many people living in Asia. Pandemic pedagogy is necessarily rapid response pedagogy, but it must not come at the expense of guiding interdisciplinary tenets such as cultural relativism.

Rapid Response Pedagogy

Immediately after revising my syllabus to accommodate a new remote learning environment, my anthropology of food students had the option of listening to and discussing a *Code Switch* episode about anti-Asian discrimination and xenophobia.[3] The intent was to provide some additional context prior to our asynchronous, chat-room-based, virtual discussions of food and COVID-19. Students subsequently shared their own articles and background research with the class—there was no shortage of articles about "bat soup" and Wuhan wet markets in March 2020. One of the first questions posed by a student after reading through our collective resources was: What is a wet market? The term racked their imaginations seemingly out of nowhere. Follow-up questions helped me redesign my course to include rapid responses to burning questions while framing the pandemic in the purview of my expertise and training.[4]

When I realized that my proposed food and commodity journaling project was no longer feasible, I asked students to instead develop a COVID-19 eating and food procurement journal. I kept my own journal alongside the class, partially to offer a working example and stimulate discussion but also out of personal curiosity. I could not help my tendency to compare pandemic buying, hoarding, and toilet paper and egg shortages in the US to the food situation in specific

Figure 1: Market in Dalat, Vietnam. Source: Unsplash,
https://unsplash.com/photos/GCbiB49XskU.

regions of Vietnam where stockpiling and hoarding were not common or even possible. The practices of hoarding and pandemic buying, however, were not uniform across Southeast Asia, or Asia for that matter. In Taipei, Hong Kong, and Singapore, for example, consumers faced shortages of many supplies and empty shelves.[5] In a "COVID-19 Dispatches" series, Tram Luong describes the pandemic atmosphere in Ho Chi Minh City, where "to dissuade people from panic buying, state-sponsored messages popped up on all citizens' mobile phones every other day" assuring people "of the steady supply of essential goods."[6] Thinking back to my own wet market experiences in Vietnam, I explained to my students what it is like to purchase fresh produce daily and how distinct it is from the bulk warehouse shopping we were largely familiar with in urban California.

While living in Dalat, Vietnam (2010–2012), to conduct ethnographic research on the commodity coffee industry, I frequented many wet markets in my neighborhood and the larger Central Highlands region. The market I frequented most often I will refer to as "Chợ Hẻm" ("Alleyway Market"). Chợ Hẻm specifically served the neighborhood I lived in. Fish, shellfish, snails, pork, and chicken made up the bulk of available meat options while fresh produce, rice, tofu, noodles, fish sauce, and flowers rounded out the other small stalls and carts. Chợ Hẻm was a wet market not because of the live fish splashing about in aerated plastic containers, but because of the requisite hosing down and cleaning at the end of every day. The use of "wet" in "wet market" implies a dichotomy: wet/dry. But markets in much of Vietnam do not fall neatly into the "wet" or "dry" category— wet markets are amalgamations of wet and dry and anything in between. Where, for example, does a locally made but neatly packaged and sealed tofu fit into the dichotomy? Wet markets in Vietnam, for all of the wet seafood sold, habitually sell dried squid and shrimp. The largest and certainly most widely recognized market in Vietnam is Chợ Bến Thành, in Ho Chi Minh City.[7] Like other markets, the wet and dry sections of Chợ Bến Thành, although spatially delineated, are still in one centralized marketplace where locals—and tourists in the case of Chợ Bến Thành—go to purchase "wet" goods (fresh meat, eggs, and produce) but also "dry" goods (rice, dried spices, cooking ware, oil, fabric, etc.). In Dalat, neighborhood residents frequented Chợ Hẻm daily and sometimes multiple times each day to purchase fresh goods for meal preparation. I often saw my neighbor rushing off before sunrise to catch the best bánh mì cart and to purchase the freshest snails, clams, and flowers. Later in the afternoon, she would return home with vegetables and pork. The wet market is also an important social space where neighbors catch up and learn about various food chain supply issues and town gossip. Above all, the wet market is the primary source of sustenance for this particular community.

Pandemic Anthropologies of Asia

If the pandemic has taught me anything about the anthropology of Asia, it is that the field is thriving and innovative. Within days of statewide university closures, colleagues and friends had posted thoughtful editor-reviewed resources—pedagogical and research-oriented—across the field's many platforms. For faculty who may be new to thinking about the cultural politics of zoonotic transfer or ethnographic perspectives about wet markets, or the politics of eating and representation in the Asian American diaspora, there are resources aplenty. Before jumping into class discussions about pangolins and wet markets, however, I encourage my colleagues to consider some of the reflective essays that have emerged in the past months. I recommend that faculty prepare themselves to frame the topic with background material about xenophobia; Orientalism; wet markets and epidemic photography in China and elsewhere in Asia; or any recent publications from your own disciplinary background and best practices.[8] The emerging literature about markets and COVID-19 in Asia are reminders of the preexisting precarity in places intertwined with both wet markets and wildlife markets. This precarity is exacerbated by the pandemic and rampant media representations of wet markets in Asia, often conflated with wildlife markets. Regardless, the introduction of wet markets and wildlife markets to our everyday vernacular engender important questions about the meaning and effects of these markets. Smith and Theriault in particular, bring up important questions about the long-term implications of wildlife markets, pointing out that, "Wherever wild lifeforms are extracted for sale in distant markets, human communities bear the direct consequences of this lost 'biodiversity' and of corresponding efforts to securitize it."[9] Beyond questioning the conflation of wet markets and wildlife markets, it is worth thinking about how these markets always operate in larger geopolitical, economic, and ecological spheres.

Lesson Plan: What's in a Wet Market?

The following lesson plan includes resources for both synchronous and asynchronous classroom spaces. It is designed to unpack the following questions:

1. How is the visual and media-based representation of the pandemic shaped by underlying xenophobia and stereotypes about food consumption?

2. What are our preconceived notions and norms about markets and food procurement—how do we procure our food and what do markets look like cross culturally?

3. What does an anthropological perspective on the wet market tell us about the everyday experiences of the novel coronavirus, COVID-19,

and why are wet markets the subject of continued scrutiny and concurrent mistrust of those who rely on wet markets as a primary source of sustenance?

Whether teaching synchronously or asynchronously, begin the lesson with a series of open-ended icebreaker questions broken into two themes: (1) wet markets and (2) food procurement. In a large-enrollment class, it is worth breaking students into groups by using virtual features such as "Breakout Rooms" and assigning each group one theme.

Theme 1: Wet Markets Discussion

The first theme requires students to reflect on the following questions: What is a wet market? What do you know about wet markets? How do you know what you know about wet markets? Chances are, students have heard the term "wet market" at some point during the pandemic, but these questions encourage them to think through the context in which they have heard past utterances of the term. Perhaps students have watched the late travel show host Anthony Bourdain visit a wet market in Asia or they have traveled or lived in a place with wet markets and already have this experiential knowledge. The student responses are important because they open the door for discussions with epistemological objectives about overgeneralizations, truths, observations, experiences, and how our preconceived norms about cultural practices shape the way we consume print and visual representations of a place and its culture.

Theme 2: Food Procurement Discussion

The second theme requires students to reflect on the following questions about food procurement: Prior to the pandemic, how did you procure food for yourself? Where did you purchase food from? Describe the accessibility and availability of food and your shopping frequency. How did these practices shift during the pandemic? These questions encourage students to think about the cultural specificity of food procurement and set the groundwork for instructors to ask about the advantages and disadvantages of supermarket shopping. It may also open the door for follow-up questions about freshness, differences in food costs, and food traceability. This is also a good opportunity to introduce anecdotes about food hoarding and panic buying in the United States.

Mini-Lecture and Collective Reading

Using their discussions as an impromptu formative assessment, you should next deliver a mini-lecture that defines or clarifies important concepts such as xenophobia, Orientalism, cultural relativism, and wet markets. By providing specific examples that draw on your own area of thematic and geographic expertise or focusing on the many unfolding examples of xenophobia and Orientalism in the era of COVID-19, you ground the class in meaningful, personal experiences. For synchronous classes, you can provide this mini-lecture in a mere seven to ten minutes.[10] After contextualizing these terms, ask students to read "Should Wild Meat Markets Be Shut Down?" The article is open-access via hyperlink and available directly through the Somatosphere website, where you can download a PDF version. As they read, encourage students to consider what experts already know about zoonotic transfers and wet markets from cross-cultural contexts (Africa in this case) and how this knowledge might shape a global response to the pandemic in Asia. After reading, return to small groups, discuss the article, and eventually share your own perspective. If wet markets or wild meat markets in Asia are beyond the scope of your experience and expertise, consider thinking about the *many* ways in which live animals circulate in everyday Asia.[11]

To end the lesson, as a class, read the 2017 VN Express International article, "A Hanoi Wet Market at the Crossroads of Modernity."[12] As students read, ask them to consider the challenges facing wet market vendors in 2017 and think about what new challenges might emerge in 2020 and beyond. Watch the video embedded in the article, "Hanoi Wet Market Draws a White Line to Enforce Social Distancing," paying close attention to the perspective of the sellers and shoppers in the market during the pandemic.[13] Conclude by asking students to think about the future of wet markets, grounded in a reflexive consideration of their own eating and food procurement norms.

Learning Outcomes

1. Distinguish "wet markets" from "wildlife markets" and reflexively think about the future of wet markets and those who rely on them for food procurement

2. Understand how COVID-19 is not experienced evenly across the world, with attention to the ways particular places are stigmatized and people questioned for their cultural practices

3. Normalize the many cross-cultural ways people procure food for household consumption

Notes

[1] For more on the subject of cultural representation through popular television, see James B. Hoesterey, "The Adventures of Mark and Olly: The Pleasures and Horrors of Anthropology on TV," in *Human No More: Digital Subjectivities, Unhuman Subjects, and the End of Anthropology*, eds. Neil L. Whitehead and Michael Wesch (Boulder: University of Colorado Press, 2012), 157–176.

[2] Tamara Giles-Vernick, "Should Wild Meat Markets Be Shut Down?" *Somatosphere*, March 6, 2020, http://somatosphere.net/forumpost/wild-meat-markets/.

[3] Natalie Escobar, "When Xenophobia Spreads Like a Virus: Code Switch." *National Public Radio*, March 4, 2020, https://www.npr.org/2020/03/02/811363404/when-xenophobia-spreads-like-a-virus.

[4] My students, above all else, wanted to know what constitutes a wet market and where they could find reliable information about zoonotic transfer and the multispecies relationships that we inhabit alongside the animals we consume. For more on these relationships and multispecies ethnography in Asia, I recommend Natalie Porter, *Viral Economies: Bird Flu Experiments in Vietnam* (Chicago: University of Chicago Press, 2019) and Frédéric Keck, *Avian Reservoirs: Virus Hunters and Birdwatchers in Chinese Sentinel Posts* (Durham, NC: Duke University Press, 2020).

[5] Shashank Bengali and Ralph Jennings, "Coronavirus Outbreak Spurs Hoarding in Asia," *Los Angeles Times*, February 12, 2020, https://www.latimes.com/world-nation/story/2020-02-12/virus-fears-asian-shoppers-hoarding-rice-noodles.

[6] Tram Luong, "COVID-19 Dispatches from Ho Chi Minh City, Vietnam," *Anthropology Now* 12, no. 1 (2020), 46.

[7] See Ann Marie Leshkowich, *Essential Trade: Vietnamese Women in a Changing Marketplace* (Honolulu: University of Hawaii Press, 2014) for a comprehensive ethnography of social life in the Ho Chi Minh City marketplace and beyond.

[8] Joey S. Kim, "Orientalism in the Age of COVID-19," *Los Angeles Review of Books*, March 24, 2020, https://lareviewofbooks.org/short-takes/orientalism-age-covid-19/; Christos Lynteris, "The Prophetic Faculty of Epidemic Photography: Chinese Wet Markets and the Imagination of the Next Pandemic," *Visual Anthropology* 29, no. 2 (2016), 118–32.

[9] Will Smith and Noah Theriault, "Seeing Indigenous Land Struggles in the 'Multispecies Cloud' of Covid-19." Covid-19, *Fieldsights*, April 16, 2020, https://culanth.org/fieldsights/seeing-indigenous-land-struggles-in-the-multispecies-cloud-of-covid-19.

[10] For asynchronous classes, I recommend recording a mini-lecture and posting it to your course site with supplemental materials and references for further study. Discussion boards are also a good space for students to share their responses to the icebreaker questions. There are numerous tools and guidelines for best practices in an asynchronous classroom, but I recommend building community through short, digestible lectures that use multimodal approaches to student learning—your lecture should point students in the direction of additional audio-visual material and accessible readings such as those provided throughout this essay. Depending on your circumstances, you may be preparing the entire lesson asynchronously. If that is the case, consider including a brief voice and/or video recording about your own wet market experiences or perspectives on pandemic food purchasing alongside supplemental materials that students can easily access for free and through a variety of access points (phone, tablet, laptop).

[11] For an ethnographic study of human-animal relations, kinship, and sacrifice, see Radhika Govindrajan, "'The Goat that Died for Family': Animal Sacrifice and Interspecies Kinship in India's Central Himalayas," *American Ethnologist* 42, no. 3 (2015), 504–519.

[12] Bao Yen, "A Hanoi Wet Market at the Crossroads of Modernity," *VN Express International*, June 12, 2017, https://e.vnexpress.net/news/travel-life/a-hanoi-wet-market-at-the-crossroads-of-modernity-3588516.html.

[13] Huy Manh, "Hanoi Wet Market Draws a White Line to Enforce Social Distancing," *VN Express International*, April 13, 2020, https://e.vnexpress.net/news/video/hanoi-wet-market-draws-a-white-line-to-enforce-social-distancing-4083886.html.

19

TEACHING COLLEGE-LEVEL ASIAN POLITICS THROUGH SIMULATIONS IN ONLINE ENVIRONMENTS

Petra Hendrickson

The COVID-19 pandemic and the shift to new educational modes has been disruptive in a number of ways and has posed significant challenges for college classes centered around active, face-to-face learning. However, disruptive does not mean disqualifying, and rich interaction can still occur in an online context. This chapter will discuss how simulations can be conducted online using synchronous and/or asynchronous technologies. Suggestions for how to implement simulations, including assignments and assessments, will be provided, followed by a discussion of how to utilize online capabilities to carry out simulations. I provide examples of two online platforms, Zoom and Slack, that can be used for simulations to provide practical options for those who have not conducted simulations online. Both platforms have rich user-support networks and relatively low learning curves. Basic features necessary for simulations, such as breakout rooms in Zoom or private channels in Slack, can be learned quite quickly and easily, either through start-up tutorials upon signing up for the service or through a brief exploration of the application.[1] A list of Asia-focused political simulations will be provided, as will resources for the use of simulations in political science classes in general, which include a number of best practices and a wide array of advice for getting the most educational benefit out of the simulations.

Planning Your Simulation

The first step to using a simulation is to decide what event or scenario you want to illustrate further with an active learning experience. The list of Asia-focused political science simulations listed below is one resource for deciding this. All simulations in that list are role-play scenarios, where students take on a particular role, be it a person, a group, or a country. For the purposes of this chapter, I will assume that you have already designed the content of the simulation or are using a ready-made simulation for your class, as designing a simulation from scratch is beyond the scope of this discussion.

Once you know what simulation you will be using, you can begin to plan the accompanying assignments and assessments that will provide structure for the students to help them prepare for the experience. First, students should be provided with an assignment that requires them to contemplate their role and goals for the outcome of the simulation. Position papers and policy memos work well here, as they require students to explicitly consider their role and how they should approach the situation or event being simulated based on that role. In addition to a more conversation-based debriefing after the simulation (more on synchronous and asynchronous discussions below), best practices suggest that students should also write a formal reflection paper considering how the simulation went. This should include discussion of their actions, where they think they succeeded or fell short in accomplishing their goals, and how they interpreted other students' actions, among other things. The real learning associated with simulations occurs during the whole-class debriefing and individual reflection, so real consideration needs to be given to how to implement them. The appendix provides examples of an assignment sheet and rubrics that I have used for simulations I have conducted, including for the pre-simulation paper, participation during the actual simulation, and the post-simulation reflection.

Conducting Your Simulation Online

In considering how to actually implement your simulation online, perhaps the biggest consideration will be whether it should be run synchronously, with everyone participating at the same time, or asynchronously, with students participating at different times. A combination of the two can also be used and may lead to the best student learning outcomes. I will discuss a platform that can be used for each type of implementation, as well as how the two may be integrated. The specific choices an instructor makes will likely depend on the idiosyncratic circumstances and logistical hurdles of their specific classes. For example, synchronous meetings will likely be easier to coordinate for smaller classes over larger ones, as individual schedules would need to be accommodated to find a mutually acceptable time, while asynchronous implementation could accommodate classes of all sizes and a variety of personal circumstances that might impede synchronous learning.

Synchronous

Perhaps the most prominent piece of software for synchronous interaction among groups of people is Zoom (zoom.us), which played a significant role in many educators' shift to online learning in spring 2020, in part because of its ability to be directly integrated into many learning management systems such as Moodle or Canvas. Although the base-level subscription limits meetings of three or more people to just forty minutes, depending on the specific simulation and the extent to which asynchronous possibilities are utilized, one live session may be sufficient.[2] For instance, I utilized a simulation of a National Security Council meeting concerning the use of drone warfare in Pakistan in a South Asian Politics class. Because these simulations were designed to take place within a single sixty-minute class period, compressing it into forty minutes was not especially onerous. Alternatively, multiple live sessions can be utilized to recreate the feeling of typical class periods, with the use of breakout rooms or the chat function facilitating both small-group and whole-class interaction in the main conference area. These small-group discussions and negotiations could be between students playing the same role or students playing different roles who want to engage in more private discussions. In order to monitor participation and role adherence, instructors can rotate among discussions and have students complete a log about their "face-to-face" interactions: who they met with, what they discussed, and what the outcome of the interaction was.[3] I utilized such a log in a simulation for an International Organization class to great success. I created a worksheet for the students with a table with all the roles and a reminder of what they should record about the meeting (who, topic, outcome). An example of this table is included in the appendix. One trade-off for using breakout rooms is that they actively take away from time spent in whole-group discussion and negotiation. If whole-group discussion is required by the simulation (for instance, multiple countries agreeing on a resolution, or the need to take a straw poll to gauge the popularity of particular proposals and discuss issues with all stakeholders simultaneously), this trade-off should be taken seriously, and perhaps further consideration should be given to asynchronous methods in tandem or as an alternative to synchronous participation.

Asynchronous

A key consideration for any asynchronous simulation platform is the ability to have multiple threads of conversation between a large number of combinations of participants. Features such as the ability to upload files to the platform may also be relevant. The platform I have used for asynchronous simulations is Slack (slack.com). Slack features the ability to create "public" channels of discussion visible to everyone in the workspace (think of it as a chat room), as well as "private" channels visible only to select participants and direct messages that can accommodate up to eight participants. These possibilities allow for general discussion to which everyone is privy, as well as more private discussions between subsets of participants, probably focused on specific issues. In order for the instructor to monitor participation and role adherence, students must add the instructor to their private channels and include him or her in their messages. This can be remedied after the fact by having students copy and paste their private conversations into a direct message with the instructor, but speaking from experience, it is easiest if the instructor is included in the initial discussion thread.

Once the workspace has been created by the instructor and the students have registered, communication can occur at any time, allowing for additional flexibility in implementing the simulation. Students can also sign into the workspace using both their real name and their role identity so that their classmates know who they are interacting with both inside and outside of the simulation scenario. This may be especially important for classes that are strictly online, to help personalize the experience rather than keeping participants as nameless, faceless role identities.

Slack has additional features that may increase its utility. First, participants can upload files to Slack for other people to review, so if there is something specific that a participant wants others to review, that can easily be accommodated. Further, apps can be added to Slack to enhance its functionality. Zoom can be added, for instance, allowing Zoom meetings to launch from the Slack workspace, and an app called Polly allows for the creation of polls within the Slack interface. The free version of Slack places a limit on the number of apps that can be added, but even the limited number is sufficient for a robust simulation experience.

Combining Synchronous and Asynchronous

Especially with the basic Zoom subscription limiting multiparty meetings to just forty minutes, utilizing both Zoom and Slack may allow for a richer simulation experience than using either platform individually. Moreover, combining them is straightforward—Zoom can be used for whole-group discussions and negotiations that would benefit from a more conversational environment (as opposed to the stilted back and forth of asynchronous chat), while Slack can be used both asynchronously and synchronously for additional dialogue during the Zoom call, allowing for side bargains to be struck in small groups or between individuals while the broader negotiation is taking place. This means that the entirety of the forty-minute Zoom session can be spent resolving whole-group issues rather than trying to coordinate numerous synchronous meetings to accommodate both whole-group and small-group discussions. Moreover, in my experience, students prefer having some face-to-face (even if virtual) interaction with each other during a simulation, so even if the bulk of the simulation occurs asynchronously,

I would encourage instructors to consider at least one synchronous session to deliberate any lingering details and questions related to "solving" the simulation. Alternatively, as happened in one of my South Asian Politics simulations, students can also coordinate synchronous meetings on their own to supplement the asynchronous interactions. If they choose to do so, they can simply record the content and outcome of these discussions in their interaction log, described above.

Asia-Themed Politics/Political Science Simulations

I have discovered three resources that have multiple simulations, each related to political science topics in the context of Asia. Below, I provide a brief overview of each as well as a list of their specific Asia-themed simulations.

United States Institute of Peace (USIP)

Basic details
Available at: usip.org/simulations
Cost: free
Overview: These simulations focus on conflict and governance. They provide "public" information about the simulation scenario and "private" information about each role. Moreover, they provide rich and complex issues that often pit members of the same "team" (such as different factions of an armed ethnic group) against each other to highlight that real-life questions might not have any easy solutions.

Asia-Themed Simulation List
Nepal: Governance, Corruption, and Conflict
The Paris Peace Talks of December 1972–January 1973 (Vietnam)
The Cambodia Peace Settlement
Peacekeeping in Kashmir: An American Choice
Sri Lanka: Setting the Agenda for Peace

Model Diplomacy

Basic details
Available at: modeldipolomacy.cfr.org
Cost: free
Overview: These simulations deal with US foreign policy and national security. Each simulation takes the form of a National Security Council meeting, with the specific actors depending on the details of the simulation. Moreover, students can be assigned specific roles, such as secretary of state, or be given the general role of "advisor to the president." Simulations provide both "public" information about the scenario and "private" information specific to a student's role.

Asia-Themed Simulation List
Dispute in the East China Sea
Cyber Clash with China
Drones in Pakistan
Korean War in 1950
North Korean Nuclear Threat

International Communications and Negotiations Simulations (ICONS) Project

Basic details

Available at: icons.umd.edu
Cost: fee-based
Overview: The ICONS Project provides simulations dealing with a variety of international issues. Simulations provide both "public" information about the scenario and "private" information specific to a student's role. ICONS simulations also come with their own native messaging system and are designed to facilitate entirely asynchronous participation.

Asia-Themed Simulation List

Border Dispute: The Temple of Preah Vihear (Thailand and Cambodia)
Crisis in North Korea
India-Pakistan Crisis
International Relations of Southeast Asia

Resources for Successful Simulations

- Asal, Victor, and Elizabeth L. Blake. 2006. "Creating Simulations for Political Science Education." *Journal of Political Science Education* 2(1): 1–18.

- Asal, Victor, and Jayson Kratoville. 2013. "Constructing International Relations Simulations: Examining the Pedagogy of IR Simulations through a Constructivist Learning Theory Lens." *Journal of Political Science Education* 9(2): 132–143.

- Baranaowski, Michael K., and Kimberly A. Weir. 2015. "Political Simulations: What We Know, What We Think We Know, and What We Still Need to Know." *Journal of Political Science Education* 11(4): 391–403.

- Butcher, Charity. 2012. "Teaching Foreign Policy Decision-Making Processes Using Role-Playing Simulations: The Case of US-Iranian Relations." *International Studies Perspectives* 13(2): 176–194.

- Glazier, Rebecca A. 2011. "Running Simulations without Ruining Your Life: Simple Ways to Incorporate Active Learning into Your Teaching." *Journal of Political Science Education* 7(4): 375–393.

- Hendrickson, Petra. Forthcoming. "The Effects of Active Learning Techniques on Student Excitement, Interest, and Self-Efficacy." *Journal of Political Science Education.*

- Kanner, Michael D. 2007. "War and Peace: Simulating Security Decision Making in the Classroom." *PS: Political Science and Politics* 40(4): 795–800.

- Kollars, Nina, and Amanda Rosen. 2016. "Bootstrapping and Portability in Simulation Design." *International Studies Perspectives* 17(2): 202–213.

- Lantis, Jeffrey. 1998. "Simulations and Experiential Learning in the International Relations Classroom." *International Negotiation* 3: 39–57.

- Lantis, Jeffrey. 2004. "Ethics and Foreign Policy: Structured Debates for the International Studies Classroom." *International Studies Perspectives* 5(2): 155–178.

- McKee, Lauren. 2017. "Modeling Asia: An East China Sea Simulation." *Education about Asia* 22(1): online supplement. Available from: https://www.asianstudies.org/publications/eaa/archives/modeling-asia-an-east-china-sea-simulation/ (accessed August 26, 2020).

- Raymond, Chad, and Simon Usherwood. 2013. "Assessment in Simulations." *Journal of Political Science Education* 9(2): 157–167.

- Starkey, Brigid, and Elizabeth L. Blake. 2001. "Simulation in International Relations Education." *Simulations and Gaming* 32(4): 537–551.

Notes

[1] For instance, if a user has the Zoom open in full-screen, icons for things like polling and breakout rooms appear at the bottom of the Zoom screen, making it easy to utilize these tools.

[2] In light of the continued possibility of remote instruction, many institutions that had previously used the base version of Zoom have upgraded to the professional version, which eliminates the forty-minute limit and adds additional features like polling.

[3] Zoom also allows participants to chat with each other and the host, and enables the host to record the meeting, which would provide another avenue for instructors to observe student participation.

Appendix: Assignment Sheet with Rubrics

Simulation Guidelines

Purpose: These simulations will provide you with the opportunity to experience firsthand the difficulties of international cooperation and the strengths and limitations of specific organizational bodies. In each simulation, you will take on the role of a country and advance that country's interest within the body being illustrated during the specific simulation—either the UN Security Council or the International Whaling Commission. You will see how realistic particular options are and the challenges of fostering agreement on and support of various proposals that may involve competing interests between other members of the organization.

This assignment will help you practice the following skills that are essential to your success in this course, your academic career, and life beyond college:

- Clear communication skills

- Interest articulation and compatibility assessment

- Taking on particular points of view and operating from those perspectives

- Tying simulation activities back to core course themes and concepts

Tasks: For each simulation, you will complete the following assignments:

1. Position paper (10% of final grade total; 5% of final grade each). In these 900–1,500 word papers, you will identify your country's role in the world and in the organization, as well as discussing your country's interests and how you will try to see that those interests are met.

2. Participation in simulation (10% of final grade total; 5% of final grade each). During the simulations, you will utilize a variety of communication methods to try to meet your country's interests and goals during the simulation. You will keep track of what other countries you meet with, your goals, and the extent to which the meeting was successful.

3. Reflection paper (10% of final grade total; 5% of final grade each). In these 900–1,500 word papers, you will critically analyze your performance in the simulation and how the simulation relates to course material. You will discuss your strategy as well as the extent to which that strategy was successful and why. You will also discuss how various aspects of the simulation relate to course material.

Criteria for Success

Simulation Position Paper Rubric

Criteria	Description	Score
Country's role in world	Paper discusses country's general position in the international system. Discussion of state's power and its general ability to exert influence in the world and why.	/5
Country's role in organization	Paper discusses country's historical and contemporary role in the organization. Discussion of country's interests in the organization and its continued participation.	/10
Country's stance on issues	Paper articulates country's specific stances on the issues/resolutions to be considered. In cases where state interests are not fully met by proposals on each issue, discussion of what would be required for approval/agreement. In cases where proposals do conform to country's interests, discussion of how other countries' approval/agreement will be encouraged.	/20
		/35 (%)

Simulation Position Paper Rubric

Criteria	Description	Score
General participation	Student is present in class each day of simulation, makes active use of online platform, and is active in face-to-face interactions.	/5
Substantive participation	Student adheres to role identity and meaningfully interacts with classmates. In interactions, student is advancing role's interests. Student uses a variety of modes of communication to reach bargains and compromises.	/15
Daily participation/ contact log	Student provides record of interactions with other members of the class on provided handout. Student details who they interacted with, what they interacted about, and the outcome of the interaction.	/10
		/30 (%)

Simulation Position Paper Rubric

Criteria	Description	Score
Strategy	Paper discusses approach to playing role. Discussion of country's goals and how the country worked to achieve its goals.	/10
Outcome	Paper discusses extent to which outcomes aligned with the country's goals, discussing both own strategy and that of others and the response of others to own strategy. When aligned, discussion of how the outcome was obtained. When not aligned, discussion of why the country was unsuccessful in advancing its interests. Paper discusses what student would do to produce more desirable outcomes if simulation were attempted again.	/15
Course content/ themes	Paper contains sophisticated discussion of how the simulation illustrates course material. Attention is paid to class discussion and readings of specific organizations and/or issues. Sophisticated discussion of the extent to which the theories were highlighted and the ways in which they were highlighted.	/30
		/55 (%)

Individual Interactions Participation Log

Country interacted with	Topic of interaction	Outcome of interaction
Role 1		
Role 2		

20

Investigating the COVID-19 Pandemic

An East Asian Perspective

Matthew Roberts

Background

March 13, 2020. Eight senior high school students arrived in ones and twos to their Asian Studies class. It was the last class of the day on a dreary Friday afternoon, but that day's discussion promised to be a lively one; should the United States have dropped the atomic bombs? Even in such a small class, I knew there was a full range of opinions on this issue—everything from the war-hawkish "teach them a lesson," to liberal doves' "the war was already won," to heartbreaking teenage apathy. The students had already read about and discussed Japan's descent into fascism, China's foreign and domestic conflicts, US imperialism in the Pacific, and the general conduct of the war. Despite their best efforts to hide it, I could tell the students were excited to engage in a healthy argument.

The announcement came twelve minutes into the period. The school was canceling in-person classes for the next two weeks. Though we did not know it at the time, two weeks would become three and a half months. While this interruption to live instruction came as a surprise to most of our students, teachers and administrators had been anticipating the change for some time. "Bridge" lessons were finalized and posted online almost immediately. Plans were developed for continuity of learning at the course, department, and building level. But one thing was obvious, my curriculum was out the window. As we have all so painfully learned, the COVID-19 pandemic touched everything, and my little Asian Studies class was no exception.

We struggled on with chapter readings, online discussions, and awkward Google Hangout meetings for the next two weeks. The novelty wore off very quickly, and it was clear that my students' interest and level of engagement was waning at an alarming rate. Keeping seniors engaged through the spring is hard enough; doing it in a remote learning environment seemed nearly impossible. When it was announced that remote learning would continue through at least May 1, I realized we needed a project that was engaging and relevant.

My students were already asking many questions about the pandemic. Not only was this virus robbing them of their senior year, it was threatening their plans for colleges and careers. Its origins in China and rapid spread throughout East Asia made for an obvious connection to the course. The topic also easily lends itself to connections with the NCSS Ten Themes and the C3 Inquiry Arc.[1] My task, then, was to build an inquiry-based project that met three requirements. First, use current events to promote historical inquiry. Second, help students understand the powerful forces that were threatening to change their lives in such dramatic ways. And finally, navigate and appropriately filter the tidal wave of information about the pandemic that was flowing through the twenty-four-hour news outlets.

Process

A good inquiry-based project always begins with a compelling question, one that forces students to dig below surface-level answers and find deep, meaningful connections to the past.[2] Typically, we would develop the compelling question together in class. Unfortunately, in the virtual learning environment, class meetings were infrequent and not mandatory. I therefore developed the following question myself and presented it to my students in a Google Meeting without any prior warning or instruction: *What historical events and cultural elements have influenced various countries' responses to the COVID-19 pandemic?*

What followed was a remarkably interesting, frustrating, and yet fruitful brainstorming session that eventually led to a detailed explication of the question. A compelling question often demands that we ask smaller, more pointed, supporting questions.[3] Which countries do we want to focus on? What do we mean by "responses"? And most importantly, how do we go about drawing lines between historical events, cultural elements, and the current situation? R. Kieth Sawyer points out that "learning sciences research has found that deep understanding occurs when a learner actively constructs meaning based on his or her experiences and interaction in the world."[4] In order to meet my second goal of deeply understanding the issue, I felt it was important for the students to play an active role in defining the parameters of the project.

The Asian Studies course is designed to follow the AP World History periodization and structure with a focus on Asia. Any experienced world history teacher will recognize the difficulty in limiting the scope of a course to one region, especially one as large and diverse as Asia. For the purposes of this course, Asia is defined as everything from Egypt to Japan and Siberia to Indonesia. Of course, Asia's influence on Europe and Europe's later influence on Asia is not ignored, but our intent is always to look at Asia from an Asian perspective, rather than the more traditional approach of looking at Asia from a European perspective. This approach positions the student in Asia, looking at inter-Asian connections and occasionally looking out from Asia toward the non-Asian world. In doing so, we "de-other" Asian people and their histories.

In this project, we further limited the scope to only East, South, and Southeast Asian countries. This decision was due to the wealth of information available on this area and the lack thereof on southwest and central Asia. At the insistence of my students, we also decided to compare the responses of two Asian countries to each other and then to that of the United States. Incorporating the US response into the project turned out to be a great way of addressing my last two requirements, those of understanding the pandemic and navigating the flow of information.

We also tackled issues such as defining "response," whether this referred to the government's actions or those of the people. We decided that this was an issue that each student needed to address directly as it related to the fundamental question of historical events and cultural elements.

This then led us to the final and most difficult portion of the project, which was to make connections between historical events, culture, and the present. While this was challenging for most students, and some fell short of the goal, it was a wonderful opportunity for them to think and write like historians. Not surprisingly, the students were worried about being wrong in their conclusions. My response was, "Welcome to academic writing. If we had more time, we would publish your papers and submit them to peer review." While this did little to settle their nerves, it did put them in the mindset of making a case and supporting it with evidence.

By the end of our first discussion, we had a compelling question, some argument stems, and several supporting questions. We could now begin to identify and filter our sources. Due to the daily torrent of information on COVID-19, I recognized that my students could very easily become swamped with information. Despite the district's best efforts, and those of many of my fellow educators, students continue

Figure 1: In gratitude for the Navajo veterans who served in the Korean War, the South Korean government donated 10,000 masks and other PPE to the Navajo Nation during COVID-19 pandemic. Office of Greg Stanton, United States Congress. Source: Wikimedia Commons.

to struggle to identify reliable sources. Most importantly, they do not easily differentiate between opinion-based, analytical, investigative, and informational pieces. Counter to my first inclination and standard practice, I decided to provide them with a resource list. Thankfully, I did not have to curate this list myself. The staff and alumni of the National Consortium for Teaching about Asia (NCTA) were of great assistance in developing an extensive list of resources to help students get started.

The students were required to have three mainstream media sources for each country they chose to discuss. At least one of the three they had to find on their own; the others could come from our resource list. For each resource, they had to identify the author, audience, claim, and evidence. This is the standard model we use in our social studies courses for grades seven through twelve. The struggle for most students, though, is to get beyond this summary technique and connect the article's key claim with their own. Therefore, about two weeks into the project, we had to take a break and go back and reevaluate some of their article choices.

I asked each student to provide a one- or two-sentence summary of how the article supported their initial claim. As one can imagine, the students were not thrilled at having to take a step back and potentially find new articles. However, this road bump proved useful in helping the students clarify their central claim. Many students discovered that rather than building a case, they were simply describing the flow of events. While this was a painful process, the results were greatly beneficial. As a result, students were better able to articulate their initial claim. For example, one student wrote:

> The COVID-19 Pandemic has been devastating to people's lives, as well as the state of nations across the world. Different countries have responded to the pandemic in a variety of methods, whether successful or unsuccessful, that reflect the state of their government and domestic nature. By looking at the responses of India and Singapore to the pandemic, it becomes evident how the nature of the country in terms of politics, economics, and cultural aspects affects its responses to a global crisis.

Another claimed that:

> The recent outbreak of COVID-19, the disease caused by the newly discovered severe acute respiratory syndrome SARS-CoV-2, took the world by storm. World leaders and health officials around the world came up with different methods to control this pandemic. Many countries made their own rules and regulations that fit their countries and people best. South Korea has been leading the fight against this virus, while Japan has quickly fallen short compared to other countries.

Admittedly, both paragraphs have some issues, but they provide the students with the opportunity to support their claim. From there, each student developed an outline and began to build their final product.

Results

Generally speaking, the students did well in using and analyzing media accounts. They used the articles to support their claims effectively. For example, one student wrote:

> When being compared to how Europe and the US responded, Max Fisher and Choe Sang-hun at the *New York Times* stated, "South Koreans, unlike Europeans and Americans, were also primed to treat the coronavirus as a national emergency, after a 2015 outbreak of Middle East respiratory syndrome in the country killed 38."

The student made a link between the South Korean response and that of Europe and the United States and tied it into a historical event, the 2015 MERS outbreak.

In our post-project meeting, most students agreed that they now had a better understanding of the virus, how it spread, and why each country's response differed so greatly. While they still expressed concern over the future, they felt that the activity was beneficial to their understanding of the issue. Most notably, several students expressed a deeper understanding of the difference between the government's response and that of the people, especially here in the United States.

Overall, the project met each of my three requirements. Students developed a better appreciation for the complexity of the issue, and they were able to analyze and filter media sources. Where the project fell short was in answering the compelling question.

No student adequately managed to link historical events and culture to the national response. Surprisingly, there was no reference to individualist versus collectivist cultures. Nor did any student make meaningful connections to environmental influences, population density, family structures, or economic activity. This shortcoming may be due to several factors. While we discussed these concepts at length throughout the course, I gave no specific instructions to incorporate them into the project. The remote learning environment, in which students were not required to attend online meetings, limited the amount of discussion about the project throughout the process. And finally, the district's decision to make all fourth-quarter grades pass/fail, while understandable and justified, led to a "just get it done" mentality.

Next Steps

It is an unfortunate reality that this project will continue to be relevant and applicable for several years. While my first attempt was only moderately successful, with some modifications I believe it can be highly effective. There are three changes I will be implementing for next year. The project will be introduced earlier in the year to serve as a primer. Considering the wide range of ability levels among my students, and the complexity of the project, a higher degree of scaffolding is necessary. Finally, students will be placed into heterogeneous ability groups.

Introducing the project early in the year, perhaps even on the first day of class, provides a compelling question that is both relevant and rigorous. Great teachers leverage their students' experiences, insights, and passions into their lessons.[5] This compelling question gives students of all ability levels something to bite into and shifts the focus of the class from performance goals to mastery learning.[6] Rather than being a one off project that "just needs to be completed," the inquiry becomes an ongoing investigation for which we, as a class, are finding evidence.

This process of building a case, based on evidence, will require a level of scaffolding commensurate to the ability level of the class. Using the *Inquiry Design Model* allows the teacher to schedule periodic check-ins and benchmark assessments. Having already provided the compelling question, and having worked with students to develop supporting questions, the project can be revisited at the conclusion of each unit. Specific performance tasks along the way will assist students in applying the learning goals of the unit to the inquiry lesson.[7] For example, at the conclusion of our unit on ancient China, students might write a brief essay comparing how Legalists and Confucians would have dealt with an epidemic. A uniform rubric for each performance task helps students organize their reflections and remain focused on the compelling question. Throughout the year, students will accumulate evidence, in both the form of sources and their own performance assessments, to assist in the final task of making connections between past and present.

As every teacher quickly learns, not every student enters class with the same level of background knowledge. Contrary to what one might think, this is particularly true in a specialized elective such as Asian Studies. A perceptive teacher also recognizes that students learn a great deal from each other, and providing students with opportunities to express their knowledge deepens their understanding.[8] Organizing students into heterogeneous groups facilitates this learning. The teacher's active participation in each group ensures that students do not draw incorrect conclusions. Late May is not the ideal time for reteaching concepts.

With these three major adjustments in mind—introducing the inquiry very early in the year, scaffolding as necessary, and heterogeneous grouping—I believe this project can be a highly effective vehicle for helping students tackle a relevant issue, filter current media sources, and connect the past to the present.

The project design can also be used to investigate similar historic events. Utilizing primary documents, students could research national responses to the 1918 influenza pandemic, the American polio epidemic, or the 1957 Asian flu epidemic for example. The compelling question might remain very much the same, while supporting questions could vary considerably. Students might focus their attention on how mass media was produced and consumed at that time and what impact it had on national responses. They may choose to consider how economic activity at that time and in that place limited or exacerbated the outbreak. What I find most valuable about inquiry-based projects such as this is the great variety of avenues that are available for students. In this way, the opportunity for engagement is high and students are more likely to retain the learning for a longer period and apply that learning to other problems.

Notes

[1] First published in 1994 by the National Council for the Social Studies, the 2010 revision provides ten interrelated themes that serve as a guide for curriculum articulation and alignment. National Council for the Social Studies, National Curriculum Standards or Social Studies: Introduction, 2010, https://www.socialstudies.org/standards/introduction (accessed July 10, 2020).

[2] The purpose of the C3 Framework is to help districts design a social studies curriculum that teaches students to develop "the intellectual power to recognize societal problems; ask good questions and develop robust investigations into them; consider possible solutions and consequences; separate evidence-based claims from parochial opinions; and communicate and act upon what they learn." Kathy Swan, "College, Career and Civic Life C3 Framework for Social Studies State Standards," in *College, Career & Civic Life C3 Framework for Social Studies State Standards* (Silver Spring, MD: National Council for the Social Studies), 6.

[3] Swan, "College, Career, and Civic Life C3 Framework," 25.

[4] Jospeh S. Krajcik and Phyllis C. Blumenfeld, "Project-Based Learning." *The Cambridge Handbook of the Learning Sciences*, ed. by R. Keith Sawyer (Cambridge: Cambridge University Press, 2006), 317–334.

[5] Kathy Swan, John Lee, and S. G. Grant, *Inquiry Design Model: Building Inquiries in Social Studies* (United States: National Council for the Social Studies and C3 Teachers, 2018), 29–30.

[6] P. R. Pintrich, "Multiple Goals, Multiple Pathways: The Role of Goal Orientation in Learning and Achievement," *Journal of Educational Psychology*, no. 92 (2000) quoted in Paul A. Kirschner and Carl Hendrick, *How Learning Happens: Seminal Works in Educational Psychology and What They Mean in Practice* (Abingdon, Oxon: Routledge, 2020), 106–111.

[7] Swan, *Inquiry Design Model, 84.*

[8] E. Z. Rothkopf, "The Concept of Mathemagenic Activities," *Review of Education Research*, no. 40 (1970) quoted in Paul A. Kirschner and Carl Hendrick, *How Learning Happens: Seminal Works in Educational Psychology and What They Mean in Practice* (Abingdon, Oxon: Routledge, 2020), 144–152.

Appendix

Designing an inquiry-based project is a collaborative process between the teacher and students. Using the format provided here can help guide the design process. This form is adapted from the National Council for the Social Studies' College, Career, and Civic Life framework (NCSS C3) and can be modified to meet the needs of almost any topic. I have provided the compelling question that we used for our COVID-19 project in Asian Studies. It may also be beneficial to track changes to the document during the process. That way, students can see the development of their compelling question, supporting questions, and sources.

COVID-19 in East Asia   Name: _____

Designing Your Report			
Your Compelling Question	What historical events and cultural elements have influenced various countries' responses to the COVID-19 Pandemic?		
The Countries you are focusing on			USA
Supporting Question 1	Supporting Question 2	Supporting Question 3	
Sources for _____	Sources for _____	Sources for _____	
My Thesis			
Major takeaways and Big Understandings			

21

CHINA IN THE AGE OF COVID-19

STRATEGIES FOR TEACHING
SURVEY STUDENTS

Tanya L. Roth

In the winter of 2020, the COVID-19 pandemic became an important touchstone for my students as they began to learn the history of modern China. We used the emerging pandemic as a starting point for our study of modern China, asking, "How did we get to where we are today?" This question is central to our World Since 1900 course, required of all ninth-grade students, but it resonates particularly well when we study places and events in the news today. Students take more interest when we study topics that they've heard about from social media or family and friends, and the learning process becomes more meaningful because they are no longer studying something that happened long ago that does not seem to matter to their own lives. Helping students see relevance and develop a sense of why the topic in question matters to their own lives is an important component of student engagement and learning.

As news of the coronavirus began to spread in January and February of 2020, we began each class by looking at the Johns Hopkins COVID-19 map to note case numbers in China (and, in time, to observe the global spread of the disease). As we did this, students began to share things they had heard in the news, and, without prompting, they asked questions about what was happening. We tailored our next steps based on these comments and questions, fact-checking

Figure 1: Taiwan President Tsai Ing-wen showing social distancing by using a traditional greeting instead of a handshake in response to the COVID-19 pandemic. Source: Wikimedia Commons.

things they had heard and following up to find answers to their questions, which largely focused on the Chinese government's response. From there, we dove into China's past so they could learn about the rise of Mao Zedong and the People's Republic of China. These historical case studies focused on Mao's larger policies, such as the Great Leap Forward and the Cultural Revolution, and the changes in China's government following Mao's death and Deng Xiaoping's later government, including the Tiananmen Square protests. Framing our historical studies with the expanding pandemic brought more buy-in from students and helped keep them interested in learning China's past so they could better understand China today.

The lesson plan below builds from that experience, offering specific strategies for using the COVID-19 pandemic to help students learn about modern China in relevant, accessible ways. The lesson divides into three independent parts: together, these create an in-depth inquiry into China today, but each part can also be used on its own. While it would be possible to condense all three portions into one longer class period of ninety minutes or more, splitting these across multiple, shorter classes would provide time for students to process what they have learned, develop new questions, and offer the opportunity for students' learning to become more concrete. The three parts of the lesson include:

- Part 1: How does the Chinese government work?

- Part 2: How has China responded to the COVID-19 pandemic?

- Part 3: How can the COVID-19 pandemic help us understand the relationship between Taiwan and China?

Each part includes a guiding question, sources, and a procedure that could be adapted for small groups, large classes, or virtual learning. While the lesson is designed for students who have little knowledge of modern Chinese history, particularly students in a survey course that emphasizes broad coverage, it would arguably be most effective as the capstone for a unit on modern China or as part of a case study of major issues in East Asia today.

Because these three parts have been designed for the introductory survey, teachers will likely encounter students' misconceptions and misinformation. By the time my students study contemporary China, we have had earlier lessons to help them understand the differences between socialism and communism, which often address their prior assumptions about communism. We have also completed activities and research projects that focus on source evaluation and how to identify and read sources critically. The lessons below provide curated materials, but teachers could alternatively ask students to source articles or videos on topics and use that as a way to talk through identifying credible news sources. Additionally, the Stanford History Education Group's Civic Online Reasoning curriculum offers free resources and lessons to help guide students through evaluating sources (https://cor.stanford.edu).

Part 1: How Does the Chinese Government Work?

Objective: to help students understand how the Chinese government functions in the twenty-first century.

In part 1, students will examine sources that help them learn about the Chinese government. The resources provided include overviews of China since Deng Xiaoping, as well as Xi Jinping's leadership prior to COVID-19, and can be curated according to class time and needs. Deng Xiaoping's government provides a useful starting point so that students with little background knowledge can better understand how Chinese communism began adapting in the late twentieth century. Xi Jinping's political rule since the early 2010s is also important for students to understand so that they can build context for understanding his government's response to COVID-19.

Discover: As a class, watch the videos below, or assign them for homework before class meets.

- "Deng Xiaoping's role in transforming China," *South China Morning Post*, November 19, 2018, https://youtu.be/9c-hDzN7lX4 (3:05 min)

- "How China Became a Superpower: 40 Years of Economic Reform," *DW News*, December 18, 2018, https://youtu.be/1SBnK9XIlZE (6:08 min)

- "China's 40 Years of Reform that Turned It into a Superpower," *ABC News* (Australia), November 29, 2018, https://youtu.be/hF__EF_yrFA (3:23 min)

- "How President Xi Jinping Is Transforming China at Home and Abroad, *PBS Newshour*, September 27, 2019, https://www.youtube.com/watch?v=O0f4o7n5UdQ (12:10 min)

Discuss: Divide students into groups to dig deeper, starting with what they just watched in the videos and adding in the articles below. Longer pieces could be divided up for different group members to investigate and share with their group.

Each group should begin by identifying and defining important concepts in the sources to ensure understanding (examples: *What is GDP? Who was Deng Xiaoping? What has Xi Jinping's approach to government been like?*). Next, each group will create one table that highlights key details of how China's government works, focusing on economic and political elements. As students work, they should compile any remaining questions they have.

- Eleanor Albert, Beina Xu, and Lindsay Maizland, "The Chinese Communist Party," Council on Foreign Relations, June 9, 2020, https://www.cfr.org/backgrounder/chinese-communist-party.

- "Deng Xiaoping," ChinesePosters.net, January 1, 2020, https://chineseposters.net/themes/dengxiaoping.php.

- "Profile: China's President Xi Jinping," *BBC News*, February 25, 2018, https://www.bbc.com/news/world-asia-pacific-11551399.

- "What does Xi Jinping's China Dream Mean?" *BBC News*, June 6, 2013, https://www.bbc.com/news/world-asia-china-22726375.

Debrief: Assign a point person from each group to share their charts and questions; debrief by comparing across groups. Revisit the central question: How does the Chinese government work?

Deduce: To wrap up part 1 and bridge into part 2, have students hypothesize a response to the following question: *Based on what you know about China's government and its vision for the country, how would you expect them to respond in the case of a national emergency?*

Part 2: How Has China Responded to the COVID-19 Pandemic?

Objective: to understand and assess the specific steps China took in response to the COVID-19 public health crisis.

Sources in part 2 inform students about how the Chinese government responded to COVID-19. Some of the sources also analyze China's response to the pandemic, providing a foundation for students to think further about the effectiveness and implications of that response.

Discover: Using Google Maps, locate Wuhan, China, and project map to help students see where COVID-19 originated in China. Spend a few moments eliciting prior knowledge from students: What do they know about when and where the pandemic began?

Project the BBC Timeline, "Coronavirus: What Did China Do about Early Outbreak?" (https://www.bbc.com/news/world-52573137). Students could also view hard copies of the timeline or view the article on their own laptops. Spend several minutes reviewing the timeline details and ask students to pinpoint two or three moments that seem most significant. Ask students to share responses, then discuss:

- Why did you choose the moments you did?
- What makes them "significant" for understanding the pandemic?
- Finally, ask students to characterize China's response using one to two adjectives, based on what they read in the timeline.

Discuss: Move students into small groups and assign each group one article from the list below. (Depending on student level and the amount of time available, articles could be edited for length, or the class could focus on one article.) Within each group, students should read and discuss the assigned article, paying particular attention to the main points in their piece. Students should be prepared to talk further about what they learned.

- Amy Qin and Vivian Wang, "Wuhan, Center of Coronavirus Outbreak, Is Being Cut Off by Chinese Authorities," *The New York Times*, January 22, 2020, https://www.nytimes.com/2020/01/22/world/asia/china-coronavirus-travel.html.

- "Coronavirus: China Admits 'Shortcomings and Deficiencies,'" *BBC*, February 4, 2020, https://www.bbc.com/news/world-asia-china-51362336.

- Li Yuan, "Coronavirus Weakens the Propaganda Machine," *The New York Times*, February 26, 2020, https://www.nytimes.com/2020/02/26/business/china-coronavirus-propaganda.html.

- Amy Qin, "China May Be Beating the Coronavirus, at a Painful Cost," *The New York Times*, March 7, 2020, https://www.nytimes.com/2020/03/07/world/asia/china-coronavirus-cost.html.

- "Xi Defends China's COVID-19 Actions, Backs 'Impartial' Review of Pandemic Response," *National Public Radio*, May 18, 2020, https://www.npr.org/sections/coronavirus-live-updates/2020/05/18/857868374/xi-defends-chinas-covid-19-actions-backs-impartial-review-of-pandemic-response.

- "Nation's COVID-19 Fight in Spotlight," *China Daily*, June 8, 2020, https://www.chinadaily.com.cn/a/202006/08/WS5edd70b6a31083481725155a.html.

- "Timeline: How Xi Jinping led China's COVID-19 Battle," *Chinese Global Television Network*, June 9, 2020, https://news.cgtn.com/news/2020-06-09/Timeline-How-Xi-Jinping-led-China-s-COVID-19-battle-RbQnYSoXKg/index.html.

Debrief: Provide each group time to report out. Consider the following options and select based on what works best for your class dynamics and environment:

- Use large paper, whiteboards/chalkboards, or similar virtual spaces (e.g., Zoom whiteboards, Google Docs or Slides, Padlet, Stormboard) to have each group write down main points, takeaways, and questions from the reading. Next, students rotate around the room (or virtual space), leaving post-its or comments to highlight things they have questions about, things that surprised them, or things that confirmed what they read in their own pieces.

- Redivide groups so that each group now has students who read different articles. In new jigsawed groups, each participant is responsible for sharing out what they learned.

Follow small-group debriefs with a full-class conversation to identify common threads of information and questions that students generated based on their reading and discussion.

Debate: Wrap up part 2 by having students debate the following questions:

- To what extent was China's approach successful?

- What are the implications or costs of the Chinese government's actions?

- How did their actions affect their relationship with the Chinese people? Other countries?

Extend: Have students evaluate China's response to past pandemics or learn more about public health campaigns in China.

- A good starting point is Robert Peckham's Foreign Affairs article from March 27, 2020, "Past Pandemics Exposed China's Weaknesses," https://www.foreignaffairs.com/articles/china/2020-03-27/past-pandemics-exposed-chinas-weaknesses. The article includes four subsections outlining China's historical response to pandemics since the late nineteenth century. This structure would make it easy to provide to students or to divide amongst students in small groups.

- Additionally, the US National Library of Medicine offers a focused lesson plan on China's public health campaigns in the twentieth century: https://www.nlm.nih.gov/exhibition/education/chinesepublichealthposters/highereducation/class4.html#:~:text=The%20theme%20of%20integrating%20public,the%20diseases%20that%20plagued%20people

  - Alternately, the National Library of Medicine has several sets of public health posters, including:

    - Chinese Public Health Posters: https://www.nlm.nih.gov/hmd/chineseposters/public.html

    - Chinese Anti-Malaria Posters: https://www.nlm.nih.gov/exhibition/chineseantimalaria/index.html

    - Chinese Anti-Tuberculosis Posters: https://www.nlm.nih.gov/exhibition/chineseantitb/index.html

Part 3: How Can the COVID-19 Pandemic Help Us Understand the Relationship between Taiwan and China?

Objective: to learn about Taiwan's relationship with China and how that relationship impacts Taiwan on the world stage.

Part 3 focuses on educating students about Taiwan by highlighting how the country's status with China has kept Taiwan out of the World Health Organization and the significance of their absence. Part 3 can be a concluding piece to a study of China today, or an extension or stand-alone lesson.

Discover: Begin by providing students with an overview of the relationship between Taiwan and China. The two sources below support this goal; the video may be more accessible for younger students, while the article may be most appropriate for advanced secondary school students or college students.

- "Taiwan and China Explained," *TRT World*, January 11, 2019, https://youtu.be/a2a4yR4P_Vk (4:18 min)

- Zhiqun Zhu, "A Unique Trilateral Relationship: The US, the PRC, and Taiwan since 1949," *Education about Asia*, Winter 2012, https://www.asianstudies.org/publications/eaa/archives/a-unique-trilateral-relationship-the-us-the-prc-and-taiwan-since-1949

Discuss: Talk through these resources with students to assess their understanding of the relationship between Taiwan and China. Once students have established a baseline for understanding the connection between Taiwan and China, ask them to compare Taiwan and China's experiences of COVID-19 using the map, table, and article below.

- Coronavirus Resource Center, Johns Hopkins University, https://coronavirus.jhu.edu

- Select "View the COVID-19 Global Map"

- "Virus Outbreak: Timeline of preventive efforts against COVID-19," *Taipei Times*, April 14, 2020, https://www.taipeitimes.com/News/taiwan/archives/2020/04/14/2003734588

- William Yang, "How Has Taiwan Kept Its Coronavirus Infection Rate So Low?" *Deutsche Welle*, April 9, 2020, https://www.dw.com/en/taiwan-coronavirus/a-52724523.

It may be helpful to have students refer back to part 2 materials, particularly to compare the timeline of China's response to the pandemic with the *Taipei Times* timeline. As students read and discuss their findings, ask them to consider these questions:

- How does Taiwan's experience with COVID-19 compare to China's?

- Why might it be useful to understand China and Taiwan's successes and challenges in combating COVID-19?

Next, introduce the World Health Organization by asking students what they know or have heard about it. Show the video below and consider having students read the overview about the World Health Organization to learn more about WHO.

- "WHO: Guardian of Health," World Health Organization, June 16, 2017, https://youtu.be/p7liQk45fFk (2:01 min)

- Peter Beech, "World Health Organization: what does it do and how does it work?" World Economic Forum, April 17, 2020, https://www.weforum.org/agenda/2020/04/world-health-organization-what-it-does-how-it-works/.

Once students understand the role WHO plays, particularly in a pandemic, give them resources to explore Taiwan's status with WHO. Students should work in small groups to examine one or more of the resources below:

- Yu-Jie Chen and Jerome A. Cohen, "Why Does the WHO Exclude Taiwan?" Council on Foreign Relations, April 9, 2020, https://www.cfr.org/in-brief/why-does-who-exclude-taiwan.

- Ben Blanchard, "Taiwan Rejects China's Main Condition for WHO Participation," *Reuters*, May 14, 2020, https://www.reuters.com/article/us-health-coronavirus-taiwan/taiwan-rejects-chinas-main-condition-for-who-participation-idUSKBN22R0HM.

- Huileng Tan, "Taiwan 'Disappointed and Angry' about Being Excluded from WHO Meeting, Says It Is Developing Its Own Coronavirus Vaccine," *CNBC*, May 19, 2020, https://www.cnbc.com/2020/05/19/taiwan-says-it-is-disappointed-and-angry-being-excluded-from-who-meeting.html.

Debrief: Ask students to take notes individually or as a group to track important facts and information they learn. Once students have finished exploring the sources, gather to wrap up by focusing on these questions:

- Why might it be useful to understand China and Taiwan's successes and challenges in combating COVID-19?

- Why does it matter that Taiwan is not included in the World Health Organization?

  - What does this tell us about...

    - China's relationship with Taiwan?

    - the global response to COVID-19?

Extend: Ask students to examine COVID-19 in Hong Kong. Like Taiwan, Hong Kong is also part of China, but both places have unique relationships to China. Prior to the COVID-19 pandemic, prodemocracy protests in Hong Kong began making international news in 2019. The sources below could be used to help students develop more context for these protests and Hong Kong's relationship with China and to evaluate Hong Kong's responses to COVID-19.

- "Hong Kong Protests One Year Later," *The New York Times*, June 9, 2020, https://www.nytimes.com/2020/06/09/world/asia/hong-kong-protests-one-year-later.html.

- "How Hong Kong and South Korea Manage to Keep Covid-19 at Bay Without Enforcing Lockdowns," *South China Morning Post*, April 22, 2020, https://www.youtube.com/watch?v=IBHGnsxEDN0 (4:55 min)

- "Officials Tighten Restrictions Again as Hong Kong Reports Record-High Covid-19 Cases," *South China Morning Post*, July 20, 2020, https://www.youtube.com/watch?v=U9d3j8M1U88 (2:51 min)

- "Hong Kong to Start Massive COVID-19 Testing from Sept. 1," *Chinese Global Television Network*, August 21, 2020, https://news.cgtn.com/news/2020-08-21/Chinese-mainland-sends-50-experts-to-HK-to-assist-COVID-19-testing-T8xkwES6DC/index.html.

CPSIA information can be obtained
at www.ICGtesting.com
Printed in the USA
LVHW012120281220
675265LV00006B/6

9 781952 636196